Welcome the Child

A Child Advocacy Guide for Churches

Shannon P. Daley
and
Kathleen A. Guy

Copyright © 1994 by Children's Defense Fund

Published by Friendship Press, Inc.

Editorial Offices:
475 Riverside Drive, New York, NY 10115

Distribution Offices:
P.O. Box 37844, Cincinnati, OH 45222-0844

Manufactured in the United States of America

Cover photo by Nita Winter
Typesetting by ediType

Library of Congress Cataloging-in-Publication Data

Daley, Shannon P.
    Welcome the child : a child advocacy guide for churches / Shannon
P. Daley and Kathleen A. Guy. — Rev. and expanded ed.
        p. cm.
    ISBN 0-377-00266-6
    1. Church work with children. 2. Child welfare — United States.
3. Children's rights — United States. I. Guy, Kathleen A.
II. Title.
BV639.C4D35 1994
261.8'3423–dc20
                                                    93-46974
                                                      CIP

Contents

Acknowledgments

This book could not have been produced without the assistance and contributions of the following people:

- Marian Wright Edelman, Margaret Schwarzer, Minerva Carcano, Ruth Fowler, Eileen Lindner, and Mary Potter Engel, who contributed sermons and other texts.

- Betty Jane Bailey, Margery Freeman, Martha Pillow, Carol Wehrheim, Belva Finlay, Alice Yang, and Brendan Goff, who helped write and edit pieces of this book.

- Stephen Wilhite and Deneice Patterson, who worked tirelessly to edit and retype hundreds of pages of text.

- Donna Jablonski, Janis Johnston, David Heffernan, Margaret Larom, Audrey A. Miller, and John Eagleson, who produced this book.

- MaryLee Allen, Lisa Mihaly, Sara Rosenbaum, Helen Blank, Kati Haycock, Ray O'Brien, and Luis Duany, who provided research and input on Section III.

- The members of the former Child Advocacy Working Group of the National Council of Churches, now called the Commission on Justice for Children and Their Families, whose commitment to children and dedicated work on their behalf helped make this book possible.

- The members of the Program Committee on Education for Mission, representing churches in the U.S. and Canada, for their insights into how this book could be the foundation for the 1994–95 ecumenical mission study theme, "Making the World Safe for Children."

Preface

Then Jesus took a little child, and put it among them; and taking it in his arms, he said to them, "Whoever welcomes one such child in my name welcomes me, and whoever welcomes me welcomes not me but the one who sent me."

Mark 9:36–37

For many of us, when we think of our church's ministry to children, or how it "welcomes the child," the examples and images that come to mind are of a baby being baptized in the arms of the minister, of children clustered around the minister for the children's sermon, or of children in Sunday School. But what of the children whose physical, emotional, social, economic, and educational conditions are depriving them of the opportunity to develop their God-given potential?

Who is one such child that we are called to welcome?

- One of the 2,860 children born into poverty each day.

- One of the 100,000 children who are homeless each night.

- One of the 145 babies born at very low birthweight each day, weighing less than 3 1/4 pounds.

- One of the 2,350 children in adult jails each day.

- One of the 7,945 children who are reported abused or neglected each day.

- One of the 2,255 children who drop out each school day.

- One of the 1,234 children who run away from home each day.

- One of the 27 children who die because of poverty each day.

These facts about children in the United States may be surprising or even shocking, to the point of seeming unreal or unimaginable. Take a moment and picture the sanctuary of your church. How many persons fill it each Sunday? Now look back to the statistics above and visualize the children the numbers represent in the pews of your sanctuary: Would the children born into poverty each day fill the pews once? Twice? Would the 100,000 children who were homeless last Sunday night fill your sanctuary seventy-five times? A hundred times? Picture now the 2,255 children who dropped out of school yesterday…the 7,400 children who will be reported abused or neglected today…the 1,234 children who will run away from home tomorrow.

It is a human and moral travesty that more than 14.6 million U.S. children are poor and 8 million lack health insurance in a nation blessed by such abundance and riches. What are the true values of a wealthy, democratic nation that lets infants and toddlers be the poorest group of citizens? We know that poverty makes children more likely to be born too small, to die, be sick, hungry, and malnourished, to fall behind in school and drop out, and to cost their families immeasurable suffering and taxpayers billions in later remedial costs and lost productivity. How do we reconcile rampant national child neglect and preventable suffering with the biblical warning that from those to whom much is given, much is expected?

The United States is afflicted by a poverty of riches unleavened by enough justice. The religious community must take the lead in guiding the nation away from the sin of child abuse and neglect and toward God's intended creation of compassion and justice. The religious community must renew and deepen its own commitment to faithful child advocacy. The problems of child and family poverty, of discrimination, of hunger and homelessness that confront every nation in the world are not problems that the religious community is required to solve alone. But they are problems on which Christians cannot turn their backs.

Every person of faith has a special obligation to help the poor and the powerless and to seek justice. As people of faith we can, and often do, make the case to others that investing in preventive programs and policies is "cost-effective." But the deepest and most enduring truth is that we must take better care of all children because it is the right and moral thing to do. Just as Christ's model of ministry sought justice for the most vulnerable and marginalized, so too must we minister with compassion and seek justice for the most vulnerable and marginalized children, until each has the opportunity to develop to her or his God-given potential. It is that to which Christ calls us with the words, "Whoever welcomes one such child in my name welcomes me, and whoever welcomes me welcomes not me but the one who sent me."

No child should grow up poor, unsafe, without basic health care, nutrition, housing, a strong early childhood foundation, or a decent education.

Child poverty and suffering can be alleviated. The challenge is to create the sense of urgency and the political will to give children first rather than last call on international, national, community, and family interests and resources. Committed individuals, organizations, and congregations can make life better for millions of children. The problems that too many children see each day are very real — but they can be fixed. Each and every one of us can help make a difference in the lives of children. And that's why your moral witness and hard work are so important.

In the Book of Micah we read: "And what does the Lord require of you, but to do justice, and to love kindness, and to walk humbly with your God?" Please use this guide to child advocacy to involve yourself and others in faithfully making a difference for children in your home, church, community, city, state, nation, and the world.

Use **Section I: Looking at Children through the Eyes of Faith** as you pray about and study the needs of children. Our hope for children, ultimately, rests with God. It is God who gives us the faith and courage and strength to nurture and protect children. It is God who forgives us when we don't. Ask God for the compassion to see the faces and hear the cries of children behind the statistics and stories.

This guide will help you involve your congregation in study and in action. Ministering through outreach in your community is vital. Look to **Section V: Giving Voice to the Voiceless,** however, to learn how you can extend your advocacy beyond the community to make your voice, and the voices of children, heard in the public policy and political process. Ask God for the wisdom to know what you faithfully and realistically can do. Then get righteously angry. Get inspired. Get involved. Demand action. Follow through.

I ask you to join with me and millions of people of faith on this journey of celebrating and loving our own, our congregation's, and all of God's children. Together, let's strive to take on their joys and sorrows, find ways to help them grow and develop to their God-given potential, and seek justice for *all* children. May God bless us on our journey. May we find joy and strength in one another as we join arm in arm with children.

Marian Wright Edelman
President, Children's Defense Fund

Standing Strong for Children

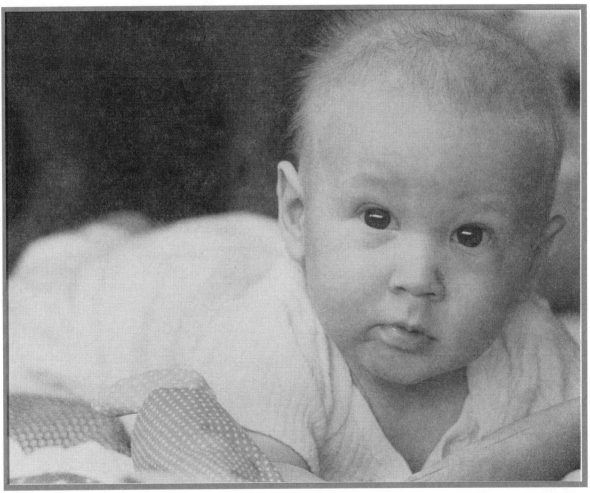

PHOTO BY KATHY SLOANE

Standing Strong for Children...

What the Statistics Report

Teen Pregnancy

- Each year one in 10 teenage girls in the United States becomes pregnant, compared with fewer than one in 20 in England, France, or Canada, and one in 30 in Sweden.

- In 1970 three of 10 teenagers giving birth were unmarried. In 1990 two out of three were unmarried.

- About 1 million teenage girls get pregnant each year, and about half a million babies (equivalent to the population of Boston) are born to teenagers.

- Teenage girls with poor basic skills are five times as likely to become mothers before the age of 16 as those with average basic skills.

Education

- Every 11 seconds of the school day an American child drops out (406,000 during the 1991–92 school year).

- The Soviet Union, Canada, and Norway spent more of their Gross National Product on public education than did the United States in 1988.

- Austria, Belgium, France, Germany, Ireland, Japan, the Netherlands, Spain, and the United Kingdom have a greater percentage of their four-year-olds in preschool than does the U.S.

- The average reading and math skills of 17-year-old Black and Latino students are comparable to those of White 13-year-olds.

Preschool

- Every $1 invested in high-quality preschool programs such as Head Start saves more than $7 in lowered costs for special education, grade retention, public assistance, and crime later on.

- The children enrolled in programs like Head Start are more likely than other poor children to be literate, employed, and enrolled in postsecondary education.

- Head Start now serves approximately one in three eligible youngsters.

Stories behind the Statistics

Dahlia's Story

Dahlia, a child of a teenage mother, could not escape the cycle of poverty. When she became pregnant at 16, she left her job and was supported by Julio, the father of her child. After her daughter Jennifer was born, Julio and Dahlia separated and Dahlia went on welfare.

Wayne's Story

Wayne was tutored at Simpson United Methodist Church in West Virginia while he was in the seventh and eighth grades. He recalls, "When I first started tutoring I used to goof off and I didn't think it would help. I sat down with my tutor and he showed me how easy it was to learn. That's when I got interested and really started learning. Without tutoring, I would have failed some classes and not graduated from high school. I would have failed seventh and eighth grades."

Anne's Story

Anne is a high school dropout who first became a mother when she was 16. She had six children by the time she was 26. She worked as a maid, and her husband worked as a store clerk.

...It Makes a Difference

Advocacy Comes in Many Forms

One Person

Through the help of a program called the Young Mothers Group, organized and run by a United Church of Christ minister, Dahlia received support and encouragement from her peers and the adult resource volunteers. "The Young Mothers Group helped me decide what I'm going to do with my life," said Dahlia. "Speakers come to talk to us about their careers and how they did it—and that encouraged me a lot. The group members are the same age as I am and they're also young mothers. It's encouraging to me because I feel I'm not the only one out there who's a teen parent."

Achievement Is Not a Statistic

Through the weekly support of the Young Mothers Group, Dahlia and the other young mothers learned parenting skills, personal hygiene, and employment skills. Dahlia started working part time, 20 hours a week, and went back to school. While completing her education and supporting her young child, she knew that personal support and help were available weekly when she gathered with other young mothers—all because one person saw a need and found a way to help meet it.

A Group of Church Women

The United Methodist Women's Local Unit of Simpson United Methodist Church recognized the need to assist with the education of children 10 years ago. The group started a tutorial program in its church building that has expanded to 22 sites. Today the program is coordinated by the Charleston District Outreach Ministries of the United Methodist Church.

Each volunteer tutor receives training and support. After the students are tested and evaluated, tutors receive a "prescription" describing where to begin and what skills need reinforcing.

"Right now, I really thank my tutor because he really helped me out," says Wayne. "He pushed me towards the things that I wanted to do and the goals that I set. It's great to have someone like that who cares and helps kids."

Wayne recently graduated from high school and is making plans to build and market low-income housing on the land his grandmother left him in her will. Wayne's is one of many lives reversed because a group saw where help was needed and did something about it.

Churches Working To Change Public Policies

Since 1965 the Head Start program, funded by the federal government, has been involving parents, teachers, and volunteers in a comprehensive child development program for disadvantaged three-, four-, and five-year-olds. Head Start also ensures that these children receive the health and supportive services they need to get off to an even start with other children in school and later in life.

The religious community has been a strong advocate for full funding of the Head Start program so that all eligible children can participate. Many churches house Head Start programs. Local congregations write letters to their members of Congress requesting continued and increased funding for Head Start.

At 26 Anne went back to school and received her high school diploma. She enrolled her children in the Head Start program and was employed by Head Start as a part-time worker.

With encouragement and guidance from the Head Start staff, Anne went on to college and eventually completed her college degree. Anne's three oldest children have completed college and are employed. Her other three children now are attending college.

How To Use This Guide

All people of faith acknowledge and practice, in various ways, the responsibility to nurture children. This book is intended in part to further that work: to help churches strengthen children; to affirm their growth, discoveries, and experiences; and to support their participation in the life of the congregation.

This book also aims to foster reflection on the many needs of children in the congregation, community, nation, and world — especially those who suffer in mind, body, and spirit. This book will help congregations develop or strengthen plans for children's ministries and child advocacy, and in so doing will deepen the congregation's understanding of our call and responsibility, as people of faith, to nurture, to protect, and to advocate on behalf of the children.

Who Will Benefit from This Guide?

This guide is for:

◆ Lay members of congregations who work with and for children in a variety of roles — through church, community, or professional involvement;

◆ Clergy and staff;

◆ Church council and committee members;

◆ Those church members not yet active on children's concerns;

◆ Mission and social justice advocacy organizations in the church;

◆ Community child advocates who want to establish relationships with congregations and religious organizations.

We hope this book will encourage networking among congregations, national religious organizations, community social service agencies and programs, and national child advocacy groups.

The Sections of This Book

The sections of this book have been written so that they build upon and strengthen each other. Together,

they provide a comprehensive approach to ministering to the varied needs of children in the church and in society. However, each section has been written so that it may be used on its own or in conjunction with another section or other resources. Your congregation may decide to use only a few of the sections or to divide them among clergy, staff, committees, groups, and individuals.

What Is Child Advocacy?

Child advocacy is standing up for children — your own and others'. It is an attitude, a process you go through, and all the steps along the way that bring about changes to help children grow and develop fully.

◆ If your child is suspended from school for being late three times and you go to the principal to discuss the problem together to get her back into school, you are doing child advocacy.

◆ If you go to the worship committee of your congregation to ask that children be included as greeters or ushers on Sunday mornings, you are being a child advocate.

◆ If you ask school authorities to properly test your child before placing him in a special education class, that too is advocacy.

◆ If you and others meet with the leadership of your congregation to present a plan to use the church building and resources for a latchkey program, you are advocating for children.

◆ If you sign a petition to get a playground with safe equipment built in your neighborhood and a traffic light on the playground corner, that also is child advocacy.

◆ If you send a letter supporting your governor's promise to sign a law creating jobs for teenagers, or if you write to your legislators asking them to vote for a bill that makes more money available for child care or health care for children, you are participating in child advocacy.

Looking at Children through the Eyes of Faith

PHOTO BY ERIC FUTRAN

How To Use This Section

The first step in becoming an advocate for children is to be aware of the place of children in the world and in the church today. Along with this awareness comes the recognition of God's love and care for all children, but especially for those who are most vulnerable and in need of care. For Christians, an important part of advocacy for children who are vulnerable and powerless is to seek God's will and guidance in prayer and meditation. So often what we do affects children, but we don't recognize either the positive or negative impact we are having at the time. God's grace can open our eyes and give us the strength and courage to do what is in our power to do for children.

This section provides meditations that can be used with committees, boards, councils, classes, or any group within the congregation to lift up the needs of children and our responsibility to them. Look through the meditations. Use those that are appropriate to your setting. Adapt them or develop your own. Reflection upon God's word and our call to discipleship on behalf of children is a necessary component of child advocacy for Christians, because every decision we make as individuals and as groups affects children in some way. These meditations and the accompanying questions for discussion will help you and the groups with which you meet consider what some of these effects may be.

In this section you also will find resources and suggestions for a Children's Sabbath. One way to bring the needs of children to the entire congregation is to plan a worship service on the theme of children. A Children's Sabbath also can be adapted to an existing event to include the theme of child advocacy. See pages 27–39 for ways to incorporate the entire faith community into this observance, including opportunities for raising awareness, involving the congregation in action, and reflecting on the mission of God.

Return to this section regularly as you stand strong for children in your congregation and community. Child advocacy is not a fad, but a lifetime commitment. To sustain your spirit and will, meditate and reflect regularly on what you are called to do on behalf of children.

For Pastors and Worship Leaders and Planners

In this section there are suggestions for hymns, prayers, scriptures, and other aspects of the liturgy. Throughout this book there are stories and informational material you may want to include in a sermon or print in the worship bulletin. A wealth of illustrations detailing ministries for children and God's call to us to care for the vulnerable and powerless in our midst can be found in the other sections.

Your interest and involvement in child advocacy will do much to encourage your congregation to participate in this ministry. Recognizing and pointing out the needs of children as you meet with committees or in prayers or sermons throughout the year not only lends support to those who work for and with children, but validates their ministry as well. Consider the children each time you prepare a sermon, lead a discussion group, or work with a committee. You are an important voice for children in the life of your congregation and your community.

CHAPTER 1

Sermons, Bible Studies, Reflections

For meditation and discussion with:

◆ Committees and boards;

◆ Governing bodies;

◆ Fellowship groups of young people or adults;

◆ Church staff.

The readings in this section can be used in a variety of ways. They can be presented as meditations to begin a meeting. With the discussion questions, they can raise a group's awareness of children's needs. By focusing the questions more specifically on your setting, you can help the group think about what is needed for the children of your congregation, your community, our nation, or the world.

In Your Heart

Focus: We teach God's word to our children as we talk with them about our faith and as we minister in God's name in the world.

Scripture: Deuteronomy 6:4–9
Matthew 22:36–40

God's promise to our earliest ancestors in the faith was that God would be their God and that they would be God's people. Through the incarnation, death, and resurrection of Christ that promise became more intimate and the people of God began to call themselves children of God, joint heirs, adopted brothers and sisters with Christ.

Scripture is full of references to God as loving parent, and many of us find great solace and strength in the vision of ourselves as God's children. These images are powerful when the parent-child relationship we have experienced is one in which as children we received love, forgiveness, protection, food, shelter, clothing, all that is needed for spiritual and physical well-being. That is what we ask of God. And that is what children need from us.

If we have not experienced a positive, nurturing, and secure relationship between parent and child, we may instead have developed a powerful vision of what that bond ought to be in its most perfect form — the image of God as loving parent.

Reflecting on our own experiences as children — whether they were positive or negative — gives us insight into the awesomely important role of human parents. It deepens our compassion for children today who are not blessed with an experience of love, acceptance, security, and nurture. And it underscores our charge to embody the qualities that God as our loving parent has revealed to us.

Each day millions of the world's children go without proper care — even in the so-called "First World." In every society, children are the poorest citizens. Every year in the United States alone, 10,000 children die of the effects of poverty. A baby born in the U.S. is less likely to reach his or her first birthday than a baby born in Singapore.

Many poor children who do survive grow up under a cloud of hopelessness. For more than 14.6 million children in the United States — one of five — childhood is a time when they and their families can think of little but basic survival.

Pervasive poverty threatens not only poor children, but also the social and spiritual fabric of a nation. The cost is dear. The very lives — the minds, spirits, and emotions — of these children are damaged and endangered. If we shut our eyes and refuse to see them we live in disobedience to God, whose word we have been commanded to teach to children — all children. Thus, our relationship with God suffers, for how do we teach a child of God's love when he or she does not know that all-embracing love through us?

God's love can be known through us in personal relationships, and in how we use the resources God has given us. Our task as Christians, whether adult, young person, or child, is to shape the world in which we live so that all people, whatever age, have what is required for spiritual and physical well-being. As we do this, we recite the word of God to children everywhere.

Love of God cannot be separated from love of neighbor. Few of our neighbors are as vulnerable as children. Children cannot fend for themselves. Children need our help, and they need our love. Children are powerless in the political decisions that shape their lives and futures. We are the ones with the ability and the opportunity to fulfill God's promise to them. As we work to improve their lives today and tomorrow, we are loving God with all our hearts, souls, and might.

Questions for Reflection and Discussion

◆ In what ways do you, individually or corporately, recite the word of God to your children? How do these actions show God's word?

◆ What more can you be or say? How can you show your love of God with all your heart, soul, and might, by acting on behalf of children?

Prayer

We join with people of God through all the ages, declaring "The Lord is our God, the Lord alone." We seek your help, O God, as we struggle to keep your word to us in this time and place. Guide us as we seek to keep our actions consistent with your word to us. Keep us ever from failing to hold your word in our hearts and conveying it to the children of your world at every opportunity. Through Jesus Christ, the embodiment of your Word, we pray. Amen.

Based on a sermon by Kathleen A. Guy
Former Religious Affairs Coordinator
Children's Defense Fund, Washington, DC

There Is a Boy Here

Focus: The adult community of faith can discover the Spirit of God through the gifts of children.

Scripture: John 6:1–14

The story of the feeding of the 5,000 is the story of God's realm made visible on this earth. Through God's mercy, the huge crowd was fed in fellowship and peace. The story is familiar, perhaps too familiar. We know it so well that we forget to listen as it is told or read. We know there were only five loaves and two fish and there were thousands to feed. But do we remember who provided the meager offering that fed the crowd? Oh, yes, a boy, according to the Gospel of John.

Jesus didn't pull the loaves and fish out of the air. It was no sleight-of-hand trick. He created a community feast by using what the community had to offer, what the boy had to offer. Jesus had the holy imagination to see the child's willingness to give and the potential abundance in his offerings.

One of the disciples, though observant enough to spot the child with his lunch, was too weary to imagine the divine potential presented. Andrew said, "There is a boy here who has five barley loaves and two fish. But what are they among so many people?"

What are they? In the story they are all that is needed. They are the ingredients touched by Jesus that would yield a bounteous feast for all gathered. Through Christ, who saw the transforming potential of the child's simple offering, the hungry and tired crowd discovered enough bread and fish to feed everyone.

Ironically, wonderfully, the belongings of one of the youngest, least powerful members of that mighty gathering turned out to be the instrument that inspired Christ's miracle that day. The wisdom of the world teaches us to focus on political power and might, but Christ points us to a child, once again.

Just as the boy and his bundle were the instruments of Jesus' miracle, we are invited to look for the potential miracles found in the hearts and souls of children, even the most unlikely children. They have gifts and talents that are waiting to be uncovered and nurtured.

The Holy Spirit has given each of us spiritual gifts of all varieties. Now it is our turn to recognize the gifts of the children in our world. It is our turn to reach out and uncover the gifts our children are offering. When we realize the potential of what children have to offer, our faith community and our nation can be transformed by the miracle of their gifts.

Questions for Reflection and Discussion

◆ When has a child been a source of the knowledge of God in your life?

◆ Think about the children you know. What gifts of the Spirit do you discern in them?

◆ What, in your congregation, helps children use their gifts for the good of the community? What hinders them?

Prayer

God of all beings, large and small, old and young, we praise you for the gift of your Son, Jesus Christ, his life and his teachings. We thank you for the children in our congregation and in our lives. Help us to acknowledge their presence and their gifts, alert us to their potential as Jesus was alert to the potential of the boy with his meager lunch of loaves and fish. Remind us in our work together that we are blessed by you a hundred-fold, as were those who came to hear your Son. Keep us mindful of all your people, young and old. Amen.

Based on a biblical reflection by Margaret Schwarzer
Former Intern from Yale Divinity School
Children's Defense Fund, Washington, DC

At the Pace of Children

Focus: When we take notice of the pace of the children in our world, we recognize our need to adjust to their pace to be on the path to the kingdom of God.

Scripture: Genesis 33:12–14
Matthew 18:2–5

At first glance, the Genesis passage gives us a positive image of Jacob carefully weighing the needs of children.

Yet, throughout the narrative of the reconciliation of Esau and Jacob, we have a vignette of people of faith using children. The children are treated as a buffer between Esau and Jacob, as chattel to be offered up as gifts in times of need, and as sacrifices in times of battle. Knowing something about the social attitude, traditions, and mores of the time gives us the broader picture of this treatment.

An ancient Pentateuchal tradition was that God would provide land and posterity for Israel. Jacob comes to be identified as the representative of the divine promise. To him are born the 12 sons of Israel, and his descendants gain hold of land in Shechem, in the area of Canaan. Land and posterity were of the highest importance, for they would determine Israel's ability to survive as a people. Children were viewed as a means to survival, not necessarily as persons of inherent worth. The meaning of the names of two of the women who bore children to Jacob illustrates the attitude toward women and children. In the ancient language the name Leah means "cow," and the name Rachel means "ewe"!

What's more, male children were considered more important than female children. For this reason we are more likely to remember that Jacob had 12 sons than we are to remember that he had 13 children, and that his twelfth child was not Benjamin, but a girl child named Dinah.

Other cultures of the time had similar attitudes toward children. For example, we know the Greeks did not want large families for fear that too many children would mean not enough food to feed everyone. So the Greek customs and laws condoned infanticide, and children often were left to die from exposure in the wilderness. In the time of Moses children often were abandoned at the Nile or Euphrates rivers.

The negative attitudes toward children had not changed significantly by the beginning of the Christian era. The Interpreter's Bible commentary on the Gospel of Matthew reports a letter written by an Egyptian laborer named Hilarion to his pregnant wife, Alis. Hilarion advises her, if she has a girl, to let the baby die.

Similarities in Jacob's and Christ's Perspectives on Children

Two statements that Jacob makes when returning home, however, point to a biblical understanding of children and our relationship with them that is positive rather than negative.

When Esau sees the company of his brother Jacob and asks, "Who are these with you?" Jacob responds, "The children whom God has graciously given your servant" (Genesis 33:5). In so answering Jacob acknowledges the sacred worth of the children, because they are from God.

The second positive statement comes when Jacob says, "...I will lead on slowly, according to the pace of the cattle that are before me and according to the pace of the children..." (Genesis 33:14). Jacob's concern for walking at the pace of the children comes from their fragility and need for protection. His comment also suggests that children need to be heard and heeded by adults. On this point Jesus also teaches us.

In the Gospel of Matthew 18:1, the disciples come and ask Jesus, "Who is the greatest in the kingdom of heaven?" Jesus responds neither with a traditional theological answer, nor with a guidebook, nor with a formula for success. Jesus instead presents them with a child: "He called a child, whom he put among them, and said, 'Truly I tell you, unless you change and become like children, you will never enter the kingdom of heaven. Whoever becomes humble like this child is the greatest in the kingdom of heaven'" (Matthew 18:2–4).

Jacob speaks of leading the children to the homeland as a father who knows what is best for them. Jesus teaches that it is the children who will lead us to the homeland of God's eternal presence, and that in the children the measure of greatness is to be found.

This paradox continues in our lifetime. Yes, we must care for the children with whom God has blessed us — truly care for them. At the same time, we must be attentive to what the children have to say to us. Children lead us daily — if only we will listen.

Knowing What To Preserve

Children do not always set the best example; they can be self-centered and selfish. The apostle Paul stresses that as we mature there are certain child-like ways we must put behind us. But there are also qualities of children, qualities of humble nature, which Jesus recommends we consider and incorporate into our lives.

Some of those qualities are relationships of equality that are to be seen among children regardless of culture, color, or social status; lack of worldly ambition; and a receptiveness to new things. Adults teach children to feel prejudice and racism, to lust for power and control, and to close their minds to the possibility of new things. Adults have set the pace for life as we know it today. Often that pace has been determined by overwhelming ambition. Adults must bear the moral and ethical responsibility for the condition of the world.

We would do well, as we approach the end of this century, to look to the children, and to learn from them. Our greatness may be determined by our ability to walk at their pace. The children may be the ones who will lead us to the kingdom of heaven.

Questions for Reflection and Discussion

- Think first about the way Jacob answered Esau. How was it a reversal of the norms of that time? How was Jesus' answer to his followers also a reversal of the norms of his time?

- As a nation, we talk about the importance of our children. Yet there are many children who are not included in that definition of importance. What would it mean to reverse the norm by which our nation lives, rather than speaks?

- What would it mean for your congregation, board, or committee to conduct its business "at the pace of children?" What changes in thinking would be necessary?

Prayer

O Thou who blesses each of us, young and old, according to your loving kindness, grant us the capacity to find the pace of our children and to match it, so that we too may be headed toward your rule of peace and justice. Forgive us our desires to be first, best, and strongest when we know that all life is in your hands. Remind us that we, too, are children in your sight. In the name of your Son, who showed us all good things. Amen.

Excerpts from a sermon by Minerva G. Carcano
Former Western District Superintendent
Rio Grande Conference United Methodist Church
Albuquerque, NM

Do Not Lose Heart

Focus: Changing an unjust law or situation requires faith and persistence.

Scripture: Luke 18:1–8

An adult, whether a parent or not, who has tried to withstand the pleadings of a child can identify with the judge in the parable. And any child who has found success by wearing down a parent, grandparent, aunt, or uncle knows the determination of the widow.

Although different from most of Jesus' parables, this one is consistent with Jewish teachings in Jesus' day and may be illustrative of Proverbs 25:15: "With patience a ruler may be persuaded, and a soft tongue can break bones."

The widow and the proverb are important to us as we seek to provide justice for the children of our congregation, our community, our nation, and our world.

But children, too, are examples to us by their persistence. When we feel downhearted for lack of progress, when we feel defeated after a hard-fought debate, when we feel overwhelmed by the magnitude of a problem, let us step back and recall the child, the widow, and the proverb. Let us remember also why the parable was told. The writer of Luke says that Jesus told this parable so his hearers would remember "to pray always and not to lose heart." This parable reminds us that God's goodness and justice, unlike the frustrated judge's, are motivated by love.

Today we are the judge. The cries of the widow are the cries of mothers throughout our land and throughout the world. When will we listen? When will we grant justice? How long will it take to wear us down?

Today we are also the widow. We cry out for children — children of poverty, children at risk, children who are abused, children who are spoiled, children who are unwanted, children who have AIDS. Like the

LOOKING AT CHILDREN THROUGH THE EYES OF FAITH

widow we must continue our pleading, for how else will the structures of power be worn down, as was the unjust judge?

As overwhelming as this may feel, to find ourselves both the widow and the judge, we persist because the parable, the proverb, and the child remind us that we can do nothing else. God is with us when we succeed, and when we fail. God both calls us to this task and supports us in it.

Thus, we are judge and widow. When our task, whether to admit complicity and need of forgiveness or to stand strong for children, overwhelms us, we turn to God who forgives us and sustains us. We are filled with new resolve and return to our calling with hope and energy.

Questions for Reflection and Discussion

- When do you feel like the judge? When do you feel like the widow?

- What causes you to lose heart?

- What helps you to keep the faith or to persevere?

- Why is this parable important to persons and groups that seek justice? What does it teach you about God?

- How does this parable relate to the life and work of your committee, fellowship group, or congregation?

Prayer

Great God of justice and perseverance, grant us the gift of determination that we may wear down the walls of injustice and the footings that hold them up. Let us not lose heart, remembering that your love ever surrounds us. Call to us so that our prayers may be constant before you. Finally, keep us aware of the cries of children around us and throughout our world, so that we don't become the unjust judge. All this we ask in your great mercy and through Jesus the Christ. Amen.

Based on a reflection by Carol A. Wehrheim
Church Educator and Curriculum Writer
Princeton, NJ

Touch the Wounds

Focus: When we speak out for children, we confess our faith as we touch their wounds.

Scriptures: John 20:19–29

This gospel passage is commonly known as the story of Thomas the Doubter. Yet a more thoughtful exegesis might suggest that this disciple, who has wandered through nearly 2,000 years of church history with the epithet "doubting," got a bad rap.

Let's recall the scene. It was the night of a terrifying day, ending a week of awe and mystery. The tomb was empty; the women claimed to have seen Jesus; the town was in turmoil. The disciples — exhausted, confused, and terribly frightened — locked themselves in a room. In the midst of this tense meeting Jesus appeared and greeted them with peace. Thomas wasn't present, and he remained unconvinced when the others told him what had happened. A week later the disciples met again, and there, in their midst, appeared Jesus. Thomas still wasn't convinced, so Jesus invited Thomas to touch his wounds. Finally Thomas was persuaded. We have always seen this story as a tale of weak faith. Many of us were taught in childhood and beyond that we should aspire to be good and strong disciples, not doubting Thomases.

However, there is another way to look at this story. Perhaps Thomas was asking the relevant question, for then and now: How will the world believe once the teacher, Jesus, is no longer with us? Doesn't our sad and doubting world ask the same question repeatedly? How are we to believe? How are those of us who neither knew Jesus personally nor witnessed his life and ministry firsthand to have faith?

In Jesus' response to Thomas we find solace and gain insight. How are we to believe? Reach out to the wounds and touch them. How are we to have faith? Put your fingers at that place where the body is wounded. This is quite a challenge in a time when our incapacity to touch has made AIDS patients pariahs and the homeless are pulled from city streets by hands covered with latex rubber gloves.

Most of us have difficulty touching wounds. It seems difficult to think about hungry or homeless children, let alone to touch them. Therefore, we must pray to God in the name of Jesus, whose gaze avoided no one and whose touch healed the sick, for the grace to overcome our reluctance, exploitation, and injustice.

We can touch the wounds inflicted by arrogance about race, class, gender, and ethnicity. We can touch the wounds of children without homes or schools or health care. We can touch the wounds of church policies and public policies that ignore the urgent needs of children. We can touch the wounds of families and communities broken by despair and poverty.

To touch such wounds is to stand with children. It is to include child advocacy in the larger mission of the church, precisely because it stands in the faith tradition of Jesus. As child advocates, to reach out and touch the wounds of the children of the world is to touch the wounds of our Savior, to remove doubts, to know faith.

Questions for Reflection and Discussion

◆ What new insights do you have into this Bible story?

◆ How have questions or doubts strengthened your faith?

◆ As you think about the children in your congregation and community, what are their wounds? What can you, your family, your committee, and your congregation do to touch these wounds?

Prayer

Holy One, Healer of all wounds, be with us as we search for faith to be your people. Help us see the wounds around us, especially those inflicted on children. Guide us to bring a healing touch of love and care, not given at a distance or hidden from view, but person to person. We pray all this in the name of Jesus Christ, whose gaze avoided no one and whose touch healed the sick. Amen.

Based on a sermon by the Rev. Eileen W. Lindner
Associate General Secretary for Ecumenical Relations
National Council of the Churches of Christ in the USA
New York, NY

Receive the Stranger

Focus: When we welcome children in the name of Jesus, we welcome the God who created us.

Scripture: Mark 9:33–37

For the people of Nepal, the two greatest sins are picking wildflowers and harming children. Disconcerting at first, the juxtaposition of these two acts calls attention to the fragile, seasonal beauty of children and our sacred duty to protect them. Children are more like wildflowers than adult human beings. Children are not like us. This same truth underlies the story from Mark.

This account in Mark, unlike other stories about Jesus and children, does not tell adults to be children or become like children in order to become part of the realm of God. Many sermons have focused on that idea, encouraging adults to be more playful, innocent, and open. Instead, this story says: If you want to be welcomed into the realm of God, you must receive children as strangers and welcome them with a holy heart of gracious hospitality.

Children, even our own, are strangers to us. We forget this, most of the time. We think we know all about them, better than they know themselves. We forget they are not like us when we confuse them with our younger selves and try to use them to make up for our own hurts, disappointments, or failures. We forget they are not like us when we expect them to be miniature versions of adults, when we expect them to be well-behaved, always fitting into our world without muss or fuss.

Because we were once children, we think we know all about childhood. We don't. Once we become adults, we forget what it is to be a child. The passage from childhood to adulthood is not like filling a balloon with air. It is more like changing from a caterpillar into a cocoon into a butterfly. It is a series of metamorphoses, of dramatic changes in which we leave behind forever our old life to take on a new one.

The point of the story in Mark is that the world is not our world. Children are already welcome in it, and not only when they play by our rules. The realm of God is a world which adults share with children, a world about which they teach us as much as we teach them. Certainly the same can be said about the faith community.

Questions for Reflection and Discussion

◆ How do you interpret the Nepalese saying? Could it be said about our nation? Why? Why not?

◆ What differences do you see between "becoming as a child" and receiving or welcoming a child?

◆ How does this story from Mark and the commentary on it relate to your mission as a church? Your work as a committee? Your calling as a disciple of Jesus?

Prayer

To the One who welcomes all creation, we give praise. To the One who sent us a Son to show us the way, we give thanks. To the One who receives us even when we fail to acknowledge that acceptance, we ask forgiveness. To the One for whom no one is a stranger, we seek mercy. Now, as we go about our lives and our work together, send your Spirit to us that we may see you in our midst and always be ready to welcome Your presence in a child. In Jesus' name we pray. Amen.

Based on a sermon by Mary Potter Engel
Professor of Historical Theology
United Theological Seminary, Minneapolis

Selling the Shadow for the Substance: What Parents and the Community Must Do for Children

Focus: We are responsible for being role models and mentors for children — *all* children.

Scripture: Proverbs 20:7
Proverbs 23:26

The wisdom of an illiterate slave woman, Sojourner Truth, has frequently guided me as I have struggled and continue to struggle to see, hear, understand, feel, and heal in my life. American parents, citizens, and leaders need to follow Sojourner's advice "to sell the shadow to support the substance," to be able to know the difference between them, and to pass on that understanding to our children. My parents, many other "ordinary" Black adults, and Black leaders taught these lessons to my generation of Black children.

Because I was the granddaughter, daughter, and sister of Baptist ministers, service was as essential a part of my upbringing as eating and sleeping and going to school. The church was a hub of Black children's social existence, and caring Black adults were buffers against the segregated prison of the outside world that told us we were inferior and unimportant. But our parents said it wasn't so. Our teachers said it wasn't so. And our preachers said it wasn't so. So the message I internalized, despite the ugly racism of my childhood, was to let no man or woman look down on you and to look down on no man or woman.

Children were taught, not by sermonizing but by personal example, that nothing was too lowly to do, and that the work of our hands and the work of our minds were of equal dignity and value. I remember a debate my parents had about whether I was too young to go with an older brother to help clean the bed and bedsores of a very sick, poor woman. I went. And I'm grateful. I learned early how much even the smallest helping hand can mean to a lonely, suffering person.

I also was taught not to ask in the face of need, "Why doesn't somebody do something?" but rather, "Why don't I do something?" As Black children, we couldn't play in public playgrounds or sit at drugstore counters and order a Coke, so my Daddy built a playground and canteen behind the church. Whenever he saw a need, he tried to respond. There were no homes for the Black aged in South Carolina so he began one across the street, and he and my mother and we children cooked and served and cleaned. I resented it sometimes, but I learned that it was my responsibility to take care of elderly family members and neighbors, and that everybody was my neighbor. My mother carried on "the old folks' home" after my father died, and one of my brothers has carried it on since our mother died in 1984.

Finding another child in my room or a pair of my shoes gone was far from unusual, and 12 foster children followed my sister and me and my three brothers as we left home. When my mother died, an old White man in my town asked me what I did. In a flash I realized I do exactly what my parents did — just on a different scale. The ugly external voices of assault of my rural segregated childhood (as a very young child I remember standing and hearing former South Carolina Senator James Byrnes railing at the local courthouse), were tempered by the internal voices of parental and community expectation and pride. My father and I waited anxiously for the *Brown v. Board of Education* decision. We talked about it and what it would mean for my future and the future of millions of other Black children. He died the week before *Brown* was decided. But I and other children lucky enough to have caring and courageous parents were able, in later years, to walk through the new but heavy doors that *Brown* slowly and painfully opened. I remember Langston Hughes coming to my small town, reading poetry and signing a book of poems I still treasure. And I remember having dinner at Benedict College in Columbia, South Carolina, with Mary McLeod Bethune, founder of the National Council of Negro Women, and hearing her boast, "The blacker the berry, the sweeter the juice!" and her stories about going into segregated shops to buy hats and overwhelming the flabbergasted White sales clerks with, "Do you know who I am? I am Mary McLeod Bethune!"

Caring Black adults at all levels, within and without my family, countered the constant negative messages of the outside world. Child-rearing and parental work were inseparable. I went everywhere with my parents and was under the watchful eyes of members of the congregation and community who were my extended parents. They kept me when my parents went out of town, they reported on and chided me when I strayed from the straight and narrow of community expectations, and they basked in and supported my achievements when I did well. Doing well meant high academic achievement, playing the piano for Sunday school or singing, participating in church activities, being helpful to somebody, displaying good manners (which is nothing more than consideration toward others), and reading. I was reminded recently that the only time my Daddy would not give us a chore ("Can't you find something constructive to do?" was his favorite refrain, and he always made sure we did have something constructive to do), was when we were reading. So we read a lot and were clear early on about what our parents and extended community parents valued.

My brother Harry, at a 1981 tribute to our mother by the Mothers Club of the Shiloh Baptist Church (which she founded), thanked her for providing us three things that he thought were instrumental in helping all of us set and reach individual goals: elementary courtesy, character, and respect; inspiring us to dream; and leading us to an awareness of the reality of God.

"Throughout our lives," he said, "we shall reflect your teaching, and you shall live as long as we shall live." And, I hope, as long as our children and their children and their children's children shall live.

Black adults in our churches and community made children feel valued and valuable. They took time and paid attention to us. They struggled to find ways to keep us busy. While life often was very hard and resources very scarce, as for so many today, we always knew who we were, and that the measure of our worth was inside our heads and hearts and not on our backs or in other people's minds. We were told that the world had a lot of problems, that Black people had extra problems, but that we were able and obligated to struggle and change them; that being poor or Black was no excuse for not achieving; and that extra intellectual and material gifts brought with them the privilege and responsibility of sharing with others less fortunate. As a result we never lost hope, like so many children have today. We learned that service is the rent we pay for living. It is the very purpose of life, not something you do in your spare time. And nobody ever promised that it would be simple or easy.

The legacies my parents and preachers and teachers left to my generation of Black children were priceless, but not material: a living faith reflected in daily service, the discipline of hard work and stick-to-it-ness, and a capacity to struggle in the face of adversity ("giving up" and "burnout" were not part of the language of my elders — you got up every morning and you did what you had to do and you got up every time you fell down and tried as many times as you had to until you got it done right). They had grit. They valued family life and family rituals and tried to expose us to good role models.

Role models were of two kinds: those who achieved in the outside world like Marian Anderson, my namesake; former Morehouse College president and Martin Luther King, Jr.'s mentor Benjamin Mays; and former Howard University president Mordecai Johnson, whose three- and four-hour speeches I sat through once a year (my parents believed in osmosis!) even before I could understand or stay awake through them; and those who didn't have a whole lot of education or fancy clothes but who taught us, by the special grace of their lives and without ever opening a book on philosophy or theology other than the Bible, that the kingdom of God is within — in what you are, not in what you have or look like. And I still hope I can be half as good as Miz Lucy McQueen, Miz Tee Kelly, Miz Kate Winston, and Miz Amie Byers (who helped me raise my three sons), "uneducated" but very wise and smart women, who were kind and patient and loving with children and with others. When I went to Spelman College,

Miz Tee sent me shoe boxes with chicken and biscuits and greasy dollar bills. And I think you and I owe our children and their children the same kind of loving support as was given to us by these and so many others like them, of every race and class in America, on whose shoulders of sacrifice and care we all stand today.

It never occurred to any Wright child that we were not going to college or were not expected to share what we learned with the less fortunate. I was 40 years old before I figured out that when my Daddy often responded to my requests for money by saying he didn't have any change, he meant he really didn't have any, rather than meaning "nothing smaller than a $20 bill." When he died, in 1954, he had holes in his shoes but two children out of college, a child in college, and another in divinity school. He knew the difference between substance and shadow.

Questions for Reflection and Discussion

◆ Who are the persons who showed you substance when you were growing up? How do you feel when you recall them?

◆ The verses from the Book of Proverbs are just two of many that remind us of the connections between children and adults and the attainment of wisdom, or the giving of substance rather than shadow. Look through this section for others. What insights relating to children do they give you about relating to children?

◆ In the meditation parents are important figures, but so too are many other adults, related and unrelated. How does your congregation encourage adults to provide substance for children outside their family or outside your congregation?

◆ What roles of leadership might your board or committee take to see that all children are provided with a variety of role models and to support families in the task of nurturing?

Prayer

God of Grace, who created us to be in community with one another and with you, hold us closely as we strain to know the difference between substance and shadow in your sight. Open our eyes and unplug our ears that we may know true wisdom. Alert us to integrity of word and deed. Then grant us the courage and perseverance both to say and do that which is wise and righteous in the presence of children. In Jesus' name, we pray. Amen.

A reflection excerpted from *The Measure of Our Success*, by Marian Wright Edelman, President Children's Defense Fund, Washington, DC

Two Meditations for the Holiday Season

The Hope of a Child

Focus: Advent is the season of hope and expectancy; all children deserve to be a part of this hope and assured of their survival.

Scripture: Luke 1:46–50

Each December wide-eyed and expectant children all over the world wait for Christmas. They wait for presents, to see Grandma and Grandpa, to visit Santa, or to be a lamb or angel in the Christmas pageant. Children also wait to celebrate the birth of the Christ child, the Savior who came with a promise to change the bitterness of a world living without reconciliation. Their eyes reflect the expectancy and hope that is the essence of the Advent season. With each day, the expectancy builds as they dream of what Christmas Day will hold for them. The prophet Isaiah told the people of God what Christmas Day would hold — the coming of One who is called Wonderful Counselor, Mighty God, Everlasting Father, Prince of Peace.

Parents awaiting the arrival of their first child are full of dreams, too. They imagine the kind of life their child will lead. They want the child to enjoy brightly lighted Christmas trees, and to know the love of God. They want their child never to be cold or hungry. During the Christmas season, many children and their families are waiting for something good that they hope will come.

During this time of Advent and through all the seasons of the year there are families who are waiting for something good that may never come. Nearly one-fifth of all children in the United States are poor, and one-third of all poor children are not covered by health insurance. How can they declare God's mercy from generation to generation?

Only children who have an even chance of survival can dream the visions of the Christmas to come. Only children for whom those dreams come true, at least once in a while, can approach Advent with the compassion and expectancy that we learn from Isaiah. Only children who know themselves to be lovingly nurtured and nourished can recognize the loving presence of God through a baby born into poverty nearly 2,000 years ago. Only we can make the dream of survival a reality for all. God grant us that courage.

Questions for Reflection and Discussion

- What hopes or dreams do you hear from the children you know? How are these related to the hope we celebrate during Advent?

- Who are the children without hope in your community? How can you minister to and with them?

- What role does your congregation or committee have in bringing hope to children in your church? In your community? In this nation? In the world?

Prayer

Almighty God, Giver of Hope, praised be your name. Provide us with the courage and stamina to be bearers of hope to the children of your world, even when we are without hope. Grant us the newness of faith that we may be filled with the hope Isaiah brought to the nation of Israel. Show us the great light that we may rejoice before you. In the name of the Messiah who is to come. Amen.

The Heart of a Child

Focus: We can turn a child's heart to God when we reveal God and emulate Christ through loving and empowering relationships with children.

Scripture: Luke 1:51–55

After the weeks of preparation during Advent, Christmas arrives and we open our hearts to celebrate the birth of Jesus Christ. We celebrate not because of the birth of Jesus Christ as a baby, even though the message of the heavenly host and the visit of the Magi mark this birth as an extraordinary one. We celebrate this birth because of what the baby has become in our lives — the Savior, the fulfillment of the promise to the people of Israel, and to all their descendants.

Christ came that our hearts and the hearts of children everywhere might be filled with love, not hate; with hope, not despair; with compassion, not selfishness. Christ came to change the hearts of humankind in that ancient time and today. Christ came to teach all creation how to love God and one another.

15

How we love our children has a powerful influence on how they will love others, and God. How we love others, seen and unseen, teaches our children our understanding of the love Christ has brought to us. What kind of love do we give our children? What kind of love do we teach by example? We can strive to love children as unconditionally as God loves us. We can give to others as wholly as Christ gave for us. We can speak out for children in places of power as courageously as Christ spoke out for children and all those who were powerless. We can welcome children into our midst as Christ beckoned them to him. When we do all this in the example of Christ, we help shape the hearts of our children, and reshape our own as well.

Question for Reflection and Discussion

◆ Who are the powerless children in your church? In your community? In your nation? In the world?

◆ How can you, your family, your committee, and your congregation represent these children to those in the seats of power?

◆ What examples do your children see of God's love in your congregation? How can you make these examples more visible to children? How can you increase the examples for children to see and participate in?

Prayer

Loving God, Shaper of the universe and Bestower of all good things, when we pause to ponder your love we know that we can never comprehend its breadth or its depth. May we daily show our children but glimpses of that love so they too will give their hearts to you. Teach us to stand up to evil and to speak for children and all others who are powerless in the sight of our ruler. For us we pray. Amen.

Based on a biblical reflection
by the Rev. Ruth Fowler, Pastor
Richboro Baptist Church, Staten Island, NY

❧

CHAPTER 2

Children and the Bible

Read through the following scripture passages for a biblical basis for ministry with and for children. Use them for personal reflection, as the basis of a sermon or Bible study, to prepare a litany, as verses for banners or posters, or to combine them in a choral reading. All of the biblical passages cited in Chapter 1 of this section are found here.

Then Esau said, "Let us journey on our way, and I will go alongside you." But Jacob said to him, "My lord knows that the children are frail and that the flocks and herds, which are nursing, are a care to me; and if they are overdriven for one day, all the flocks will die. Let my lord pass on ahead of his servant, and I will lead on slowly, according to the pace of the cattle that are before me and according to the pace of the children, until I come to my lord in Seir."

Genesis 33:12–14

You shall not wrong or oppress a resident alien, for you were aliens in the land of Egypt. You shall not abuse any widow or orphan. If you do abuse them, when they cry out to me, I will surely heed their cry....

Exodus 22:21–23

Hear, O Israel: The Lord is our God, the Lord alone. You shall love the Lord your God with all your heart, and with all your soul, and with all your might. Keep these words that I am commanding you today in your heart. Recite them to your children and talk about them when you are at home and when you are away, when you lie down and when you rise. Bind them as a sign on your hand, fix them as an emblem on your forehead, and write them on the doorposts of your house and on your gates.

Deuteronomy 6:4–9

O Lord, you will hear the desire of the meek; you will strengthen their heart, you will incline your ear to do justice for the orphan and the oppressed, so that those from earth may strike terror no more.

Psalm 10:17–18

Yet it was you who took me from the womb; you kept me safe on my mother's breast. On you I was cast from my birth, and since my mother bore me you have been my God. Do not be far from me, for trouble is near and there is no one to help.

Psalm 22:9–11

Father of orphans and protector of widows is God in his holy habitation. God gives the desolate a home to live in; he leads out the prisoners to prosperity, but the rebellious live in a parched land.

Psalm 68:5–6

Happy is everyone who fears the Lord, who walks in his ways. You shall eat the fruit of the labor of your hands; you shall be happy, and it shall go well with you. Your wife will be like a fruitful vine within your house; your children will be like olive shoots around your table. Thus shall the man be blessed who fears the Lord. The Lord bless you from Zion. May you see the prosperity of Jerusalem all the days of your life. May you see your children's children. Peace be upon Israel!

Psalm 128

O Lord, my heart is not lifted up, my eyes are not raised too high; I do not occupy myself with things too great and too marvelous for me. But I have calmed and quieted my soul, like a weaned child with its mother; my soul is like the weaned child that is with me. O Israel, hope in the Lord from this time on and forevermore.

Psalm 131

May our sons in their youth be like plants full grown, our daughters like corner pillars, cut for the building of a palace.

Psalm 144:12

The righteous walk in integrity — happy are the children who follow them! *Proverbs 20:7*

Train children in the right way, and when old, they will not stray. *Proverbs 22:6*

My child, give me your heart, and let your eyes observe my ways. *Proverbs 23:26*

Speak out for those who cannot speak, for the rights of all the destitute. Speak out, judge righteously, defend the rights of the poor and needy. *Proverbs 31:8–9*

For a child has been born for us, a son given to us; authority rests upon his shoulders; and he is named Wonderful Counselor, Mighty God, Everlasting Father, Prince of Peace. *Isaiah 9:6*

A shoot shall come out from the stump of Jesse, and a branch shall grow out of his roots.... His delight shall be in the fear of the Lord. He shall not judge by what his eyes see, or decide by what his ears hear; but with righteousness he shall judge the poor, and decide with equity for the meek of the earth.... The wolf shall live with the lamb, the leopard shall lie down with the kid, the calf and the lion and the fatling together, and a little child shall lead them. *Isaiah 11:1, 3–4, 6*

Is not this the fast that I choose: to loose the bonds of injustice, to undo the thongs of the yoke, to let the oppressed go free, and to break every yoke? Is it not to share your bread with the hungry, and bring the homeless poor into your house; when you see the naked, to cover them, and not to hide yourself from your own kin? Then your light shall break forth like the dawn, and your healing shall spring up quickly; your vindicator shall go before you, the glory of the Lord shall be your rear guard. Then you shall call, and the Lord will answer; you shall cry for help, and he will say, Here I am. *Isaiah 58:6–9a*

If you remove the yoke from among you, the pointing of the finger, the speaking of evil, if you offer your food to the hungry and satisfy the needs of the afflicted, then your light shall rise in the darkness and your gloom be like the noonday. The Lord will guide you continually, and satisfy your needs in parched places, and make your bones strong; and you shall be like a watered garden, like a spring of water, whose waters never fail. Your ancient ruins shall be rebuilt; you shall raise up the foundations of many generations; you shall be called the repairer of the breach, the restorer of streets to live in. *Isaiah 58:9b–12*

And the streets of the city shall be full of boys and girls playing in its streets. *Zechariah 8:5*

When Herod saw that he had been tricked by the wise men, he was infuriated, and he sent and killed all the children in and around Bethlehem who were two years old or under, according to the time that he had learned from the wise men. Then was fulfilled what had been spoken through the prophet Jeremiah:
"A voice was heard in Ramah, wailing and loud lamentation, Rachel weeping for her children; she refused to be consoled, because they are no more." *Matthew 2:16–18*

"Ask, and it will be given you; search, and you will find; knock, and the door will be opened for you. For everyone who asks receives, and everyone who searches finds, and for everyone who knocks, the door will be opened. Is there anyone among you who, if your child asks for bread, will give a stone? Or if the child asks for a fish, will give a snake? If you then, who are evil, know how to give good gifts to your children, how much more will your Father in heaven give good things to those who ask him!" *Matthew 7:7–11*

At that time the disciples came to Jesus and asked, "Who is the greatest in the kingdom of heaven?" He called a child, whom he put among them, and said, "Truly I tell you, unless you change and become like children, you will never enter the kingdom of heaven. Whoever becomes humble like this child is the greatest in the kingdom of heaven. Whoever welcomes one such child in my name welcomes me.
"If any of you put a stumbling block before one of these little ones who believe in me, it would be better for you if a great millstone were fastened around your neck and you were drowned in the depth of the sea. Woe to the world because of stumbling blocks! Occasions for stumbling are bound to come, but woe to the one by whom the stumbling block comes!" *Matthew 18:1–7*
See also Mark 9:33–37, 42 and
Luke 9:46–48

"Teacher, which commandment in the law is the greatest?" [Jesus] said to him, " 'You shall love the Lord your God with all your heart, and with all your soul, and with all your mind.' This is the greatest and first commandment. And a second is like it: 'You shall love your neighbor as yourself.' On these two commandments hang all the law and the prophets." *Matthew 22:36–40*

LOOKING AT CHILDREN THROUGH THE EYES OF FAITH

People were bringing little children to him in order that he might touch them; and the disciples spoke sternly to them. But when Jesus saw this, he was indignant and said to them, "Let the little children come to me; do not stop them; for it is to such as these that the kingdom of God belongs. Truly I tell you, whoever does not receive the kingdom of God as a little child will never enter it." And he took them up in his arms, laid his hands on them, and blessed them.

Mark 10:13–16
See also Matthew 19:13–15 and
Luke 18:15–17

And Mary said, "My soul magnifies the Lord, and my spirit rejoices in God my Savior, for he has looked with favor on the lowliness of his servant. Surely, from now on all generations will call me blessed; for the Mighty One has done great things for me, and holy is his name. His mercy is for those who fear him from generation to generation. He has shown strength with his arm; he has scattered the proud in the thoughts of their hearts. He has brought down the powerful from their thrones, and lifted up the lowly; he has filled the hungry with good things, and sent the rich away empty. He has helped his servant Israel, in remembrance of his mercy, according to the promise he made to our ancestors, to Abraham and to his descendants forever."

Luke 1:46–55

Then Jesus told them a parable about their need to pray always and not to lose heart. He said, "In a certain city there was a judge who neither feared God nor had respect for people. In that city there was a widow who kept coming to him and saying, 'Grant me justice against my opponent.' For a while he refused; but later he said to himself, 'Though I have no fear of God and no respect for anyone, yet because this widow keeps bothering me, I will grant her justice, so that she may not wear me out by continually coming....'" And the Lord said, "Listen to what the unjust judge says. And will not God grant justice to his chosen ones who cry to him day and night? Will he delay long in helping them? I tell you, he will quickly grant justice to them. And yet, when the Son of Man comes, will he find faith on earth?"

Luke 18:1–8

After this Jesus went to the other side of the Sea of Galilee, also called the Sea of Tiberias. A large crowd kept following him, because they saw the signs that he was doing for the sick. Jesus went up the moun-

tain and sat down there with his disciples. Now the Passover, the festival of the Jews, was near. When he looked up and saw a large crowd coming toward him, Jesus said to Philip, "Where are we to buy bread for these people to eat?" He said this to test him, for he himself knew what he was going to do. Philip answered him, "Six months' wages would not buy enough bread for each of them to get a little." One of his disciples, Andrew, Simon Peter's brother, said to him, "There is a boy here who has five barley loaves and two fish. But what are they among so many people?" Jesus said, "Make the people sit down." Now there was a great deal of grass in the place; so they sat down, about five thousand in all. Then Jesus took the loaves, and when he had given thanks, he distributed them to those who were seated; so also the fish, as much as they wanted. When they were satisfied, he told his disciples, "Gather up the fragments left over, so that nothing may be lost." So they gathered them up, and from the fragments of the five barley loaves, left by those who had eaten, they filled twelve baskets. When the people saw the sign that he had done, they began to say, "This is indeed the prophet who is to come into the world."

John 6:1–14

But Thomas (who was called the Twin), one of the twelve, was not with [the disciples] when Jesus came. So the other disciples told him, "We have seen the Lord." But he said to them, "Unless I see the mark of the nails in his hands, and put my finger in the mark of the nails and my hand in his side, I will not believe."

A week later his disciples were again in the house, and Thomas was with them. Although the doors were shut, Jesus came and stood among them and said, "Peace be with you." Then he said to Thomas, "Put your finger here and see my hands. Reach out your hand and put it in my side. Do not doubt but believe." Thomas answered him, "My Lord and my God!" Jesus said to him, "Have you believed because you have seen me? Blessed are those who have not seen and yet have come to believe."

John 20:24–29

Let mutual love continue. Do not neglect to show hospitality to strangers, for by doing that some have entertained angels without knowing it. Remember those who are in prison, as though you were in prison with them; those who are being tortured, as though you yourselves were being tortured.

Hebrews 13:1–3

CHAPTER 3

Prayers, Litanies, Poems, Stories, and Songs

Prayers and Litanies

The prayers and litanies in this section are samples for you to use as you find them, to adapt, or to use as models in preparing your own. Additional prayers and litanies are found in the sample Children's Sabbaths on pages 30–37. For the litanies, the leader's words are in regular type, and the people's response in **boldface**.

Call to Worship

Let us praise God who has brought us together.

With one voice we give praise.

Dear friends, the gift of children is both a joyous and a solemn treasure with which we have been entrusted. We are gathered together today to celebrate and to honor children and to remind ourselves of our responsibility to them. It is an occasion for rejoicing and for remembrance. Let us join in giving thanks to God, the Giver of life, for the gift of children; and raise our voices, together in prayer, for our children's many needs.

From *Recognizing and Celebrating Children*
Congregations Concerned for Children, Minneapolis

Call to Worship

"[Jesus] called a child and put it among them, and said, 'Truly I tell you, unless you change and become like children, you will never enter the kingdom of heaven.' "

We come together today seeking within ourselves the faith, hope, and love of a child.

"[Jesus said] 'Whoever welcomes one such child in my name welcomes me.' "

We come together today seeking the vision, understanding, and commitment to "welcome" the children as you would have us.

Be with us now in our worship, O God, that we may both find the trusting faithfulness of children and assume our adult responsibility to nurture and protect all children.

Written by Shannon P. Daley
Director of Religious Affairs
Children's Defense Fund

Prayer of Confession (in unison)

God, forgive us for being asleep so often when you need us. You writhe in the agony of the world's hungry, while we worry over the menu. You weep with the soul of one who is friendless, while we fret over whom to invite to some social occasion. God, forgive us for sometimes taking our children, your children, for granted, and not hearing their special needs, for not loving them as you require. Wake us up to the needs of our sisters and brothers everywhere. In Christ's name we pray. Amen.

Assurance of Forgiveness

"The mercy of God is everlasting." Such is the witness of our heritage, which, being interpreted for our times, means: Now and in every moment our past is accepted, our future is opened, our present is offered to us afresh. This is the truth that sets us free. In Jesus Christ we are forgiven and set free. Amen.

Written for the closing service of worship for the
Child Advocacy Conference
Presbyterian Church (USA), Tampa, FL

A Litany for Children

O Lord of light and Source of all creation, we praise and glorify you for the children you have given us.

Accept our thanksgiving, O Lord.

For their lives, their inquiring minds and receptive spirits, for their health and growth,

We humbly praise you, O God.

For their beauty and innocence, their laughter and tears, their joyous ways that fill us with wonder and delight,

We humbly praise you, O God.

For their youthful vision by which you lead them trustingly into the future,

We humbly praise you, O God.

For your constant protection, which keeps them safe from harm,

We humbly praise you, O God.

&

For our families and for your loving forgiveness which allows parents and children to make mistakes and, confessing them, to continue to live in harmony,

We humbly praise you, O God.

O God of Abraham, Isaac, Jacob, of Sarah, Rachel, and Rebecca, of your prophets and teachers in every time and place, generation after generation you call your children forth to honor and obey you.

In awe and gratitude we praise you, O Lord.

For our children's growth in faith and their simple trust in you in these complex and troubled times,

We thank you, O Lord.

That your Spirit will remain with them as they grow, guiding them in the ways of justice, righteousness, and peace,

We pray to you, O Lord.

For all those who in the faith minister to and teach our children and are models of truth and goodness,

We thank you, O Lord.

&

Defender of the oppressed and the orphan, we pray for all children in our nation and our world who suffer from poverty, injustice, and fear.

Hear the cries of your children, O Lord.

For children who are runaways, homeless, in institutions or jails,

In your tender mercy, protect them, God.

For children who are disabled in mind or body,

In your tender mercy, encourage and strengthen them, O God.

For children who this day will not have enough to eat,

In your tender mercy, provide them food, O God.

For babies born at risk, for children who are sick, and for those who lack proper health care, especially pregnant teenagers,

In your tender mercy, help and sustain them, O God.

For children who are victims of race or class discrimination, poor education, drug or alcohol abuse, and hopelessness,

In your tender mercy, grant them lives of hope and a future, O God.

For children who daily experience the fear and pain of war and civil strife, especially in the countries of _____,

In your tender mercy, defend and protect them, O God.

&

O God, Loving Parent, we pray for our families and the families of our nation.

Open our hearts, O Lord.

For children and parents forced to live apart because of poverty, illness, jail sentences, or migratory work,

Embrace and uphold them, Spirit of God.

For children and parents enduring the pain and grief of death or divorce,

Send your comfort, Spirit of God.

For families facing loss of jobs or the anxiety of an uncertain future,

Give them hope, Spirit of God.

For children and parents who live in conflict and misunderstanding,

Give them your peace and truth, Spirit of God.

For single mothers and single fathers who experience the burden of raising children alone,

Grant them courage and love, Spirit of God.

&

PRAYERS, LITANIES, POEMS, STORIES, AND SONGS

O Ruler of all, our sure defense, we pray for the world our children live in and will inherit.

Have pity on us, O Lord.

For the sake of all children, bring an end to the buildup and proliferation of nuclear weapons. Preserve us from attitudes and acts that threaten the annihilation of all life and the future we hold in trust for the children.

We cry to you, Creator of all.

For the sake of all children, bring an end to conflict and war between nations. Give us hearts and minds of peace and help us to teach peace to our children.

We cry to you, Creator of all.

For the sake of all children, bring an end to our misuse and pollution of the land, air, and water of the Earth. Teach us to be stewards and guardians of your creation.

We cry to you, Creator of all.

For the sake of all children, bring an end to the injustices caused and abetted by those in places of power. May our hearts and minds be changed by the cries of your hungry and suffering children.

We cry to you, Creator of all.

❧

O Holy God, through whom all things are transformed and made whole, grant us and our children newness of life. Refresh and sustain us with the glorious vision of your world to come in which all children will live in peace and harmony, all children will be filled with good things to eat, and all children will rest secure in your love.

O God Most High, whom we name Yahweh, Lord, and Our Father, Creator, Redeemer, and Sanctifier of the world, we ask these things on behalf of our children and generations yet unborn who will live to praise your Holy Name, world without end. Amen.

Written by the Children's Defense Fund for
National Children's Day, June 1982
The Washington Cathedral, Washington, DC

Prayer of Intercession

Pray always, and do not lose heart. For the millions of children who are living in poverty, that they might receive the basic necessities to develop their potential,

O God, hear our prayer. Help us not to lose heart.

For the children who cried themselves to sleep last night, stomachs tight with hunger, that they be nourished and comforted,

O God, hear our prayer. Help us not to lose heart.

For the children who will tuck themselves into bed tonight, while their parents burrow into briefcases or newspapers, that families make time to enjoy and celebrate each other,

O God, hear our prayer. Help us not to lose heart.

For the parents who struggle to make ends meet, find jobs, and clothe and feed their families, that they find support and compassion,

O God, hear our prayer. Help us not to lose heart.

For those in positions of power, that their hearts will not be like that of the unjust judge, but instead be moved by your mercy and justice,

O God, hear our prayer. Help us not to lose heart.

For ourselves, that we are moved from complaisance about poverty and that we find the faithful persistence of the widow to challenge injustice,

O God, hear our prayer. Help us not to lose heart.

"Will not God grant justice to [God's] chosen ones who cry to [God] day and night? Will God delay long in helping them? I tell you, [God] will quickly grant justice to them."

O God, hear our prayer. Help us not to lose heart.

Written by Shannon P. Daley
Director of Religious Affairs
Children's Defense Fund
Based on Luke 18:1–8

Benediction

Into your hands, O God, we place ourselves, the guardians of your children. Support and strengthen us as we seek to make the world a more welcoming place for them. Unify us in our concern and respect for them.

Into your hands also we place the children of our homes, our cities, and the world. Support them in their joys and in their sorrows, strengthen their families, enlighten their governments, shelter them from evil. Through your guidance, may we respond to their needs that they may discover the joy of your creation and know the bounty of your unending love. All this we ask in your name. Amen.

From *Recognizing and Celebrating Children*
Congregations Concerned for Children, Minneapolis

Poems

Greenless Child

I watched her go uncelebrated into the second grade,
A greenless child,
Gray among the orange and yellow,
Attached too much to corners and to other people's
    sunshine.
She colors the rainbow brown
And leaves balloons unopened in their packages.
Oh who will touch this greenless child?
Who will plant alleluias in her heart
And send her dancing into all the colors of God?
Or will she be left on the kitchen table —
like an unwrapped package —
Too dull for anyone to take the trouble?
Does God think we're her keeper?

Ann Weems, from *Reaching for Rainbows:*
Resources for Creative Worship
Copyright 1980, The Westminster Press
Reprinted and used by permission of
The Westminster/John Knox Press

The Cry of the Children

Do ye hear the children weeping, O my brothers,
Ere the sorrow comes with years?
They are leaning their young heads against their
    mothers,
And that cannot stop their tears.
The young lambs are bleating in the meadows,
The young birds are chirping in the nest,
The young fawns are playing with the shadows,
The young flowers are blowing toward the west —
But the young, young children, O my brothers,
They are weeping bitterly!
They are weeping in the playtime of the others,
In the country of the free.

Elizabeth Barrett Browning (1843)

The Child's Name Is "Today"

We are guilty of many errors and faults
but our worst crime is abandoning the children,
neglecting the fountain of life.
Many of the things we need can wait.
The child cannot.
Right now is the time bones are being formed,
blood is being made, senses are being developed.
To the child we cannot answer "Tomorrow."
The child's name is "Today."

Adapted from a poem by Gabriela Mistral
Nobel Prize-winning poet from Chile

Children Learn What They Live

If children live with criticism, they learn to condemn.
If children live with hostility, they learn to fight.
If children live with ridicule, they learn to be shy.
If children live with shame, they learn to feel guilty.
If children live with tolerance, they learn to be patient.
If children live with encouragement, they learn
    confidence.
If children live with praise, they learn to appreciate.
If children live with fairness, they learn justice.
If children live with security, they learn to have faith.
If children live with approval, they learn to like
    themselves.
If children live with acceptance and friendship,
    they learn to find love in the world.

Adapted from Dorothy Law Nolte
Baptist Leader, July 1972

A Child

Bitter are the tears of a child: sweeten them.
Deep are the thoughts of a child: quiet them.
Sharp is the grief of a child: take it from him.
Soft is the heart of a child: do not harden it.

Lady Pamela Wyndham Glenconner
(nineteenth century)

Child Hunger

Every night it's the same old thing. We go to the
church for dinner, walk home to our one bedroom
apartment and go in bed for a night full of bad dreams.
In the morning we walk around town looking for food
in garbage cans. We find cereal boxes with a little cereal left in it and a rotten apple. At six o'clock we
start walking to the church for our dinner. I made a
poem that expresses my feelings about the way the
day crawls by:

Cereal and a rotten apple for breakfast
Nothing for lunch
A dinner at the Baptist church
And that's the way my day goes by.

Cathy, a fifth-grader from New Mexico
Reprinted from *Child Poverty in America*,
Children's Defense Fund, 1991

PRAYERS, LITANIES, POEMS, STORIES, AND SONGS

Stories

For Their Sake

When Israel stood to receive the Torah,
The Holy One, blessed be He, said to them:
I am giving you my Torah.
Bring me good guarantors that you will guard it,
and I shall give it to you.
They said:
Our fathers are our guarantors.
The Holy One, blessed be He, said to them:
Your fathers are unacceptable to me.
Yet bring me good guarantors,
and I shall give it to you.
They said to him:
Master of the Universe,
our prophets are our guarantors.
He said to them:
Your prophets are unacceptable to me.
Yet bring me good guarantors,
and I shall give it to you.
They said:
Behold, our children are our guarantors.
The Holy One, blessed be He, said:
They are certainly good guarantors.
For their sake, I give you the Torah.

Canticles Rabbah (Midrash)

The Story of the Children's Fire

The whole community sits around a circle called a Medicine Wheel. Around that wheel are representatives of all the different aspects of the community. In the East, there's the fool. In the West, there's the witch. In the South, there's the hunter. In the North, there's the creator. Others positioned around the circle are the shaman, the politician, etc. And in the center of the circle is the children's fire. Next to the children's fire sit the grandfather and grandmother. If you want to build a condominium in the community of Spirit Lake, you have to enter the Medicine Wheel in the East, at the position of the fool. The question you ask is, "May I build a condo on Spirit Lake?" The fool takes your question, turns it around backwards and asks, "What would Spirit Lake say about such a condo?" You then have to take the question the fool gives you to everyone around the Medicine Wheel. Each will respond to you according to their position in the community. The last people you must ask the question to are the grandmother and grandfather who guard the children's fire. If these two decide that the request is not good for the children's fire, then the answer is "no." They are the only ones in the circle who have veto power. The concept of the ultimate question is simple. Does it hurt or help the children's fire? If it can pass the test of the children's fire, then it can be done.

Excerpted from materials
by Congregations Concerned for Children.
(This story was told to Magaly Rodriguez Mossman
by Robin Van Doren, who heard it from elders of
the Hopi Nation. It could be the basis of a role play
by youths or others.)

A Ten-Year-Old's Story

I was asked to tell you what it's like to live in a single-parent home with no money.

Sometimes it's sad because I feel different from other kids. For instance, when other kids get to go to fun places and I can't because I don't have enough money and they do.

Most of my friends get an allowance but I don't because my mom doesn't have enough money to pay me. They get to get the things that they want and need and I don't.

The other day in school we had this balloon contest, and it only cost one dollar and out of three years I haven't been able to get one.

Me and my brother are a little hard on shoes. This summer the only shoes we had were thongs, and when church time came, the only shoes we had to wear were one pair of church shoes. The one that got them first got to wear them. The one that didn't had to wear a pair of my mom's tennis shoes or my sister's.

I have a big brother. He is not my real brother. He is with the Big Brothers and Big Sisters Association. Once I tried to tell my big brother about welfare. It was so embarrassing I was about to cry. I don't like Joe just because he takes me to a fun place every week; I like Joe because he makes me feel special.

Sometimes I pray that I won't be poor no more and sometimes I sit up at night and cry. But it didn't change anything. Crying just helps the hurt and the pain. It doesn't change anything.

One day, I asked my mom why the kids always tease me and she said because they don't understand, but I do understand about being on welfare and being poor, and it can hurt.

An anonymous 10-year-old

LOOKING AT CHILDREN THROUGH THE EYES OF FAITH

Hymns, Songs, and Anthems

"All Things Bright and Beautiful," by C. F. Alexander (LHS 827, PH 267, UMH 147)

"All Who Love and Serve Your City," by Erik Routley (BP 165, LBW 436, PH 413, UMH 433)

"Bring Forth the Kingdom" (LHS 821)

"Called as Partners in Christ's Service," by Jane Parker Huber (PH 343)

"Canto de Esperanza" (PH 432)

"Child of Blessing, Child of Promise," by Ronald S. Cole-Turner (PH 498, UMH 611)

"Child of Wonder," by Marty Haugen (GIA)

"Christian Women, Christian Men," by Dorothy Diemer Hendry (PH 348)

"Come Now, You Blessed," by Ruth Duck (BP 207)

"The Church of Christ, in Every Age," by F. Pratt Green (LBW 433)

"Everybody Is Somebody's Child" by Doug Peters, adapted by Jerry Leggett (BWM)

"For Courage to Do Justice" (UMH 456)

"For the Beauty of the Earth" (LBW 561, PH 473, UMH 92)

"For the Healing of the Nations" (UMH 428)

"God of Justice, God of Mercy," by Jane Parker Huber (BP 86H)

"God, Who Stretched the Spangled Heavens" (LBW 463, PH 268, UMH 150)

"Guide My Feet" (traditional African-American song, PH 354)

"Help, O Lord, the Thrown Away," by Bob Russ (BP 150)

"Help Us Accept Each Other," by Fred Kaan and Doreen Potter (BP 186, PH 358, UMH 560)

"Here I Am, Lord," by Daniel L. Schutte (BP 129, PH 525, UMH 593)

"He's Got the Whole World in His Hands" (SNG)

"Hope for the Children," by Douglas Clark (BP 90)

"Hosanna, Loud Hosanna" (PH 89, UMH 278)

"How Happy Is Each Child of God" (PH 239)

"If We're Going to Walk Together," by R. Tiffany Bates

"In Christ There Is No East or West" (BP 87, LBW 359, PH 439, 440, UMH 548) Text by T. Oxenham. Adaptation by Grace Moore, Nancy Krody, and Ruth Duck.

"Jesu Came and Laid Down His Life for Us," by Tom Colvin (BP 172)

"Jesus Loves Me!" by Anna Bartlett Warner (PH 304, SNG, UMH 191)

"Kum ba Ya" (traditional, BP 216, PH 338, UMH 494)

"Let the Whole Creation Cry" (LBW 242, PH 256)

"Let Us Talents and Tongues Employ" (BP 213, PH 514, LHS 770) Text: Fred Kaan

"Live into Hope," by Jane Parker Huber (BP 217, PH 332)

"Lord of Our Growing Years" (PH 279)

"The Lord of the Dance" by Sydney Carter (SNG)

"Lord, You Give the Great Commission," Jeffrey W. Rowthorn (BP 106, LHS 748, PH 429, UMH 584)

"Love Them Now," by Richard Avery and Donald Marsh

"Morning Has Broken," by Eleanor Farjeon (SNG, PH 469, UMH 145)

"Now in This Banquet" (LHS 775)

"Now Praise the Hidden God of Love," by Fred Pratt Green (PH 402)

"O Day of God, Draw Nigh," by Robert B. Y. Scott (BP 120, PH 452, UMH 730)

"O for a World," by Miriam Therese Winter (PH 386)

"O God of All the Years of Life," by Jane Parker Huber

"Our Parent, by Whose Name," by F. Bland Tucker (UMH 447)

"Pass It On" (replace "friend" in verse 3 with "child"), by Kurt Kaiser (SNG, UMH 572)

"The Prayer of St. Francis" (Make Me A Channel of Your Peace), music by Sebastian Temple

"Seek Ye First," by Karen Lafferty (SNG, UMH 405)

"Sing Out Earth and Skies" (LHS 839)

"Tell Me the Stories of Jesus" (UMH 277)

"There's a Spirit in the Air" (BP 214, PH 433, UMH 192)

"Today We All Are Called to Be Disciples" (PH 434)

"We Are Your People," by Brian Wren (PH 436)

"We Lift Our Hands, O God, in Praise," by Gregory Smith (BP 171)

"We Shall Overcome," by Frank Hamilton, Guy Carawan, Zilpia Horton, and Pete Seeger (SNG, BP 222, UMH 533)

"We Thank You God for Strength of Arm," by Robert Davis

"What Does the Lord Require" (PH 405, UMH 441)

"You Made Your Human Family One," by Davie A. Robb (BP 119)

BP   *Banquet of Praise.* Gary P. Davison, Editor. Washington, DC: Bread for the World. Copyright 1990.

BWM *Songs to End the Silent War.* Jerry Leggett and Friends. Available from Better World Music, P.O. Box 1477, San Marcos, CA 92079.

GIA   GIA Publications, 7404 South Mason Avenue, Chicago, IL 60638.

LBW *Lutheran Book of Worship.* Minneapolis: Augsburg Publishing House. Copyright 1978.

LHS   *Hymnal Supplement.* Chicago: GIA Publications, Inc. Copyright 1991.

PH   *The Presbyterian Hymnal.* Louisville: Westminster/John Knox Press. Copyright 1990.

SNG   *Songs.* Compiled by Yohann Anderson. Songs and Creations, Inc., P.O. Box 7, San Anselmo, CA 94960. Tel: (800) 227-2188.

UMH *The United Methodist Hymnal.* Nashville: The United Methodist Publishing House. Copyright 1989.

Prayer for Change

Tune: Dix: "For the Beauty of the Earth"

1. For the beauty of the earth,
   For the glory of the skies,
   For the children ev'rywhere,
   With their sad or joyful cries,
   God of All, to Thee we raise
   This our hymn of grateful praise.

2. For the beauty of the earth,
   For the glory of the skies,
   For each child whose life of worth
   May be missed by human eyes,
   God of All, to Thee we raise
   This our hymn of grateful praise.

3. For the hungry, homeless ones
   Seeking life despite despair,
   For the nations buying guns
   While the children wait for care,
   God of all, this plea we raise:
   Help us change our hurtful ways.

4. Thanks for gifts the children bring:
   Love and trust and open hands.
   Help us give them songs to sing,
   Meet their needs as love commands.
   God of all, this prayer we raise:
   Let us bring forth better days.

Virginia Sargent
American Baptist Churches in the U.S.A.

CHAPTER 4

෭෧

Celebrating Children's Day and Organizing a Children's Sabbath

Involving children in the life of the church and lifting up their needs and gifts are vital ways in which your congregation acts as an advocate for children. The gifts and the needs of children can be integrated, regularly, into the worship and programs of every congregation.

There are two special times to highlight and focus attention on children, however: Children's Day in the summer and the National Observance of Children's Sabbaths in the fall.

Annual commitment to participating in Children's Day and the National Observance of Children's Sabbaths is an important signal to both children and adults that the "children's ministry" to which we are called includes both recognizing and celebrating the God-given gifts and specialness of children, and opening our eyes and responding to the vulnerability and urgent needs of children.

Children's Day

Children's Day, celebrated in many parts of the U.S. on the second Sunday in June, provides an opportunity to celebrate the special contributions of children and to thank those who have worked with or for children throughout the year, such as church school teachers and youth group leaders.

The first Children's Day in the United States was celebrated in June 1856 at the Universalist Church in Chelsea, Massachusetts. It followed the European tradition of Confirmation Day in the Roman Catholic and Lutheran churches, when all the children of the congregation carried bouquets of spring flowers into the church. By 1868 Children's Day was recognized officially by the Methodist Church as the second Sunday in June, and soon other denominations began observing it. Children's Day is now part of the calendar of the National Council of the Churches of Christ in the USA.

For some congregations, a Children's Day (also known as Rally Day) is an annual tradition. For others, it may be a new celebration. Whatever your congregation's situation, use this occasion to celebrate children as an integral part of your faith community and to thank all of those who have worked with children throughout the year.

National Observance of Children's Sabbaths

The National Observance of Children's Sabbaths is an important time to raise awareness about the needs of children and to involve all ages of the congregation in activities that help meet them. The National Observance of Children's Sabbaths is designated for the third weekend of October. (Churches whose congregational calendars conflict with this date are urged to find a more suitable weekend; what is most important is setting aside time to focus on and respond to children's needs.) Throughout this weekend, a wide range of denominations, congregations, and individuals participate according to their own faith tradition and make a common commitment to the well-being of children. The National Observance of Children's Sabbaths joins congregations in lifting a united voice of concern for children, exploring the faith-based imperative to speak out on behalf of the vulnerable, and encouraging a commitment to help children and families through prayer, education, service, and advocacy.

Beginning with Friday night services in synagogues and concluding with church services on Sunday, congregations across the nation focus worship services, religious education programs, and congregational activities on the needs of children and how people of faith can help to meet those needs. Many congregations develop a special theme for their own service, some join others for interfaith services, and some plan community-wide activities.

Planning a Children's Sabbath

Considering a Theme and Format

As you think about planning this special day, use one of the meditations from pages 7–16 and reflect on the importance of children in your life and in the life of your community of faith. Jesus often pointed to children as models for our spiritual development. They are the source of our hope for the future. Their care and welfare are the responsibility of every adult Christian.

A Children's Sabbath can introduce a specific scriptural theme, such as "Let the Children Come to Me." A Children's Sabbath can inform and involve the congregation in a social issue especially pertinent to the children in your local area, whether that be child poverty or adoption and foster care.

Once you have selected a possible theme for the Children's Sabbath, consider the format. Although your congregation may wish to observe Children's Sabbath exclusively through the worship service, you can use the resources and suggestions throughout this book to extend the scope of the celebration and its purpose.

Forming a Planning Committee

When you have given some thought to the theme and format, take the idea of a Children's Sabbath to your church staff or the appropriate board or committee of your congregation. Once you have their agreement, your planning begins in earnest. Recruit a committee to help plan and carry out the day. Invite children and young people to join you. If you are trying to raise the awareness of the congregation about a particular issue, invite someone with relevant information and experience to work with you.

Convening the Planning Committee

Take time at the first meeting to get to know one another and to be clear about your task. Select a meditation or prayer from pages 7–16 to use in beginning your work together. Adapt it as necessary.

Present any preliminary decisions that have been made regarding the theme, format, and scope for the Children's Sabbath. If the scope is still flexible, look at the worship service, the church school hour, and the fellowship time. Plan for one segment or for all three. Consider having a congregational meal or picnic as a part of the day. You may concentrate all your efforts on a single day or use the Children's Sabbath as either the kickoff or the culmination of an education series on a theme related to children.

After you have determined the basic range of activities, recruit other volunteers to assist. Be sure to allow plenty of time to publicize this special day.

Promotion

Enthusiastic promotion is vital to build support, participation, and enthusiasm for the Children's Sabbath. Alert those in responsible positions, such as the choir director or church school teachers, to any changes in the usual schedule well in advance.

Introduce the upcoming Children's Sabbath to the congregation through announcements in your church newsletter and worship bulletin. Prepare a press release for the religious affairs section of the local newspaper. Ask children to create posters and display them throughout the church to publicize the event. Reminders from the pulpit a few Sundays prior to the day are helpful as well. Plan to place bulletin inserts such as those found on pages 122–126 in your church bulletin one week in advance of the actual day.

Suggestions for the Worship Service

- Use the bulletin insert found on pages 38 and 39 in your Sunday church bulletin.

- Select scriptures that focus on children. See pages 17–19.

- Name specific needs of children during the liturgy. Include prayers for the needs and suffering of children, specifically naming needs that will be familiar to the congregation and praying for ministries with which the congregation is involved.

- In the prayer of confession, acknowledge our lack of compassion for or complacency about the suffering of children. Allow a few moments for the worshipers to meditate in silence on our failure to protect and sustain all of God's children.

- Include a special offering to meet the needs of children or to support a program serving children. The offering could be money, food, or other material goods such as toys or hats and mittens, or letters to be sent to legislators. A mission project chosen by the children could be the recipient of the offering.

- During the worship service, project slides of the children of your congregation on a blank wall as statistics about children in need are read. This can be part of a sermon or the call to confession.

- Decorate the sanctuary with banners or posters made by the children.

- The children and young people could enter the church in the processional at the beginning of the worship service carrying the banners they have made.

- The children and young people could read prayers and scripture lessons.

- The children could lead hymns or responsive readings.

- The children could greet worshipers as they arrive in or leave the sanctuary.

- A group of older children and young people might present a short drama for the sermon.

At the end of this section you will find four sample worship services for a Children's Sabbath. Use them or adapt them with the suggestions above and your own ideas.

Suggestions for Church School Groups

These suggestions can be used in church school groups or during a special time of celebration following worship, such as a congregational meal or picnic.

For all ages

- Select a mission project that provides services to children, such as a program for homeless children, a child care program, or a maternal and child health clinic. Contact the staff and find out how you can help promote or participate in its work. Introduce the project to the congregation with photographs or slides or with an on-site tour. Develop activities based on the suggestions from the staff to promote or support the program. Some of the introduction can be done in church school groups prior to the Children's Sabbath.

- Hold a poster party or essay contest on the focus of your Children's Sabbath. Include age categories from young children through adults. Display the entries throughout your church building or in the community. The prizes could be donations to a children's program of the winners' choice.

- Ask each church school group, including adults, to prepare a specific part of the service of worship for the Children's Sabbath. Provide them with options from this book. One person from the planning committee should be responsible for coordinating the service.

Young children (ages 3 to 5)

- Have the children decorate posters that are pre-printed with the slogan, "Please remember children in all that you do." Crayons, markers, or pictures cut from magazines can be used. Send the posters to elected officials in local, state, and national offices. Include a cover letter explaining the Children's Sabbath.

- Take a photograph of the children with their posters before you mail them. Display the photograph where your congregation will see it. If possible, have prints made for the children.

- Concentrate on helping the children see themselves as part of the congregation. They can help in the publicity for the Children's Sabbath by drawing pictures for flyers or the worship bulletin cover.

Older children (Grades 1 through 6)

- Make posters as suggested in the activity for young children.

- Talk with the children about the things for which they are thankful, including families, friends, homes, good health, and safety, as well as pets, toys, and favorite foods.

- Help them write prayers of thanks. Display them for the congregation to see. Print them in the church newsletter or worship bulletin from time to time. Credit the authors.

- Make mobiles of their prayers of thanks. Have the children write them on cardboard shapes. Hang them with yarn or string from dowels. Balance a shape on each end of the dowel.

- Help them write a litany of thanks. The line for the response of the worshipers can be: "For this, we give you thanks, Loving God." See the litany on pages 21–22 for a sample format.

- Have the children write new words to a familiar hymn tune, using the focus for the Children's Sabbath as the topic. Sing this hymn as part of the service of worship for Children's Sabbath.

Young people (Grades 7 through 12)

- Use the meditations from pages 7–16 to begin church school or fellowship group meetings. Include time to discuss the meditation, using the questions provided or questions of your own. Focus on how young people can participate in speaking out for themselves and all children.

- Have them create a large banner for the Children's Sabbath.

- With the young people, create a list of ways they can act on behalf of children in your congregation, community, state, or nation. The list could include writing to legislators, volunteering at a children's shelter or child care center, tutoring, and working in a food pantry or emergency shelter. Check with programs in your area for some specific suggestions to offer the young people.

- As soon as possible, provide ways for the group to volunteer, either together or individually.

- If the young people want to focus on teen pregnancy or AIDS or violence, work carefully on how their concerns may be lifted up in the group and in the congregation.

Adults

- Develop a short-term study course on the needs and rights of children, to begin or conclude on the Children's Sabbath (see **Section III**).

- Organize an adult forum, "A Moral Witness for Children," and ask representatives from the standing committees to highlight their committee's concern for and involvement with children. Include young people or parents of young children in your planning.

- Invite persons from the congregation or the community to be on a panel to discuss the unmet needs of children and families in your community, in your state, or around the nation. Highlight effective programs. Provide a list of ways the group can support these programs.

- Secure copies of resolutions or statements passed by your congregation, regional body, or denomination regarding the rights and needs of children. Study them and talk to the appropriate committees or boards of your congregation about their implementation. (Refer to **Section VI** for ordering information.)

An All-Church Dinner and Program

Many of the previous suggestions can be incorporated into a program following a meal together. The planning committee will want to answer these questions:

- How can children and young people be involved in the planning and leadership?

- Will everyone participate in the same activities, or will some activities be for specific age groups?

- Will the meal be a potluck, or will a group prepare it?

- Will the program begin with a presentation for everyone, or will people go to workshops first and gather together at the conclusion?

Building on the Children's Sabbath

After your Children's Sabbath, try to further your congregation's involvement with children and young people.

If you have made the congregation more aware of the needs and rights of children, keep them informed and encourage them to speak out for children locally, nationally, and internationally. Distribute information about pending federal and state legislation affecting children. Urge members to write letters expressing their opinions to the appropriate legislators.

A Sample Children's Sabbath #1

Theme: God calls each of us, young or old, to action and service on behalf of others, especially of children.

Order of Worship

Prelude: Children's bell choir or youth duet on piano and flute.

Call to Worship

Reader 1: From the quiet retirement of Abraham's and Sarah's old age, when we feel too weary, too old, too weak, God calls us.

Reader 2: From Peter's fishing net and Levi's tax concerns, when we feel too busy with jobs or school or routines, God calls us.

Reader 3: From the disciples' arms holding back the children, when we feel that we are the wrong age, gender, race, or social status, God calls us.

All: And so we assemble here now to heed God's call and seek God's empowering Spirit.†

Hymn: "Colors of Day," by Sue McLelland, John Pac, and Keith Ryecroft, or "Let There Be Love Shared among Us," by Dave Bilbrough.

Prayer of Confession: (first through Litany, then in silence)

Each day in our nation, when 100,000 children are homeless, living on the street or in shelters,

God, we confess that we avert our eyes, and pass by on the other side.

Each day, when the air is filled with the cries of more than 790 babies born at low or very low birthweight,

God, we confess that we cover our ears, and pass by on the other side.

Each day, when more than 7,400 reported neglected or abused children yearn to be hugged,

---

†The people's response appears in bold face type throughout.

God, we confess that we withhold our hugs, and pass by on the other side.

Each day, when 27 children die from poverty, and 44 die or are wounded by guns,

God, we confess that we harden our hearts, and pass by on the other side. God, open our eyes, ring in our ears, throw wide our arms, and soften our hearts, that we may receive these children in Christ's name, and so receive you who sent Christ. Amen.

Assurance of Pardon

Christ came that we might know ourselves to be God's children. And so we are! Children of God, believe the Good News: through Jesus Christ, we are forgiven.

Old Testament Lesson: 1 Samuel 3:1–19

(Read in parts: young person [Samuel], older person [Eli], narrator, and voice of God.)

New Testament Lesson: Luke 10:25–37

("Modern day" enactment of the Good Samaritan story by a youth group or intergenerational group.)

Brief Reflection or Sermon on Theme

God calls all of us, young and old, to use our unique gifts and skills in service of others, especially of children in need. What can each of us offer?

Anthem: "Here I Am, Lord" by Daniel L. Schutte.

Offering

Collect monetary offering as usual, perhaps designating it for a particular children's group or program. In addition, invite all present to write, on a slip of paper inserted in the bulletin, a skill, action, talent, or amount of time they can give to help meet the needs of children. Young children could draw their offering, such as helping a new child in class. Gather these "offerings" in a basket and bring them to the altar as well.

Offertory Anthem: "Ubi Caritas," from the Taizé community (Where Love and Caring Are, There Is God).

Prayer

O God of infinite love and unending challenge, help us to listen to your call. Inspire us to use the varied gifts with which we have been blessed in the service of others, especially of children in need.

Keep us ever mindful, we pray, that when we provide adequate nutrition for the children who are hungry, we will have fed Christ.

When we welcome the "strangers" who are children without safe and loving homes, we will have welcomed Christ.

When we donate warm, well-made clothing for the children who are ill-clad, we will have clothed Christ.

When we have immunized all children against preventable disease and ensured adequate health care for all, we will have visited Christ.

When we care for juveniles in custody or the children of people in prison, then, too, we will have come to see Christ.

Help us to meet your challenge and reflect your love, so that one day it might be said that when we did this to the least of them, truly we did it to you. Amen.

Hymn: "The Prayer of St. Francis" (Make Me a Channel of Your Peace), music by Sebastian Temple, or "Let Us Talents and Tongues Employ," by Fred Kaan.

Benediction

Let us go out to love our neighbors, especially children in need, and in so doing love God with all our heart, all our soul, all our strength, and all our mind. Amen.

Written by Shannon P. Daley
Director of Religious Affairs
Children's Defense Fund, Washington, DC

A Sample Children's Sabbath #2

The following service can be used or adapted by a single congregation or by an interfaith group of congregations. Up to eight religious leaders from Catholic, Jewish, Muslim, and Protestant traditions can lead various portions of the service.

"A MORAL WITNESS FOR CHILDREN"

Prelude

Procession of Religious Leaders

Call to Worship (based on Jeremiah 31:15–17)

Child 1: Every day in our nation, more than 2,700 babies are born into poverty.

Child 2: Every day in our nation, more than 7,400 children are reported abused or neglected.

Child 3: Every day in our nation, more than 675 babies are born to mothers who received late or no prenatal care.

Child 4: Every day in our nation, more than 790 babies are born too small to be healthy.

Child 5: Every day in our nation, more than 100 babies die before their first birthday.

Leader: "A voice is heard in Ramah, lamentation and bitter weeping. Rachel is weeping for her children; she refuses to be comforted for her children, because they are no more."

We come together with hearts that weep for our nation's children.†

"Thus says the Lord: Keep your voice from weeping, and your eyes from tears; For there is a reward for your work, says the Lord:"

We come together to be moved from weeping to hear the promise of the work we can do.

"[The children] shall come back from the land of the enemy; there is hope for your future says the Lord: your children shall come back to their own country."

We come together to glimpse your vision of homecoming that would bring our nation's children from an experience of need to one of safety, plenty, and love.

Be with us in our worship and in our work, O God. Prepare us by the power of your spirit that we may commit our hearts and hands and minds to realizing your vision of homecoming for the children of our nation. Amen.

---

† The people's response appears in bold face type throughout.

*Hymn: "Here I Am, Lord" by Daniel L. Schutte

Litany Adapted from the Hoshanot Service

Please save! For Your sake, Our God

Please help us to save our children — for their sake.

Please save! For Your sake, Our Creator

Please help us to save our children — for our sake.

Please save! For Your sake, Our Redeemer

Please help us to save our children — for the future's sake.

Please save! For Your sake, Our Advocate

Please help us save our children — for the sake of the world.

As you saved Noah and his children

Help us save our children now.

As you saved Isaac on the altar

Help us to save our children now.

As you saved the children of Jacob from famine

Help us to save our children now.

As you saved the children of Israel at the sea

Help us to save our children now.

As you have saved us so many times, O Lord,

Help us to save our children now.

Adapted from the Hoshanot Service
by the Religious Action Center of Reform Judaism

Reading: Isaiah 43:1–13, 18–21

Reflection on the Text

How might we bring our nation's children out of exile in a barren wilderness of poverty and need? How might we work toward a vision of a more loving and just order for our nation's children? What is the "new thing" that we are called to do to help all children develop to their God-given potential?

Prayer of Intercession

For the millions of children who are living in poverty, that despite our society's rejection and inaction, they might feel loved and valuable in your sight.

O God, hear our prayer.

For our nation, that we are moved from tolerance of child poverty to passionate work for justice.

O God, hear our prayer.

---

*All who are able may stand.

LOOKING AT CHILDREN THROUGH THE EYES OF FAITH

For the parents who struggle each day to provide food, pay the rent, keep their families together and just survive, that they might find community supports that enable them to nurture, enjoy, and spend time with their children.

O God, hear our prayer.

For the children whose needs are unmet, whose cries go unheard, and whose lives hold little joy, that we might fill their needs, respond to their pain, and seek to enrich their lives.

O God, hear our prayer.

For the children who are born too soon or too small, that they will receive the special care that they need, and that our nation will learn from their pain to invest adequately in prenatal care.

O God, hear our prayer.

For the children who are sick and for their parents who don't know how they can pay the bills, that they find care and healing and their parents respite from worry.

O God, hear our prayer.

For our nation's leaders, that they might make children the nation's highest priority, and fulfill the promises that they make to the children.

O God, hear our prayer.

For ourselves, that we might continue, with renewed determination, to serve and advocate on behalf of all children and see that no child is left behind.

O God, hear our prayer.

Anthem: "The Sea Is So Wide" by John Jacobson or "For the Beauty of the Earth" by John Rutter.

Charge to the Congregation

The Charge should express the moral responsibility to care for the most vulnerable children of our nation through our personal, religious, professional, and public lives. The Charge should also inspire the religious community to be a powerful and prophetic voice to the nation, stirring it to fulfill its responsibility to the children.

*Act of Commitment

Leader: In the Book of Micah, we read:

"[God] has told you, O mortal, what is good; and what does the Lord require of you, but to do justice, and love kindness, and walk humbly with your God?"

In this time and in this place, let us covenant together to renew our commitment to the children, knowing that when we strive to do these things for the most

vulnerable of our nation, we are seeking to do what is good in the eyes of God.

What does the Lord require of you? To do justice!

We covenant to do justice for the children of our nation, as we work to change policies that allow one in five to live in poverty.

Do justice!

We covenant to do justice, as we insist that the needs of our nation's voteless children are not ignored in the election process.

Do justice!

We covenant to do justice, as we work as leaders in our communities to ensure the well-being of children.

What does the Lord require of you? To love kindness.

We covenant to love kindness, as we nurture the children in our lives, and remember to listen to them.

Love kindness!

We covenant to love kindness, as we spend time with children, teach them right from wrong, and are good role models for them.

Love kindness!

We covenant to love kindness, as we reach out to support children and families through our work or personal involvement, ensuring that their needs are met in relationships that foster dignity and respect.

What does the Lord require of you? To walk humbly with your God.

We covenant to walk humbly with our God, as we seek God's guidance to know what is right for the children we touch and those on whose behalf we work.

Walk humbly with your God.

We covenant to walk humbly with our God, as we see God in each child, and as we respect all children as created equal and equally cherished by God.

Walk humbly with your God.

We covenant to walk humbly with our God, as we celebrate the gifts of children and lift up their needs in our places of worship.

And finally, we covenant to walk humbly with our God as we strive to do all of these things, knowing that we, as well as the young, are children of God and ultimately in God's care.

*Closing Hymn: "Guide My Feet," choir and congregation.

*Benediction/Sending Forth

May we go forth
   to celebrate the gifts of each child;
May we go forth
   to heal the hurts of each child;
May we go forth
   to seek justice for each child.

This we ask
as ones who are claimed
as God's children.
Amen.

*Postlude

Written by Shannon P. Daley
Director of Religious Affairs
Children's Defense Fund, for the 1992
National Observance of Children's Sabbaths

A Sample Children's Sabbath #3

A sampling of worship resources developed for Healthy Baby Weekend 1990 by Indianapolis-area clergy and lay people.

Options for Scriptural Texts and Themes

2 Samuel 12. Nathan confronts David with his sin. David's child dies for the father's misdeeds. The story interprets the death as a sign of the covenant violated. What does our city's constantly high infant mortality rate say about the quality of our covenant? What other injustices are connected with our high infant mortality rate? What must we do to restore the covenant?

Genesis 15. God and Abram enter into covenant. Abram is to be our blessing for all the earth. All our children are gifts, signs of the eternal covenant, signs of blessing.

Call to Worship

The Good News is this:

    ◆ Pain and suffering have limits.
    ◆ We are not lost.
    ◆ The poor are loved.
    ◆ Resurrection is real.

Our world has other news. Bad news.

    ◆ Babies die.
    ◆ Parents grieve.
    ◆ Poverty grows.
    ◆ People blame others.
    ◆ Violence occurs.

Between the Good News and the bad news is the presence of God's people. We are called to let light illumine darkness, to elevate joy over gloom, and to struggle for truth to dispel evil. Come, let us be God's people today. Amen.

Litany

Christ has brought good news to the poor.

Let us be partners in spreading this message.†

Christ has proclaimed liberty to the captives.

Christ has set us free.

Christ promises sight to the blind.

Open our eyes that we might see.

Christ uplifts the downtrodden.

Let us look up, then, to proclaim the year of the Lord.

Written by the Rev. Duane Grady
Northview Church of the Brethren, Indianapolis

Litany

We give you thanks, O God, for your life-giving power!

Thank you, God!

We give you thanks, O God, for those parents who nurtured us in the womb of their love!

Thank you, God!

We give you thanks, O God, for doctors, nurses, midwives, and those who lovingly brought us forth into the world!

Thank you, God!

We give you thanks, O God, for the many loving family members and neighbors who surrounded us with their loving touch and words as we first encountered our new earthly environment!

Thank you, God!

We lift up our prayers, O God, that every child of yours will be able to fully experience your joyful gift of life.

Hear our prayers, O God!

---

*All who are able may stand.

†The people's response appears in bold face type throughout.

We lift up our prayers for those parents who struggle daily to care for their child, and for their own well-being.

Hear our prayers, O God!

We lift up our prayers for the medical professional community, that they will be able to use the gifts that you have given them so that they may sustain every newborn's life to maturity.

Hear our prayers, O God!

We lift up our prayers for ourselves, O God, and we ask that you sustain us and remind us of our calling to care for every person, young or old, so that we may all enjoy the fullness of life that you have given us and experience the fullness of your blessing.

Hear our prayers, O God! Amen!

Written by the Rev. Phil Tom
Westminster Presbyterian Church, Indianapolis

Dedication to New Life

In the tradition of the Disciples of Christ, a service of Dedication to New Life is performed for children and their families shortly after a new baby comes. Such a service could be planned for all children in the congregation on this day. Or a similar service could be held for all the unnamed children, that they might no longer be at risk. Here is a litany that could be used for such a dedication ceremony.

In the face of the increasingly complex, nearly overwhelming problem of infant mortality in our city, this day has been designated Healthy Baby Sunday.

As members of the human family, as believers in a God who affirms life, and as participants in the life of this city, we rise to the challenge of making this city a healthier place for babies and their families.

The problem of infant mortality is not a problem with individuals. It is not a problem of the poor. It is not a minority issue. It is society's problem.

We understand that if we are to do our best to make the world a place where babies are healthier, we must first recognize and learn the widespread causes of infant mortality.

While study is important, it means nothing if it is not accompanied by advocacy and action on behalf of those who have no voice.

We confess that advocacy and action often scare us, but we are willing to risk status and reputation if

that is what it takes to make the world a safer place for babies and their families.

There is a resource available to all persons of faith that feeds and sustains all that we do.

We are busy people, but not too busy to pray for babies who are conceived and born at risk, to pray for the families that care for those children, to pray for the church that is called to offer the sustaining grace of God to all who are in need, and to pray for ourselves, that our response might be pleasing in the eyes of God.

Today is Healthy Baby Sunday in Indianapolis.

Those of us who are woven into this community commit ourselves this day to each thread that makes us who we are — a beautiful, colorful, vibrant tapestry that reveals nothing less than the majesty of God.

Written by the Rev. Rick Powell
Centenary Christian Church, Indianapolis

Prayer

O God, Creator and Sustainer of all life, we come to you in prayer knowing that our individual prayers are heard, believing that our corporate prayers have power.

God, be with us this day. Comfort us as a mother comforts her child. Protect us from harm. Nourish us with word and with bread. Open our hearts. Guide our steps. We remember that prayer is a time to be encouraged and renewed as we seek the directing voice of our God.

Hear us now, O God, and lead us in the ways of justice so that as we pray for your protection and strength we might also seek this good news for others. We know that there are many for whom comfort seems a distant and abstract thing. God, you have created life and you bid us to protect and develop it.

In our midst and in our world, we hear the cries of those who suffer and of those who have not enough. Teach us to respond as you would have us, with compassion, with grace, and with hands that heed your vision of Shalom.

God, we recognize you as the author of life, hating nothing which you have made. Teach us to see your love in those for whom life is not a joy. We pray for the innocent, the lonely and pained. We pray for justice with all of its implications for those who suffer and for those who can change this suffering.

God, hear our prayers. Amen.

Written by the Rev. Duane Grady
Northview Church of the Brethren, Indianapolis

A Sample Children's Sabbath #4

The following service can be used or adapted by a single congregation or by an interfaith group of congregations. Up to eight religious leaders from Catholic, Jewish, Muslim, and Protestant traditions can lead various portions of the service.

"CHILDREN OF PROMISE"

Prelude

Procession of Religious Leaders

Processional Music

Call to Worship

Child:
To sit and dream, to sit and read,
To sit and learn about the world
Outside our world of here and now —
Our problem world —
To dream of vast horizons of the soul
Through dreams made whole
Unfettered, free — help me!
All you who are dreamers, too,
Help me make
Our world anew.
I reach out my dreams to you.

Langston Hughes

Leader: For I am about to create new heavens and a new earth; the former things shall not be remembered or come to mind....No more shall the sound of weeping be heard in it, or the cry of distress. No more shall there be in it an infant that lives but a few days, or an old person who does not live out a lifetime. (Isaiah 65:17, 20a)

People: We come together to listen for the dreams of children and to hear the promise of God's vision for our world. Guide us and renew us, O God, that we might be partners in your new creation. Amen.†

*Congregational Hymn: "Hope for the Children," words by Douglas Clark, with help from Polly Mattson. Tune: St. Catherine

Litany: O God of All Children

O God of the children of Somalia, Sarajevo, South Africa, and South Carolina, of Albania, Alabama, Bosnia, and Boston, of Cracow and Cairo, Chicago and Croatia,

Help us to love and respect and protect them all.

O God of Black and Brown and White and Albino children and those all mixed together,

Of children who are rich and poor and in between,

Of children who speak English and Russian and Hmong and languages our ears cannot discern,

Help us to love and respect and protect them all.

O God of the child prodigy and child prostitute,

Of the child of rapture and the child of rape,

Of runaway or thrown-away children who struggle every day without parent or place or friend or future,

Help us to love and respect and protect them all.

O God of children who can walk and talk and hear and see and sing and dance and jump and play and of children who wish they could but can't,

Of children who are loved and unloved, wanted and unwanted,

Help us to love and respect and protect them all.

O God of beggar, beaten, abused, neglected, AIDS-, drug-, and hunger-ravaged children,

Of children who are emotionally fragile, of children who rebel and ridicule, torment and taunt,

Help us to love and respect and protect them all.

O God of children of destiny and of despair, of war and of peace,

Of disfigured, diseased, and dying children,

Of children without hope and of children with hope to spare and to share,

Help us to love and respect and protect them all.

Reading from the Torah (e.g., Jeremiah 1:4–8)

Reading from the New Testament (e.g., Mark 10:13–16)

Reading from the Qur'an (e.g., Chapter 2 Verse 177)

Reflection on the Text

How does our faith remind us of the precious, irreplaceable value of each child? How does our faith impress on us our responsibility to nurture and protect children?

Anthem

Prayers of Intercession

Let us come before God with our prayers, trusting in a God of love and of hope, of justice and of forgiveness.

For the babies born too soon or too small, that they will receive the special care that they need.

O God, hear our prayer.

---

†The people's response appears in bold face type throughout.
*All who are able may stand.

For the children who are left behind to care for themselves or who don't receive good quality care, that they will receive the nurturing they need to develop their potential.

O God, hear our prayer.

For the youths who don't feel loved or hopeful, that they will find adults who share your love for them, who open doors of possibility, value and support them.

O God, hear our prayer.

For the parents who struggle to provide for and nurture their children in the midst of poverty, violence, and racism, that they will find support in you and through their communities.

O God, hear our prayer.

For our nation, that we will reorder our priorities to manifest a just and more caring reflection of your vision for creation.

O God, hear our prayer.

For ourselves, that we might find renewed inspiration and guidance in our efforts with and on behalf of children and families.

O God, hear our prayer.

Charge to the Congregation

*Act of Commitment

God calls to us through the prophet Isaiah: "Is not this the fast that I choose: to loose the bonds of injustice?"

We covenant with God's help to be a voice for children and families bound by the poverty, racism, and violence in our society.

"[Is not this the fast that I choose:] to undo the thongs of the yoke, to let the oppressed go free, and to break every yoke?"

We covenant to work for justice with families trapped without hope or opportunities.

With God's help, we will work to lift the burden of despair from children who feel that no one cares.

"Is it not to share your bread with the hungry, and bring the homeless into your house?"

We covenant to reach out to children who are hungry, and to families who are homeless.

We covenant, as well, to change the policies that have failed them.

"When you see the naked to cover them, and not to hide yourself from your own kin?"

We covenant with God's help to protect the vulnerable, especially children who are abused or neglected.

We covenant to build a nurturing society for all of God's family — all races, all colors, all incomes and all ages.

"Then your light shall break forth like the dawn, and your healing shall spring up quickly; your vindicator shall go before you, the glory of the Lord shall be your rear guard....

"Your ancient ruins shall be rebuilt; you shall raise up the foundations of many generations.

"You shall be called the repairer of the breach, the restorer of streets to live in."

*Congregational Hymn: "Here I Am, Lord"
by Daniel L. Schutte

*Closing Prayer/Sending Forth

Child:
    All you who are dreamers, too,
        Help me make
        Our world anew.
    I reach out my dreams to you.

Leader: Let us go forth to make the world safe for the dreams of children; may we be partners in manifesting God's promised new creation of compassion and justice. Amen.

Recession

Recessional Anthem

Postlude

The litany "O God of All Children" was written by Marian Wright Edelman, founder and president, Children's Defense Fund, Washington, DC. All other prayers written by Shannon P. Daley, Director of Religious Affairs, Children's Defense Fund.

Bulletin Insert (see next two pages)
How to Use This Bulletin Insert
- Duplicate both of the following pages and create a two-sided bulletin insert. Make enough copies for Sunday worship or your event.
- If appropriate, list a contact person in the space provided to assist those who want to get involved or learn more.

- Use the bulletin insert as a tool to announce an upcoming Children's Sabbath or study into action program on children.
- Include an explanation of the purpose of the insert in the bulletin and during announcements.
- Be creative! Design your own bulletin insert and make copies for Sunday worship and special programs and events.

Welcome the Child

Then [Jesus] took a little child and put it among them; and taking it in his arms, he said to them, "Whoever welcomes one such child in my name welcomes me, and whoever welcomes me welcomes not me but the one who sent me."

Mark 9:36–37

Who is one such child in our nation that we are called to welcome?

One of the 2,868 children born into poverty each day...

One of the 100,000 children who are homeless each night...

One of the 145 babies born at very low birthweight each day...

One of the 2,350 children in adult jails each day...

One of the 7,945 children reported abused or neglected each day...

One of the 2,255 children who drop out each school day...

One of the 1,234 children who run away from home each day...

One of the 27 children who die because of poverty each day...

(Copy and use this as a bulletin insert)

What does the Lord require of us?

To do justice...

♦ Call the mayor's and governor's offices to learn the extent of child poverty, homelessness, school dropout, teen pregnancy, and child abuse or neglect in our community or state. Ask what government measures or programs are addressing these problems. Express support for funding and expanding programs that work.

♦ Call or write our members of Congress to learn what steps they have taken or what legislative measures they support to address the needs of children, particularly those at risk or born into poverty. Urge them to make children one of our nation's highest priorities.

...and to love kindness,

♦ Visit a local program or organization that meets children's needs (such as an after-school tutoring program, shelter for homeless families, or a health clinic offering prenatal care classes for pregnant teens and low-income mothers), and ask how you can help.

♦ Support worship, education, and service opportunities to celebrate children, lift up their needs, and lead our congregation into deeper involvement in meeting those needs.

...and to walk humbly with our God. (Micah 6:8)

♦ Read Psalm 131:1–3, Proverbs 31:8–9, and Matthew 18:1–7. Reflect on what we, as God's people, are called to do to remove the "stumbling blocks" before America's children.

♦ Pray for the children who are not faceless statistics, but who are known and cherished by God, and whom we are called to welcome in Christ's name.

To learn more about what our congregation is doing to meet the needs of children, and how you might become involved, contact:

_____

CHILDREN'S DEFENSE FUND   or   NCC COMMITTEE ON JUSTICE
25 E Street, N.W.   FOR CHILDREN AND THEIR FAMILIES
Washington, DC 20001   c/o Margery Freeman
Telephone (202) 628-8787   1119 Dauphine Street, #5
                                                 New Orleans, LA 70116
                                                 (504) 522-9895

(Copy and use this as a bulletin insert)

Making a Difference for Children—Step by Step

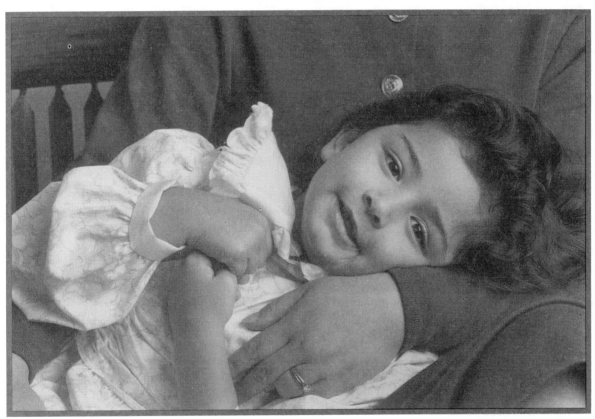

PHOTO BY NITA WINTER

A Guide for Involving Your Congregation

The opportunities for helping and empowering children are endless. However, no single congregation can do everything, nor is it appropriate for it to try. The key to effective action is to gain congregational support and determine a realistic plan.

This section provides suggestions for developing an effective, sustainable congregational effort to help children and families. In this section, and in the video developed to go with it (see page 158), you will find suggestions to help you:

1. Get started by involving key people.

2. Decide how to proceed within your congregation.

3. Assess existing interest and involvement in children's concerns in your congregation.

4. Determine resources available in your congregation to meet the needs of children.

5. Assess the needs of children that are not being met in your congregation or community. Do an inventory of organizations and individuals in the community that already are working with or on behalf of children and families.

6. Match your congregational resources to existing needs.

7. Build partnerships to become effective advocates for children and their families.

8. Raise awareness and issue a call to mission.

9. Educate congregation members for action.

For each of these initial planning steps a basic process is described and suggestions are presented that can help you. Because each congregation and community is unique, you may find other ways to streamline this process to use your congregation's resources to meet the needs of children in a concrete, effective way.

Each congregation has its own personality and style of work. Part of that style is determined by the polity of the congregation and denomination, part by the leadership. Be clear about the channels that you must use to gain approval and official sanction. Know the system for your congregation and work through it. Find an interested committee already at work or a few people to work with you. Talk with your pastor or a staff person concerned about children and families. Child advocates work together. Find them in your congregation and go over this section together. Use it to help the children in your midst.

The Congregation: A Vital Role

◆ The congregation is a community already committed to love of God and neighbor.

◆ Members know each other and work on projects together.

◆ There is a willingness to listen to the individual's ideas.

◆ Congregations can bring together a variety of skills and talents — manual trades, business experience, public service, expertise in communities — that are essential in running any project.

Step 1: Involve Key People

Whether you are a minister, a committee chairperson, or a concerned member of the congregation, don't try to initiate a new effort for children alone! Your first step should be to identify and involve others, and gain sanction for your first effort. Start by identifying the key persons and committees that have jurisdiction over and share your interest in children's issues. These committees might include: Social Concerns, Christian Education, Mission and Outreach, Global Concerns, and the Women's Association. Meet with appropriate clergy, professional staff, and lay leaders if they're not already a part of a committee. Find out what concerns they see within the congregation and the community. They can provide you with a wealth of information about the congregation's ministry and a list of interested members in your congregation.

Step 2: Decide How To Proceed

You need to decide how to proceed. You may not want to make this decision firmly until you have determined your congregation's resources (see Step 4), but now is the time to consider it. You already have talked with the key persons and committees in your congregation. You may be ready to act. Four possibilities are:

- ◆ Work through an existing committee, such as Social Concerns or Children's Ministries. The latter may be appropriate if you want to include children and youths more fully in the life of your congregation.

- ◆ Combine two committees for a broader look, such as Community Outreach and Christian Education. They could work together to provide educational programs and opportunities for action within your community.

- ◆ Organize a task force made up of representatives of standing committees, one or two persons from the congregation at large, and even the community outside. This is often a good way to proceed when you hope to develop a new program or ministry.

- ◆ Organize an ad hoc committee (as small as two or three persons) to proceed until another plan for organization is needed. This is usually an interim group that will keep things going as more information is sought or support developed.

Step 3: Assess Existing Interest and Involvement

The questionnaire on the following page can help your committee assess the level of interest and concern for children in the total life of your congregation — in worship, education, mission, and advocacy. You may want to ask additional questions, or the answer to one question may prompt another. The questionnaire is intended as a starting point for considering the range of activities through which your congregation acts, or might act, as a corporate child advocate.

The questions begin with issues closely identified with the life of every congregation and broaden until the concern is about social change throughout the nation and world. As you answer the questions, watch for the ones that are more difficult to answer and keep them in mind as you move ahead, because they indicate a stretching point for your congregation.

You Are Needed!

"Now there are varieties of gifts, but the same Spirit," wrote Paul in 1 Corinthians 12:4.

We are not all called to do the same kind of work, but everyone is called to do something to help others. The commitment may be large or small, the job may be at center stage or behind the scenes. Everyone has a role to play.

Step 4: Determine Your Congregation's Resources

In Step 3 you may have discovered changes you can make within the life of your congregation that will help children grow in wisdom and faith. You probably have begun to identify some needs of children that go beyond your congregation's. Now it's time to identify interested members of the congregation and determine the existing or potential support for programs to help children and families within your congregation and community.

Find out about the resources available within your congregation. Much of the information may be readily available from clergy and staff.

To gather the information, invite representatives of various age groups and committees to help you complete the Congregational Resources Assessment on page 51. Ask your clergy, lay leaders, and staff members for suggestions as you put this group together. If staff members are not on your committee, asking them will provide an important connection between you.

Human Resources

A church's most valuable resource is, of course, its people! By identifying their areas of interest and experience, you can tap a wealth of support for a new effort for children and their families. Design your own chart, listing the individuals' names and indicating their particular area of interest. If you develop a questionnaire to include in a Sunday bulletin or your church newsletter, keep in mind that people generally prefer to check off items you've listed rather than make up their own answers.

Make sure that your list includes those persons who have professional expertise, such as social work, medicine, nonprofit organization management, politics, or journalism, or those who have worked on a particular issue in the past. Don't overlook grandparents, parents, church school teachers, social ministry committee members, volunteers in community programs for children, and anyone else who has expressed a concern for

Your Congregation, Children, and Families

Worship

- How are the needs of children and families included in prayers or worship?

- How frequently are concerns of children and families mentioned in sermons? Are illustrations about children used primarily as amusement?

- What displays, such as banners or photo exhibits, reflect the talents of the children in your congregation? When was the last time they were displayed publicly?

- In the past three years has your congregation conducted a service of worship, such as a Children's Sabbath, that celebrates the special contributions and needs of children?

- How are children and youths encouraged to participate in the life of the congregation? Is their role primarily as observers? Are they usually age-segregated?

Education

- How does your congregation provide appropriate educational programs for children and youths?

- Has your congregation, or a group representing it, offered a program to heighten awareness about children at risk in the past three years and offered ways to minister to such children?

- In the past three years has any course in the adult education program focused on children's issues and the Christian mission?

- What books or other materials does your congregational library or resource table offer on children's issues and child advocacy?

Mission/Outreach

- How does your congregation provide programs and other activities for children and youths?

- What regularly scheduled activities are designed to help children build a spirit of giving and cooperation?

- Have the Christian education and social ministry committees ever worked together on a program affecting children in the congregation, community, nation, or world? Might they?

- Does your congregation, or a group within it, provide volunteers or financial support to a program serving children in your community? The nation? The world?

- Does your congregation conduct or house a Head Start or child care program or other service for children, youths, and families?

Advocacy

- Does any committee or other group of your congregation work at political advocacy for children and families as an expression of your Christian mission?

- Does your congregation participate in political advocacy activities on domestic and international issues, for example by studying issues, writing letters, or joining groups such as Interfaith IMPACT or Bread for the World?

- What methods, programs, and events have been most successful in motivating and empowering members of your congregation to act on behalf of others? Does your congregation respond most readily and strongly to an issue through worship, education, outreach, or advocacy?

children. Keep this list handy. Put it on a computer, if possible. Update the list regularly, adding new names and additional information. Refer to the list when you need committee members, particular expertise, or information and volunteers.

Financial Resources

Arrange a time to talk to your congregation's treasurer to assess the current and potential financial resources that are available to meet the needs of children and families. What monies are budgeted currently for mission and outreach in your congregation? What proportion of that supports programs for children and families? Determine also the monies budgeted for child and youth programs in your congregation, as well as special offerings or appeals to the congregation for programs related to children and youths. Finally, estimate what untapped financial resources in your congregation might be directed to efforts for children and youths.

Later, when you have decided what new program or effort your congregation will initiate to help children, explore what financial resources are available in the community or other congregations that might supplement the financial resources in your church. For instance, consider community foundations, seminaries, and charities, or organizations such as the Junior League, United Way, and Rotary.

Physical Resources

A congregation's physical resources are a valuable but often overlooked source of support for children and families. Walk through your church with a fresh eye and creative mind, and take stock of your church's physical resources. Consider first the church building(s). Are there unused classrooms that could house a child care, Head Start, tutoring, or after-school program during the week? Is there a gymnasium or auditorium that could provide constructive recreational alternatives for youths in the evening or on weekends? Is there a large meeting room that could be opened up to a parenting education and support group, or an occasional immunization clinic? Is there a kitchen that could be used for a nutrition and cooking class for teenage or first-time parents? Don't forget to consider the church grounds; is there a playground or other outdoor area that could be made available to a children's program?

Then assess other physical resources. A van could be used to transport pregnant women to prenatal care appointments. A VCR, books, and games could be used for an after-school program. Toys could be part of a toy-lending library for home-based family child care providers. Also consider your church's office equipment: could the photocopier, computer, or other equipment be made accessible to a program serving children or working on their behalf?

Step 5: Assess the Unmet Needs, and Identify Those Who Help

You probably don't have to look very hard to find children and families in your community or city who are struggling to survive. But how do you find information on the problems that exist for children in your area, or the agencies, organizations, and programs that serve children and their families?

Fortunately, you don't need to undertake a time-consuming research project. First, talk with staff and members of your congregation who have an interest in children's concerns. Keep in mind that you are looking for organizations and individuals to help you determine the most critical needs of children and teens in your community and ways your congregation can complement existing programs and efforts. A few well-placed phone calls can simplify the gathering of information and can build your connections within the community.

A Community Assessment

- How many children need child care? Is child care available? Are there waiting lists at area programs?

- How many teenagers drop out of school?

- What proportion of our children grow up in poverty?

- How many incidents of child abuse are reported each year? Are the cases increasing or decreasing?

- Are teenage drug and alcohol abuse, gangs, or crime a problem in our community?

- What is the infant mortality rate in our city or state? What is the rate of low-birthweight births? What proportion of pregnant women receive early prenatal care?

- How many teenagers become parents each year?

- Does our community have work opportunities for teens?

- How many of our children and families go without adequate public or private health insurance, or have none at all?

Here are some suggestions to find the answers to those and other questions about the status of children and families in your community, and to identify the organizations and individuals who help them:

- Make photocopies of the "Information Resources Worksheets" in **Section III: Developing a Study into Action Program.** Each worksheet is designed to help you identify organizations and individuals in your community or congregation who can serve as information resources. The worksheet gives tips

One Example: A Church with a Small Membership, Staff, and Resources

Like many urban churches, Bethany Presbyterian Church in Trenton, New Jersey, has a small congregation of perhaps 90 active, worshipping members in a large church building that once housed a congregation of 1,500 and numerous activities and programs.

Bethany has a long tradition of ministering to area children by providing space for a Head Start program. As the new sole pastor, Reverend Patricia Daley, and others realized, however, the needs of the children extend beyond Head Start. In particular, many of the children who had begun attending Bethany's church school, like a large number of other children in Trenton, have additional pressing needs for safe, supervised enrichment activities during the summer while their parents work.

In assessing Bethany's interest and expertise, it became clear that the most widespread and sustainable support would be for concrete, visible neighborhood outreach programs. A review of the available resources revealed that Bethany's greatest assets are plenty of available space and equipment, a committed pastor, and an energetic core of volunteers.

As a small congregation, Bethany's financial resources are modest. However, a $2,000 seed grant, donated by an individual, made the dream of an outreach program for neighborhood children seem realizable, if it could be supplemented by creative identification of other resources. Bethany teamed up with Westminster Presbyterian Church, as well as other area and suburban churches with considerable financial resources.

In addition to the resources and support found in partnership with other churches, Bethany identified the federal breakfast/lunch program as already helping children and was able to utilize it to supply free lunches. Princeton Theological Seminary offered to provide another valuable resource — a seminary student to work with the program all summer.

Bethany has found one of its greatest resources, however, in the neighborhood teenagers. By using 13- to 15-year-olds as junior counselors, Bethany simultaneously provides these older children with constructive activity and leadership skills development while filling its need for additional staff. Other churches in the Presbytery are invited to sponsor a junior counselor and pay her or his modest stipend. This, again, provides dual benefits, by supporting the teenagers while encouraging the involvement of a broader range of churches.

The success of Bethany's outreach program can be found in its creative approach to assessing needs and resources of the congregation and community, developing ongoing partnerships with area churches, and building on the strengths of the children themselves.

For more information, contact Reverend Patricia Daley, Bethany Presbyterian Church, 400 Hamilton Avenue, Trenton, NJ 08609, (609) 393-6318.

---

for how to identify these contacts, as well as basic questions to elicit critical information. You may want to complete each worksheet, or focus on the worksheet on the issue of greatest interest to your committee.

- Contact the departments of health, welfare, social services, and youth services; police and law enforcement agencies; and state vital statistics bureaus to find out which city, county, and state agencies can provide statistics and information on public programs and services for children and families.

- Find out which local organizations deal with the problems of children and families by looking in your telephone book or local newspapers for child advocacy organizations and coalitions, child care resource and referral groups, child care licensing agencies, community youth programs, child service organizations, the March of Dimes, Scouts, and others.

- Learn what roles the public schools and teachers play in meeting and identifying the needs of children and families by checking with your school board, PTA, teachers' unions, and the departments of education at local colleges and universities.

- Find out which local organizations and agencies deal with children as part of a broader mission

Another Example: A Church with a Large Membership, Staff, and Resources

All Souls Church in New York City is a Unitarian Universalist congregation of more than 1,000 members. Its membership has considerable professional and volunteer expertise in children's issues. In the fall of 1987 a Children's Taskforce was formed to respond to the growing crises affecting children in New York City and the United States generally.

In its first year, the programming of the task force consisted of a Foster Care and Adoption Project, an Education and Advocacy Committee, a Welfare Hotel Project, a Tutoring Project, and a Boarder Babies Project. In the years since, these projects have been evaluated and changed to better serve the needs of the children as well as help the volunteers who serve them.

Because All Souls is a large congregation, it can afford to invest finances and personnel in a wide variety of children's projects. Still, the leadership of the Children's Taskforce knew the importance of matching the projects to the resources they had. They used essentially the same process advocated here, working at a small number of specific projects and using their volunteers and resources wisely. Their first goals were simple and the time frames for projects short. Their expectations were realistic. By keeping their minds and hearts open to adapting and adjusting programs as they developed, they were able to create successful programs that met the needs they had recognized. Though their profile may look overwhelming to you, their process and plan of work is within your reach.

For more information, contact the Children's Taskforce, Unitarian Church of All Souls, 1157 Lexington Avenue, New York, NY 10021, (212) 535-5530.

---

by contacting the interfaith council or ministerial alliance, religious charities, United Way, hospitals, Association of Junior Leagues, YMCA, YWCA, Church Women United, League of Women Voters, the American Association of University Women, NAACP, Girl Scouts, Boy Scouts, or any of the many good local groups.

- Identify key people in your community with whom you want to establish and maintain contact. Consider elected officials and those running for office, public housing tenant leaders, school board members, reporters who cover children's issues locally, and retired persons who have been active in children's issues.

As you are involved in this process, develop a three-part list: the needs of children you are identifying; the contact information for organizations, agencies, and individuals who are helping to meet children's needs; and suggestions from those contacts about what children need most.

Step 6: Match Resources To the Needs

By now you have assessed your congregation's existing interest and involvement in children's concerns, your church's human, physical, and financial resources, the range of problems facing children in your community, and the organizations and individuals that are helping to meet them. It is time to synthesize this information to decide upon an effective, sustainable response. This response should draw upon your congregation's greatest resources and complement existing efforts or organizations that are already in place.

1. Look at the children's needs you have identified. Which needs are most pressing?

2. Look at the congregation's resources you believe to be available. Which are the greatest resources? Do you have enough resources and potential support to work on the priorities you have identified? If not, can you begin searching for others with whom you can join forces? Keep in mind your congregation's profile (completed in Step 3) as you determine the best starting point for a new effort for children.

3. Review the existing programs, agencies, and organizations in the community. Did any ask for some specific support? Is that support something that draws on your congregation's strongest resources?

4. Put this information together and determine what effort or programs you will pursue. Use the work-

sheets on pages 52–53. Plan a time, after an appropriate initial period, to evaluate your new effort and make any necessary adjustments.

For example, did you identify:

- Teen parents who need support and parenting skills? Congregation members with counseling or social work experience? Then consider organizing a parents' group, with child care when it meets. Or work in partnership with an organization that provides counseling and parenting training.

- Latchkey children who need after-school care? An unused room in the church, and adults or older teens with tutoring or camp counseling experience? Start an after-school program in the church. Borrow or buy a VCR and show movies; plan recreation activities; plan a quiet space for homework.

- Children failing in school? A youth fellowship group or singles' group eager for a weekly service activity? Set up an after-school tutoring program.

- Foster children who need permanent, loving families? Families in the congregation that would be interested in foster care or adoption if given emotional and material support from the church? Set a goal for one adoptable child in foster care to be placed with an interested family, and set up a support system. Hold a series of meetings on foster care to encourage families in your congregation to care for foster children.

- Families needing safe and affordable child care? Available financial resources in your congregation? Build a financial partnership with a child care program serving low-income families and their children. Or set up a scholarship fund for families that need child care.

- Preteens and teenagers who need support and guidance? Members in your congregation who like to volunteer? Involve members in Big Brothers and Big Sisters organizations in your area.

- A high infant mortality rate in your city or state? A congregation with a strong emphasis on education? Organize an adult forum on maternal and child health issues. Invite local speakers and end with a plan of action.

- A high child poverty rate in your area? Congregational interest in changing policies? Organize a letter-writing campaign to local, state, or national elected leaders on the need for more public investments in children and families.

Step 7: Build Partnerships To Help Children and Families

As you have researched programs in your community and as you have learned how other congregations have ministered to and with children at risk, you probably have realized that there is much to be done. Perhaps you have found programs that are doing good things. There is no need to reinvent the wheel and come up with another program to serve the same children when you could help improve or expand an existing program. Perhaps you have identified a serious need, but you cannot find the resources in your congregation to provide a program. Don't give up; look for partners from other congregations or community groups. Pooling resources for the good of the whole community is good stewardship. Build on one another's strengths. Perhaps an after-school program is sorely needed and you have a group of retired teachers willing to work in it, but your church building is not convenient to the school. Ask congregations nearer the school to plan the program with you.

Begin a partnership small, but dream big. Working together for the first time takes some getting used to and adjusting to one another's styles. Partnerships demand equality. Be clear about the resources, both material and human, that each partner will provide. Put decisions in writing so they can be communicated to others.

As you look for partners, another congregation may be your first thought, but consider nonprofit agencies that serve children and youths, religious social service agencies, ecumenical organizations, and child advocacy coalitions as well.

There are various forms of partnerships. Some provide a financial base for a program. Others provide a pool of human resources, both volunteer and professional. Partners may offer in-kind services. If you are open to the possibilities, you can come up with other ways to forge partnerships to help children and families.

Communication is an important element in working with other groups. Plan from the beginning ways that the membership of each group will be informed and encouraged to support the program. Report to each group regularly. Encourage their questions and interest.

Step 8: Raise Awareness and Issue a Call to Mission

Your next step will be to raise the awareness of the congregation in general and to present a call to mission to individual members. There are several avenues for this:

- Ask the worship committee or clergy to hold a worship service that focuses on children and their needs. (See **Organizing a Children's Sabbath**, pages 27–39.)

- Ask boards and committees, Bible study, and women's groups to use the meditations and discussions in this book.

- Offer to present programs for the various fellowship groups. Provide them with the meditations and discussion suggestions from pages 7–16.

- Ask to speak about the needs of children during the time for announcements in the worship service. Describe one area of the needs of children that you have discovered through your initial research.

- Provide inserts for your church newsletter and worship bulletins from this book.

Raising this awareness can help you gain initial support for whatever you decide to do later. However, your congregation changes over time. People come and go. Their interests and concerns also change. The single adult who listened with only mild interest last year suddenly will be all ears when married and pondering parenthood. Adults whose children are on their own may listen with concern but little motivation until they are grandparents. Keep awareness of the needs of children and families in your congregation and community alive by providing information and stories regularly.

Step 9: Educate Congregation Members for Action!

Once you have identified the problem facing children that you plan to address, formulated an action response, and begun to raise awareness, it's important to educate congregation members for action! Use **Section III: Developing a Study into Action Program**, to educate and engage your congregation. If possible, offer occasional speakers or forums after church to further inform congregation members and encourage broader participation in your effort for children and families.

As your congregation becomes involved in your initial project or effort, you may discover that this experience leads to new responses. Perhaps you will uncover additional problems that relate to the original issues that you decided to address. Because your congregation is already involved, it is more likely that it will want to extend its help to meet these newly discovered problems.

Or your church's involvement in an outreach program for children, such as housing a Head Start program, may lead it into advocacy, such as writing letters to increase funding for the Head Start program so it can serve every eligible child.

Finally, you may find that your efforts to address a local problem, such as the lack of affordable housing for families, may increase interest in responding to a related problem, such as street children in Brazil.

Site Visits and Tours

One means of raising awareness, building motivation, and choosing a specific program to support is a site visit and tour.

A newspaper may quote statistics about infant mortality, but words on a page can be erased mentally. Seeing a three-pound infant connected by tubes to life-support systems leaves a much more profound impression. Personal experiences can set hearts on fire.

If you invite members of your congregation to visit a program, also invite community leaders and policy makers. Such visits can stimulate a sense of urgency about children's needs and a willingness to becomes involved and involve others.

Suggestions To Make the Most of Site Visits and Tours

- **List all the potential sites and visits related to the area of concern you have chosen.** If you have chosen health care, show both the problem, such as babies in neonatal intensive care units, and attempts to prevent the problem, such as a prenatal care program for low-income women. If your guests become too depressed, they will be unable to act at all.

- **After you have chosen the sites you wish to visit, determine whether you have any connection with these sites through members of your congregation.** If so, ask them to help you make the contact or to assist you in planning the trip.

- **Call each program.** Ask the director for permission to visit, and how large a group the site can accommodate.

- **Visit the site and talk with the director before the tour is planned.** Be clear about your purpose and the type of information needed. For example, if you are visiting a soup kitchen, is your concern about how it handles food donations, or is it the number of children fed each day? Work with the director so that the greatest impact can

be made in a short amount of time. Encourage the director to tell an anecdotal story to illustrate the need for and impact of the program.

- **Ask for written materials from each of the sites.** Provide the participants with some basic information ahead of time. Suggest that they read it and note questions they have.

- **Coordinate the logistics of the visit carefully.** If possible, travel in one vehicle. Be sure the driver is clear about where you are going and how to get there. Provide name tags for the participants.

- **Make the trip as valuable as possible for the director, the program, and you.** Directors are very busy people, often running understaffed and underfunded programs. Be considerate about the time you are taking.

- **Prepare the participants before you begin.** Site visits and tours are learning experiences, not spectator sports. It is difficult for a group touring a program not to appear to be "looking at the poor people receiving services." Ask the participants to be as unobtrusive as possible. Discuss the need to be sensitive to the privacy of the patients or guests at the programs you visit. Should a participant recognize someone, it is better that he or she make no move unless the other person speaks. Needless to say, the identity of the service recipients should not be discussed after the visit.

- **The visit is not over when you walk out the door.** Plan to use the time between sites to talk about what you saw and how you felt. At the conclusion of the visits, plan time to talk over the experience and to discuss possible next steps. Consider these questions: How can we work in partnership with one or more of the programs we visited? How can we use the knowledge we have gained to help children and families? What actions are needed to support these programs — writing letters to legislators or newspapers, providing financial support, or volunteering, for example?

A Congregational Resources Assessment

Human Resources

Name	Address	Phone	Interest/Expertise	Availability

(use additional paper if needed)

Financial Resources

- Monies budgeted currently for mission and outreach:

  $_____

- Amount of that money that supports programs for children and families:

  $_____

- Monies budgeted for child and youth programs in your congregation:

  $_____

- Special offerings or appeals to the congregation for programs related to children and youths:

  $_____

- Your estimate of untapped financial resources in your congregation for children and youths:

  $_____

Physical Resources

What, in each category below, is available for programming for children and youths? What existing resources could be made available if needed by a program?

- Church building: _____
- Outdoor space: _____
- Audio-visual equipment: _____
- Toys and other play equipment: _____
- Office equipment (such as computers and photocopiers): _____
- Vehicles: _____

Putting It All Together: Matching Your Congregation's Resources with Children's Needs

Level of Congregation's Interest and Expertise

	High	Low	Comments
Education			
Community Outreach			
Advocacy			

Available Resources

Financial: _____   Property: _____

_____   _____

_____   _____

_____

Equipment: _____   _____

_____   _____

_____

People, Skills, Time
(Continue on additional paper)

_____ _____ _____

_____ _____ _____

_____ _____ _____

_____ _____ _____

_____ _____ _____

_____ _____ _____

(Copy and use this as a hand-out)

Most Critical Problems Facing _____

Children and Their Families _____

(Local and National) _____

_____

_____

Congregations, Organizations, and Programs Making
a Difference for Children

Name   Address   Phone Number

_____

_____

_____

_____

Resource Persons in the Congregation and Community

_____

_____

_____

_____

_____

_____

_____

_____

_____

Other Items of Interest: _____

_____

_____

_____

Developing a Study into Action Program

PHOTO BY SUSIE FITZHUGH

How To Use This Section

This section provides both a framework and resource materials for developing a Study into Action program for your congregation, designed to engage participants in:

♦ Exploring the theological basis for involvement in social issues affecting children;

♦ Learning about specific issues as they affect children locally, regionally, and nationally;

♦ Developing corporate or individual action plans to help make a difference in the lives of children.

You may choose one issue, such as child care, on which to focus a four-week Study into Action program, or you may decide to study a number of different issues in succession. Whichever format you choose, the framework and resource materials provided in this section will help you:

♦ Stimulate theological reflection on a particular issue or issues affecting children;

♦ Raise questions to consider throughout the course of study;

♦ Identify human resources in your congregation and community (as well as written and visual materials) to inform your Study into Action group about the particular issue or issues; and

♦ Plan action steps for further education, community involvement, or public policy advocacy.

Chapter 1 sets out a format (and Leader Suggestions) for developing a Study into Action program for an adult education forum, a youth group series, or an intergenerational program.

The remaining chapters contain materials on major issue areas (child care and Head Start, education, vulnerable children and families, education, homelessness and housing, maternal and child health, youth development and teen pregnancy prevention, and family income). For each issue you will find the scriptural and secular quotations; sample reflection questions; a brief introduction to the current problems, goals, policies, and programs related to the issue area; a worksheet to help you identify sources of information in your community; and examples of action steps.

A Four-Part Format for a Study into Action Program

Week 1: The Faces of _____ *(the issue, for example, Homelessness)*

Begin the session by presenting one of the suggested scriptural or secular passages. Raise the questions that will encourage members to reflect on the faith basis for addressing the issue.

If the introductory text was distributed prior to the first session, allow time for initial questions or discussion. If it was not, distribute the text now and either summarize the key issues or allow time for the group to read through it.

Invite a person who is part of the community you want to learn about — for example, a member of a homeless self-help group. Or invite someone with personal, hands-on experience working with those affected by the issue. Contact a social or community service organization, or perhaps an area church with a program related to your issue. Ask the speaker to describe, with anecdotes, the real impact of the issue on children. Invite the speaker to show slides or share photographs. A short video may also help to personalize the issue.

If possible, arrange for a site visit (see page 50) of a facility or program dealing with the issue. If the visit will take place directly after the education hour or worship service, arrange for extended child care of group members' children. Alert group members in advance of the scheduled site visit.

Week 2: _____ *(the issue) in Our Community*

Begin with prayer, or by collectively writing a litany based on what group members saw and felt and learned in the first week.

Invite a speaker from a local agency who can educate your group about the scope of the problem in your community and particular programs currently available. Ask the speaker if there are materials you can photocopy and distribute ahead of time or at the conclusion of this session.

Alternatively, you may want to incorporate the worksheet provided for each issue area as part of your Study into Action course. At the end of the first week, distribute the sheet and have group members select which agency, program, person, or aspect of the problem they will research between the first and second session. Make the second session one in which each member shares what she or he has learned.

Plan an activity for the end of this session, or for during the week. For instance, participants may want to write letters to the mayor describing their interest in the issue and requesting further information. A sample letter may help. Alternatively, some group members may want to write letters to the editor of your local newspaper.

Week 3: The Larger Picture of _____ (the issue)

Begin with prayer, or with a brief time of reflection and discussion on a scriptural passage.

Invite speakers from, or informed about, state- and federal-level agencies to discuss the national scope of the problem and state and federal policies and programs.

Learn ways that people can effect legislative change on the state and national level. For this session's action, the group may decide to make telephone calls or write members of Congress to ask that children's needs be at the top of their agenda. If the group learned about a particular piece of legislation, it may want to focus on that. (See **Section V** for ideas and reproducible materials.)

At the end of this session the group should decide whether it will pursue collective action on behalf of children, or whether each member individually will advocate based on individual interests and schedules.

Week 4: From Study into Action

Invite a trio composed of an educator, an outreach person, and a public policy advocate to present alternatives for action.

In the resource materials for each particular issue you will find specific examples of how education, outreach, or public policy advocacy action might be tailored to a particular issue. Photocopy the pages and distribute them to group members to stimulate brainstorming.

If the group has decided on collective action, use this time to determine what it will focus on and make concrete plans to follow through. You may want to invite key church leaders, staff, or committee members to attend this session to help plan what the group will do as it moves from study into action. Refer to **Section II: Step by Step** and **Section V: Giving Voice to the Voiceless** to help you plan.

If group members have decided not to pursue action collectively, but instead individually, to engage in some form of child advocacy, use the Pledge of Commitment form on pages 60–61 for this last session. Make a photocopy for each member. Have each group member decide which form of action — education, outreach, or public policy advocacy — she or he will pursue, and fill in the appropriate line of the pledge. Have the entire group sign the back of the pledge, to affirm the corporate spirit and support. The important final component of the pledge, indicating which organization or individual a group member will work with, moves the pledge beyond a statement of good intentions to a starting point of action.

Set a date in the next month or two to get together for a potluck dinner or a group breakfast before church to share what action each of you has undertaken on behalf of children.

Plan time for reflection and sharing about this Study into Action program, and for evaluation. You may wish to develop other activities as the group moves from study together into action.

Leader Suggestions for Developing a Study into Action Program

Stimulate Theological Reflection on the Particular Issue Affecting Children

Using the scriptural and secular passages at the beginning of sections for issue areas (or from **Section I** of this book), you may want to spend the first 15 or 20 minutes of each session in prayerful consideration and discussion of our God-given mandate to protect children, focusing particularly on the issue at hand.

Raise questions that not only will help your group reflect on the scriptural passages but also will guide your study of the issue area. Good questions prepared by the leader will help the group see the connection.

For instance, if the Study into Action program is about youth development and teenage pregnancy prevention, have the group read Psalm 144:12: "May our sons in their youth be like plants full grown, our daughters like corner pillars, cut for the building of a palace."

Then ask them to reflect upon and discuss the following questions:

◆ What kind of environment, or what supports, do the sons and daughters of our nation need to flourish "like plants full grown" and to be as solid and stable as corner pillars of a palace?

◆ What kind of education, job preparation, and information on issues related to sexuality and family life do they need?

Identify Education and Information Resources for Your Study into Action Program

The descriptions of issue areas in the following chapters are intended as general introductions and may be reproduced. If possible, distribute photocopies to group members before the first session.

However, you will need to identify sources of more detailed, in-depth information on issues as they relate to your community. You don't have to be an expert yourself to plan this Study into Action program. You just need to identify, invite, and involve knowledgeable people in your congregation and community.

The resource materials for each issue area include a worksheet-style page to facilitate this process. As the program leader, you can use the worksheet to help you plan and prepare this Study into Action program. Alternatively, you may want to distribute the worksheet to group members during the actual program, so they can participate in identifying information resources and researching the issue.

Either way, when you have identified a useful organization, you may decide to invite someone to address your group, to request written material on the issue or the organization, or to obtain information over the phone. Refer to **Section II,** pages 45–47, for sources of information and key people to contact regarding community problems, programs, and policies.

Plan for Your Group to Decide into What Action This Study Will Lead

You can incorporate small, immediate actions into your program while laying the groundwork for a more substantial and sustained course of action. Making a site visit after church (see page 50) the first Sunday, telephoning your state legislator's office the next week to learn about his or her voting record on children's issues, and writing to your members of Congress on the third Sunday are all immediate actions the leader can plan and incorporate into the group program. Think through the actions in advance to determine what group members will need (addresses and phone numbers, sample letters, pens, and stationery, for example).

Another desired outcome of the program of study is continued action on behalf of children. Some groups may choose to initiate a sustained corporate action. For other groups, however, moving from study into action may mean that each member, with the newly gained knowledge of the problem and programs in the community, decides upon an action which she or he will pursue independently. Either way, some possibilities for the group to consider are:

◆ **Further education,** of yourselves, the broader congregation, the community, or public leaders.

◆ **Outreach involvement in the community,** through existing programs in your own church or community organizations, partnering with other churches, or by establishing a new program.

◆ **Advocacy in the public policy arena,** on the local, state, or federal level.

Pledge of Commitment

Now there are varieties of gifts, but the same Spirit; and there are varieties of services, but the same Lord: and there are varieties of activities, but it is the same God who activates all of them in everyone. To each is given the manifestation of the Spirit for the common good.

1 Corinthians 12:4–7

To one is given through the Spirit the utterance of wisdom, and to another the utterance of knowledge according to the same Spirit....

1 Corinthians 12:8

I pledge myself to help educate others about the needs of children and how we can minister to those needs. Specifically, I pledge to:

_____

_____

_____

Then the righteous will answer him, "Lord, when was it that we saw you hungry and gave you food, or thirsty and gave you something to drink? And when was it that we saw you a stranger and welcomed you, or naked and gave you clothing? And when was it that we saw you sick or in prison and visited you?"

And the king will answer them, "Truly I tell you, just as you did it to one of the least of these who are members of my family, you did it to me."

Matthew 25:37–40

I pledge myself to undertake an outreach activity to minister to children's needs. Specifically, I pledge to:

_____

_____

_____

Speak out for those who cannot speak, for the rights of all the destitute. Speak out, judge righteously, defend the rights of the needy.

Proverbs 31:8–9

I pledge myself to advocate for public policies that benefit children. Specifically, I pledge to:

_____

_____

_____

The name, address, and telephone number of an organization or individual with whom I will work to fulfill my commitment to a ministry of child advocacy:

_____

_____

_____

As a community of faith, we are called to support each other in our ministries. The following people pledge to support me in my ministry to children in need, as I will support them in theirs:

Jesus said, "I will not leave you orphaned; I am coming to you. In a little while the world will no longer see me, but you will see me; because I live, you also will live. On that day you will know that I am in [God], and you in me, and I in you. They who have my commandments and keep them are those who love me; and those who love me will be loved by [God], and I will love them and reveal myself to them.

"I have said these things to you while I am still with you. But the Advocate, the Holy Spirit, whom [God] will send in my name, will teach you everything and remind you of all that I have said to you."

John 14:18–21, 25–26

_____

Signature   Date

CHAPTER 2

Child Care and Head Start

Look on my right hand and see—
there is no one who takes notice of me;
no refuge remains to me;
no one cares for me.

Psalm 142:4

As the major provider of child care in the United States, the church has a special responsibility to help raise ethical questions about child care. It is the obligation of the church to advocate a coherent, comprehensive, inclusive, and, above all, equitable public policy regarding child care. As it approaches public advocacy for child care, the church must be guided by its concern for all sectors of society.

National Council of the Churches of Christ in the USA
Policy Statement on Child Day Care

For every child in Sunday school, eight children are in church-housed child care on Monday.

Called to Act: Stories of Child Care Advocacy in Our Churches, Ecumenical Child Care Network, 1986

If the child is safe, everyone is safe.

G. Campbell Morgan, "The Children's Playground in the City of God," *The Westminster Pulpit,* page 262 (circa 1908)

Whoever welcomes one such child in my name welcomes me, and whoever welcomes me welcomes not me but the one who sent me.

Mark 9:37

Reflection Questions

◆ Ordinarily we think of adults as the authors of the Psalms, and thus tend to identify as adults with their writings. Try reading Psalm 142 as though a child is speaking. How does this help you understand the need of a child for security and self-esteem? How is safe and affordable child care connected to self-esteem?

◆ Churches and synagogues are the major providers of child day care in this nation, according to statistics gathered by the National Council of the Churches of Christ in the USA. What theological and biblical basis can you give for the church involving itself in child day care? Consider the two scripture quotations above in regard to this question.

◆ Jesus admonishes his followers to receive children in his name. What does that mean to you? What requirements does it place on the church? On individual members of each congregation?

◆ Today, one of two mothers is in the work force. What support is needed for them and their children? How can your congregation "take notice" and provide "refuge" for children?

Child Care

On a rainy day in Cincinnati, Ohio, Marquise Freeman woke at 5:30 a.m. to dress and feed her two children, one and two years old. At 6:30 she and the children boarded the first of two crosstown buses to her cousin's house. After leaving the children with her cousin, Marquise took another bus downtown to her office job. That evening she reversed the trek, arriving back home at about 8:00 p.m.

Marquise and her children are exhausted by this daily commute. She dreams of sending her children to a child care center near her apartment, but she can't afford it. She is in the midst of a divorce, receives no child support, and earns just $6.07 an hour. She has applied for a subsidized child care "slot" from the state, but there are 3,000 names on the list already. Meanwhile, Marquise and her children spend long hours each day riding buses to and from her cousin's house.

Hundreds of thousands of working parents like

Marquise need safe, accessible care for their children but can't afford it. Many others, especially parents of infants, are having trouble finding good quality child care at any price.

The child care crisis reflects the radical changes that have occurred in America's family and work life in the past two decades. The number of mothers in the work force is increasing every year, and most of these mothers work because they must. Nearly one out of four of today's employed mothers is the primary wage earner for her children. Many two-parent families now need two salaries in order to afford the basic necessities.

As a result, more than half of all mothers with preschool-age children now are employed, and that includes mothers of infants. Three-quarters of mothers of children ages three through 13, and two-thirds of mothers with children younger than 18, have jobs outside the home.

While many employed parents traditionally asked relatives to care for their children, that option has become far less available as more and more grandparents and other relatives are either in the work force themselves or live too far away. Today, working parents rely on a variety of child care arrangements, depending on what they can afford and what is available. An increasing number of parents are choosing center-based child care, particularly for older toddlers and preschoolers.

While communities and schools increasingly recognize the importance of offering before- and after-school care for school-age youngsters, an alarming number of children — an estimated 3.4 million between the ages of five and 12, according to the National Child Care Survey — take care of themselves. The true number of such "latchkey" children left unsupervised may be much larger than the reported number, however, since many parents find it difficult to admit that they are leaving their children alone.

Even very young children sometimes are left unsupervised by working parents who fear they will lose their jobs if they stay home with their children when their child care arrangements fall through. Linda Gonzales of San Antonio recently found herself in this predicament. Gonzales often left her children at home alone while she went to work at her hotel job because she could not find affordable child care. On one such day in 1993, 13-month-old Matthew died in a house fire that his four-year-old brother accidentally started while playing with a cigarette lighter.

The High Cost of Child Care

In 1990 the U.S. General Accounting Office reported that the average annual cost of care for a four-year-old in a good quality, accredited child care center was $4,797, more than half the total full-time income of a parent earning minimum wage. Today, many low-income families spend 25 percent of their income on child care. Other families, unable to pay so much, often are forced to settle for the cheapest child care available, even though they may not be satisfied with the quality. A few years ago in a neighborhood near Chicago, 47 youngsters were discovered being cared for in a basement by only one adult. It's unlikely that any of the parents of those children were happy about the arrangement, but, at $25 a week, the program cost only one-third as much as most child care in the community.

Although many parents cannot stretch their paychecks far enough to meet their family's basic needs and pay for decent child care, only a small proportion of low-income parents are lucky enough to receive child care assistance. In almost every state the money available for subsidized child care is grossly inadequate.

Families' Needs Are Not Being Met

Even if every family could afford decent child care, their child care problems would not necessarily be over. In many communities there simply isn't enough good quality child care to meet the demand.

Among parents of young children who were polled nationally in 1989, two of every five said there were not enough programs for preschoolers. And only one in four parents said there was a sufficient supply of child care for infants. Union Bay Child Care in Seattle, for example, recently had 18 infants and toddlers enrolled in its child care program, but it had a waiting list of 233.

More child care is available for preschool children than for infants, but many preschool programs operate only part-day. Young children in part-day programs may have to shuttle among as many as three caregivers in a single day, a stressful regimen that child development experts say is not good for young children.

The lack of reliable, affordable child care prevents many parents from going to work to support their families. In a 1986 study of welfare participants, nearly two-thirds of those who responded said that child care was their primary problem in seeking and keeping jobs. Another study found a similar situation among parents in general: an estimated one-fourth of mothers ages 21 to 29 who were out of the labor force in 1986 were not working because of child care problems.

Quality Is Critical

Child care must be more than a parking place for children while their parents work. Children and society both benefit when child care assures children's safety and provides a solid foundation for healthy social development and school success. Child development experts say that young children should be cared for in small groups with a high ratio of staff to children, in order to assure close adult supervision and adult-to-child interaction. Good child care includes activities geared to a child's age and skill level, proper health and safety practices, good communication between caregivers and parents so that children's individual needs are met. Since young children need predictable routines and relationships in order to feel secure and develop the ability to trust, there should be little turnover among a child's caregivers. But caregivers need to earn adequate wages, so they do not have to leave the field for better-paying jobs. Moreover, they need basic training to help them understand the special needs of young children, deal with parents effectively, and cope well with emergencies and stress.

Good programs also help ensure that children and their families get needed services beyond child care, such as help with housing, nutrition, health care, job training, or substance abuse programs. Although some child care and early childhood programs offer families help in meeting some of these broader needs, either by providing services directly or by helping families connect with other community agencies and services, such programs definitely are in the minority. With the exception of Head Start and a few similar state programs, neither state or federal programs have been designed or funded to take into account the full range of family needs.

The Response to the Child Care Crisis

To make sure that every child who needs it has good child care, our society must actively engage the child care crisis on many levels — public and private, local, state, and national. Such a far-reaching commitment requires new thinking about children and child care.

Traditionally, Americans have viewed child care simply as something that allows parents to work. But such thinking is too limited. Child care must serve the developmental and educational needs of young children just as school does for school-age children. And just as it is society's responsibility to educate school-age children, it is society's duty to see to it that young children are nurtured in a way that gets them ready for school and for lifelong learning and achievement.

Our whole society benefits when we nurture and develop our human resources as fully as possible. Since good child care contributes to our children's development, it is in our national interest to make it a public priority, not just a family concern.

Community organizations and employers have an important role to play in responding to families' needs for good child care. Historically, no community organization has responded more actively than churches. America's churches are the single largest provider of child care in the country. In addition, many nonprofit organizations sponsor child care programs, and local United Way chapters have both invested in child care

and earmarked funds for child care scholarships for low-income children.

Government's Role

Although some states have taken steps in recent years to address the problems of cost, quality, and supply of child care, the resources for such efforts generally have been very limited. Investments also range widely among states. State expenditures for child care and early childhood development in FY 1990 ranged from $152.04 per child in Massachusetts to $0.24 per child in Idaho. Half of all states spent less than $25 per child.

As it became increasingly apparent during the 1980s that states could not solve the child care problem without greater help from the federal government, child care advocates around the nation began working together to develop federal child care legislation and to strengthen existing federal efforts in the area of early childhood development. They achieved some landmark gains. Here are the major federal sources of child care funding today:

♦ Head Start provides quality child development and comprehensive services to low-income and disabled children, primarily through part-day, part-year programs.

♦ The Child Care and Development Block Grant provides child care subsidies for low-income children. A portion of the funds must be used to improve the quality of care and to provide early childhood or school-age child care services.

♦ The "At-Risk" Child Care Program provides child care assistance to low-income families "at risk" of going on welfare.

♦ The Family Support Act (FSA) Child Care Programs provide child care assistance for any parent on Aid to Families with Dependent Children (AFDC), or welfare, who is employed or participating in approved education or training programs. To ease the transition from welfare to self-sufficiency, child care assistance also is available for up to one year for employed parents leaving the AFDC rolls.

♦ The Social Services Block Grant (previously known as Title XX) supports a wide range of social services. Most states use at least some of these funds to provide child care subsidies.

♦ The Dependent Care Block Grant supports the start-up and operation of school-age child care programs and child care resource and referral agencies.

♦ The Dependent Care Tax Credit helps parents with a portion of their child care expenses. It is available on a sliding scale, with lower income families receiving slightly larger credits. But since the tax credit now is nonrefundable, families owing little or no federal income tax benefit little or not at all.

These are important steps toward developing a child care system that is of consistently high quality in every state. But they are just first steps. There is still much to be done before all American children have the kind of child care experiences that contribute to their full physical, emotional, and cognitive development.

Head Start

In Head Start, the nation has a highly successful preschool program for disadvantaged children. Head Start was launched by the federal government in 1965. The goal was to help break the cycle of poverty by preparing low-income preschool children for school success. What makes Head Start so unusual is the way it goes about that task.

Instead of concentrating just on increasing children's basic skills, Head Start makes sure the children are healthy and well-fed, giving them health checkups and treatment and feeding them a nutritious hot meal every day.

Instead of focusing only on the child, Head Start focuses on the whole family, making sure parents get help with a wide range of family needs, from housing to employment to parenting education.

And instead of relying completely on teachers and other professionals to run the programs and work with the children, Head Start teaches parents to see themselves as the primary teachers and advocates for their children. The program asks parents to participate through Head Start policy councils and trains parents to help in the classrooms and fill other Head Start jobs.

Over the years it has become clear that Head Start's approach works. Studies show that every $1 invested in Head Start-type programs saves more than $7 down the road in costs related to school dropout, teenage pregnancy, welfare, and crime.

Study after study shows that Head Start children start school healthy and ready to learn. They make gains on tests measuring cognitive skills and social and emotional development and are less likely to be placed in special education classes or held back a grade in school. Eighty percent of Head Start parents volunteer to help in the program. At home, Head Start parents typically read to their children and take an interest in their education. And thanks to Head Start's health services, Head Start children get treatment for medical problems and are up-to-date on their shots. With its mounting proof of solid success, Head Start has earned respect and support from all sectors of American society.

Head Start Is Facing New Challenges

Today the changing needs of Head Start families are presenting Head Start with new challenges. More and more mothers work or go to school full-time. Because Head Start typically operates half-day and only during the nine-month school year, many poor working families cannot participate. Head Start families increasingly are headed by very young and inexperienced single mothers who need parenting education. More Head Start families are struggling with substance abuse than in Head Start's early years. More families and homeless, and more live in violent, crime-ridden neighborhoods.

The first thing Head Start must do to respond to these realities in the 1990s is expand to serve every eligible child whose parents want to participate. Despite its record of success, Head Start now receives only enough funding to serve a portion of all eligible children.

At the same time, Head Start programs everywhere must be able to maintain the quality of their services. Given the tremendous odds many Head Start families face today, it's more important than ever that Head Start programs have enough good teachers and well-trained health and social service workers to give children the prompt individual attention they need. For years, however, programs have been pushed to expand enrollment without enough concern for quality. The result was that many Head Start centers were denied the flexibility and resources they needed to make sure their services were top notch.

Congress took a step in addressing these challenges in 1990 when it passed a bill that created the potential for enough funding to serve all eligible children. It also set aside money for quality improvements. Funding for Head Start was increased to $3.3 billion in 1994, yet the program still serves less than half of the eligible children.

In the 1990s, child advocates must support presidential and congressional initiatives to:

◆ Extend Head Start services to full-day and full-year for families in which parents work or go to school full-time.

◆ Enable Head Start to offer more services to families of infants and toddlers to keep babies developing at a strong pace and get them ready for Head Start when they turn three.

◆ Give children continuing help after they leave Head Start to make a smooth transition to kindergarten and the primary grades.

- Offer more extensive job training, literacy classes, housing assistance, and other social services to Head Start families.

If all this sounds like a big investment of money, time, and talent, it is. But good investments pay off, and there is no doubt that Head Start is a good investment for the U.S. Every sector of society and every individual must pitch in to support Head Start, for it provides children a good start in life through a good quality preschool experience.

What Can You Do To Meet the Urgent Needs for Child Care and Head Start?

Educate Yourself and Others

- Write an article for your church newsletter summarizing what you have learned about the child care needs of families in your congregation and community. This is important information to present to people who have no need for child care and may be unaware of the stress that finding it places on families.

- If your church already houses a child care program, discuss with the director how that child care ministry can become more visible to the congregation. Perhaps a small bulletin board could display class photographs, with a description of the program and periodic events or needs.

- Write an article for your local newspaper summarizing what you have learned about the child care needs in your community. Or talk with the staff of the newspaper and suggest that such an article or series be developed.

- With other congregations and child care organizations, sponsor a community-wide Child Care Day to focus attention on existing programs and services.

- Write a letter to the editor of your local newspaper explaining what Head Start does, why it works, and why it's in everyone's interest to expand Head Start so all eligible children can participate.

Get Involved in Your Community

- Enter into a partnership with a congregation providing child care and Head Start for low-income families. Provide toys and equipment, financial support, or volunteer assistance. You also can call your local Head Start center directly to find out what kind of help from the community is needed.

- Organize a fund raising activity to benefit a child care program, or set up a scholarship fund to help parents who cannot afford child care.

- Develop or house an after-school child care program, a full-day child care program, or a Head Start program in your church building. Excellent resources to assist you are available from the Ecumenical Child Care Network (see page 144).

- Call the Children's Defense Fund for information on how you can organize a Child Watch visit (a guided tour) for local leaders and citizens to a Head Start center.

Advocate for Affordable and Quality Child Care

- Write to your members of Congress about the child care needs in your community and urge them to increase critical funding for Head Start and child care. Do the same with your state legislators. States can supplement federal funds for Head Start and child care. Let your state legislators know how important this supplemental funding is.

- Join a child care coalition in your community or state.

- Speak with groups of business leaders or individual executives, encouraging them to take an active role in providing and advocating for quality child care and Head Start. Provide information for them about the advantages to them when workers need not worry about care for their children.

Child Care Information Resources Worksheet

Child development expert (try professors at a local community college or university): _____

_____

Speaker: yes ❑ no ❑   Send materials: yes ❑ no ❑

Ask about: what child care or preschool education should be; what environment, activities, nurturing, and discipline young children need for optimal development.

Comments/information: _____

_____

_____

_____

Local child care or Head Start program: _____

Speaker: yes ❑ no ❑   Send materials: yes ❑ no ❑   Site visit: yes ❑ no ❑

Ask about: number served; number on waiting list; costs; needs; resources; regulatory requirements and provider's opinion and enforcement of them; barriers and limitations programs face; services to low-income, minority, and special-needs children.

Comments/information: _____

_____

_____

_____

Church sponsor of child care or Head Start program: _____

Speaker: yes ❑ no ❑   Send materials: yes ❑ no ❑   Site visit: yes ❑ no ❑

Ask about: process and costs to sponsor/partner a child care or Head Start program, as well as those questions listed above.

Comments/information: _____

_____

_____

_____

(Copy and use this as a hand-out)

Community advocates for child care (look in the telephone book under Child Care Information and Referral, ask the three previous contacts, or talk with parents):

_____

Speaker: yes ☐ no ☐   Send materials: yes ☐ no ☐

Ask about: local issues, differences in providers in the community, view of the child care needs in the community, current legislative push or desired actions, membership, etc.

Comments/information: _____

_____

_____

_____

State department of social or human services: _____

Speaker: yes ☐ no ☐   Send materials: yes ☐ no ☐

Ask about: state policy on quality and regulatory issues, affordability issues and policies, relevant statistics, current legislative items, etc.

Comments/information: _____

_____

_____

_____

Child Care Action Campaign, 330 Seventh Ave., New York, NY 10001, (212) 239-0138.

Send materials: yes ☐ no ☐

Ask about: information on child care, state child advocacy contacts.

Comments/information: _____

_____

_____

_____

Ecumenical Child Care Network, 1580 N. Northwest Highway, Park Ridge, IL 60068-1456, (708) 298-1612.

Speaker (from local affiliate): yes ☐ no ☐   Send materials: yes ☐ no ☐

Ask about: membership, local affiliates/contacts, policies.

Comments/information: _____

_____

_____

(Copy and use this as a hand-out)

National Council of Churches Committee on Justice for Children and Their Families, 1119 Dauphine Street, #5, New Orleans, LA 70116, (504) 522-9895.

Speaker (from local affiliate): yes ❑ no ❑   Send materials: yes ❑ no ❑

Ask about: membership, local affiliates/contacts, policies.

Comments/information: _____

_____

_____

_____

National Head Start Association, 1220 King Street, Suite 200, Alexandria, VA 22314, (703) 739-0875.

Send materials: yes ❑ no ❑

Ask about: information on Head Start.

Comments/information: _____

_____

_____

_____

Children's Defense Fund, Child Care Division, 25 E Street, N.W., Washington, DC 20001, (202) 628-8787.

Send materials: yes ❑ no ❑

Ask about: current agenda, legislative items, desired actions.

Comments/information: _____

_____

_____

_____

National Association for the Education of Young Children, 1834 Connecticut Avenue, N.W., Washington, DC 20009, (202) 232-8777.

Send materials: yes ❑ no ❑

Ask about: information on child care, and state and local contacts who may be working on advocacy.

Comments/information: _____

_____

_____

_____

CHAPTER 3

Education

Train children in the right way, and when old, they will not stray.

Proverbs 22:6

The U.S. invests a smaller portion of its gross domestic product in education than 13 other industrialized countries.

Economic Policy Institute

Reflection Questions

◆ Read "Greenless Child" and "Children Learn What They Live" on page 23. What does the biblical passage above and the contemporary poetry have in common? How do they relate to the education of children? At home? In the church? In the community?

◆ What kind of environment does each child require so as not to be a "greenless child"? What kind of environment should our schools provide to help all children achieve their greatest potential? What prevents schools from fulfilling this goal? What part does the church have in assuring this environment for all children?

◆ Read aloud "Children Learn What They Live." Which children in your community live with criticism? With hostility? With ridicule? With shame? Tolerance? Encouragement? Praise? Fairness? Approval? Acceptance and friendship? What do these children have in common? How are they different?

◆ Read Matthew 18:1–7. Think about what you do in one day's time — at home, at work, in recreation. How much do you depend upon your ability to read, write, and communicate effectively to hold your job, to parent, to care for others, to enjoy leisure time? How would an inadequate education be a stumbling block in your day-to-day activities? How would it be a stumbling block to reaching life goals?

Education

Technical sophistication, adaptability, and problem-solving skills — not stamina and strong backs — will drive the economy in the 1990s and beyond. If we reserve the benefits of an excellent education for only some children, our nation not only will betray its democratic ideals, it will sacrifice its future.

During the 1980s, as the gap between rich and poor families widened, far too many children attended inferior schools persistently segregated by income and race. But not only poor children and children of color are being cheated of a first-rate education. Even many middle- and upper-income White children receive an inadequate education.

◆ Fewer than half (41 percent) of the 17-year-olds in the U.S. can understand, summarize, and explain material found in encyclopedias.

◆ In the latest international math and science tests, 13-year-olds from the U.S. placed thirteenth in math achievement and twelfth in science achievement among students from 14 other nations. Canada ranked eighth in both math and science tests.

Evidence of the need for change in U.S. education has been mounting for at least a decade, culminating in 1990 with President Bush's announcement of six national education goals for the decade. These ambitious goals point in the right direction, but we have a long way to go to achieve them by the year 2000.

A Nation's Future Depends on a Fully Educated Work Force

In the coming decades, the mismatch between the needs of U.S. employers and the number of qualified workers will grow worse as a result of several

The Education Goals: Where We Stand

Goal 1. All children will start school ready to learn.

As many as 35 percent of kindergarten children come to school unprepared for formal education.

Goal 2. The high school graduation rate will increase to at least 90 percent.

The proportion of young people completing high school has remained stagnant for more than a decade, with almost one in five 19- and 20-year-olds in the U.S. lacking a high school diploma.

Goal 3. Students will leave grades 4, 8, and 12 showing competency in English, math, science, history, and geography.

Fewer than one in five students in grades 4, 8, and 12 has shown math "competency" on the National Assessment of Educational Progress (NAEP).

Goal 4. U.S. students will be first in the world in science and math achievement.

Fewer than half of twelfth-graders taking the 1990 NAEP showed a detailed knowledge of science, could design experiments, or could interpret graphs and tables.

Goal 5. Every adult will be literate and will possess the knowledge and skills necessary to compete in a global economy and exercise responsibilities of citizenship.

Most twelfth-graders in the U.S. have a basic knowledge of civics, but only about half understand such specifics as separation of powers, and just 6 percent have a detailed knowledge of such government institutions as the president's Cabinet and the judiciary.

Goal 6. Every school will be free of drugs and will offer a disciplined environment conducive to learning.

About three in 10 high school seniors reported in 1989 that alcohol and marijuana were easy to obtain in their schools.

---

trends. First, the economy is exploding with jobs that require high-level skills. There is less and less need for unskilled workers. Second, the proportion of young workers in the U.S. is shrinking. By 2000 there will be 14 percent fewer workers between the ages of 18 and 24 than in the mid-1980s. And third, between now and 2000 nearly one-third of those who enter the work force will be people of color, and thus disproportionately poor and undereducated.

Students Who Need the Most Get the Least

Big-city school systems became increasingly segregated during the 1980s, according to a National School Boards Association study. Eighty percent of Latino students in the South and Northeast now attend schools that are predominantly minority. Half of all Black students in the Northeast attend schools with fewer than 10 percent Whites, and one-third attend schools that are at least 99 percent minority.

These schools typically have far fewer resources and much weaker academic programs than schools with more White and higher income students. For example, only half of the schools whose enrollment is 90 percent minority offer even one section of calculus, compared with 80 percent of mostly White schools. In 1989, the

Texas Supreme Court cited one low-income school district as evidence of the "dramatic" difference in the quality of education programs between wealthy and poor districts. The low-income district had "no foreign language, no prekindergarten program, no chemistry, no physics, no calculus, and no college preparatory or honors program," much less extracurricular activities such as a band or debate club.

Poor and minority students who attend wealthier suburban schools may not be much better off, however, for often they are tracked into nonacademic courses. Across all U.S. schools, for example, almost twice as many Black eighth-graders as White eighth-graders take no science class. Latino eighth-graders are almost two-and-a-half times as likely to take no science class as their White peers.

Given these disparities in educational opportunity, it is hardly surprising that White students from higher income backgrounds outscore minority and lower income students in all subjects — although the achievement of more advantaged students often is nothing to be proud of. While only a discouraging 19 percent of White twelfth-graders demonstrated "competency" in mathematics on the NAEP, a mere 6 percent of Latinos, 4 percent of Blacks, and 5 percent of Native Americans achieved at that level.

Schools That Help All Students Achieve

While far too many schools fail to provide students with an adequate education, some exceptions already are paving the way toward educational excellence for poor and minority students. Although most efforts to increase parental and community involvement in schools are relatively new, James Comer's School Development Program in New Haven, Connecticut, has existed long enough to show well-documented increases in student achievement and social skills when parents and the community become involved.

Schools following the Comer model adopt a form of school-based management in which parents, teachers, and teacher's aides become a team that establishes the school's curriculum, activities, attitudes, and values. Another program involves parents in classroom and school activities.

Elementary school students in New Haven pilot programs using the Comer model during the late 1970s showed marked improvement in attendance and academic achievement. And graduates of a pilot school scored considerably higher than their seventh-grade peers from another elementary school in language, math, and work-study skills.

The Comer Schools and New York City's Community School District Four in East Harlem have been leaders in supporting children both in and out of the classroom. Their efforts provide solid evidence that children's academic and social skills improve when schools, parents, and communities all work together to reinforce the messages that learning is important and every child can achieve at high levels.

In Baltimore's inner-city Dunbar neighborhood, the entire community united in 1990 to pursue a common goal of increasing its children's achievement. School principals, parents, and business leaders met with local police and representatives from the health department and social service agencies to discuss the Dunbar school's successes and challenges.

Out of that meeting emerged a wealth of creative community projects to support and supplement the school's efforts. For example, the local senior citizens' center adopted a second-grade classroom, AT&T paid to install an electronic hookup between the high school and a public library to give students access to its resources, and the American Friends Service Committee began offering a program to teach students nonviolent ways of settling problems.

The Characteristics of Effective Schools

Researchers and practitioners suggest that parents and other concerned citizens look for the following characteristics to judge whether a school is providing a quality education for all its students:

- The teachers and administrators believe that all of their students can succeed academically, and members adapt to the differing needs of the children and families they serve.

- The children themselves believe they can succeed as a result of hard work and persistence.

- Every classroom is a lively place, where:

  - The curriculum is rich, complex, and related to all students.

  - Lessons require the students' active participation and promote their working together.

  - Problem-solving and thinking skills, not rote learning, are emphasized.

  - Evaluation and grading are private, focusing on the specific learning the child has or has not accomplished, de-emphasizing comparison with others.

In addition, effective schools:

- Have access to sufficient resources for decent teacher salaries, a well-maintained physical plant, and adequate educational supplies and facilities, including libraries, lab equipment, and computers.

- Consistently initiate efforts to include parents in their children's learning and in decision-making for the school.

- Reach out to coordinate school efforts with larger community efforts to support children and families.

What Can You Do To Improve the Public Educational System?

Educate Yourself and Others

- Attend school functions. Go to the open house or student events and productions. Meet the teachers and administrative staff.

- Sit in on school board meetings. Find out the issues first-hand.

- Study the school budget. Does each school in your area have adequate resources? How well is education funded?

Get Involved in Your Community

- Volunteer to tutor children who need extra help. Select a subject you like. Talk to teachers in your congregation to find out how to proceed. Perhaps you can tutor at school during the day or in the evening in an existing tutoring program.

- Work with others to raise funds for special needs in the school. Hold a carnival or auction to provide equipment that is not in the school budget. You will have fun and meet other parents, too.

- Walk the routes that children take to school. Are they safe? Do traffic signs alert drivers to the daily presence of children? Are there crossing guards at difficult corners? If not, talk with the school principal to find out how to correct the situation.

- Ask the children you know about their schooling experiences. What is fun? What is difficult? Become a listener for their concerns. Take an interest in their homework. Provide encouragement when the child is down. Your interest and encouragement will let the child know that you think education is very important.

- Set up a literacy lab. The illiteracy rate in the U.S. is appallingly high for a developed country. Work with schools to set up programs where adults can learn to read, and learn English, and where children can get help in reading.

- Meet with representatives of the school board to organize an "adopt a school" program. Open up the possibility to congregations, businesses, and service organizations.

Advocate for the Improvement of Education for All Children

- Get involved in school board elections.

- With the help of other community groups concerned about education, plan a one-day conference for local and state educational leaders and decision-makers to focus on particular educational issues, such as the high drop-out rate among minority students or the involvement of business and community groups in the educational process.

- Know how your school board members are chosen. If they are elected, vote in school board elections. If they are nominated, submit names of qualified persons. Then stay informed about the actions of the board. Let the board know of your satisfaction as well as your displeasure.

Education Information Resources Worksheet

Church-sponsored or other local tutoring program: _____

Speaker: yes ☐ no ☐   Send materials: yes ☐ no ☐   Site visit: yes ☐ no ☐

Ask about: number served, number on waiting list, resources, description of students' needs. Who supports program? How was it established?

Comments/information: _____

_____

_____

_____

Local Parent Teacher Association: _____

Speaker: yes ☐ no ☐   Send materials: yes ☐ no ☐

Ask about: what members see as the pressing problems, needs. What have the successes been? Innovative programs? Is there tracking? Are all parents involved?

Comments/information: _____

_____

_____

_____

School board superintendent or member: _____

Speaker: yes ☐ no ☐   Send materials: yes ☐ no ☐

Ask about: current issues on agenda; how funding compares with other schools; how school's skills/ achievement level compares statewide, nationwide; dropout rate; etc.

Comments/information: _____

_____

_____

_____

National Education Association state chapter: _____

Speaker: yes ☐ no ☐   Send materials: yes ☐ no ☐

Ask about: issues on the agenda, desired action from members/nonmembers, etc.

Comments/information: _____

_____

_____

_____

American Federation of Teachers state chapter: _____

Speaker: yes ☐ no ☐   Send materials: yes ☐ no ☐

Ask about: same as above.

Comments/information: _____

_____

_____

_____

Also consider contacting: school principals, teachers, or students in your congregation; ask them what is working, what is needed. Think about a site visit to an urban school; walk the halls, flip through the textbooks, look at the playground.

CHAPTER 4

Vulnerable Children and Families

Father of orphans and protector of widows
  is God in his holy habitation.
God gives the desolate a home to live in;
  he leads out the prisoners to prosperity,
  but the rebellious live in a parched land.

Psalm 68:5–6

Speak out for those who cannot speak,
for the rights of all the destitute.

Proverbs 31:8

Every 26 seconds of each day in the United States, a child runs away from home. Every 13 seconds, a child is abused or neglected. Every seven minutes, a child is arrested for a drug offense.

Children's Defense Fund analyses

A child's tears move the heavens themselves.

Traditional saying

Imagine our surprise now to turn and see that despite our great defenses our homes have been pillaged again. Our children abused. Our wives battered. Our parents abandoned. Our homes infected with strange diseases: anorexia, bulimia, alcoholism, drug abuse, the suicide of adolescents. The bonds of our most solemn commitments are put to the test in our homes.

James Carroll, "Our Homes, God's House"
speech at Cathedral Church of St. John the Divine
New York City, 1985

Whoever welcomes you welcomes me, and whoever welcomes me welcomes the one who sent me. Whoever welcomes a prophet in the name of a prophet will receive a prophet's reward; and whoever welcomes a righteous person in the name of a righteous person will receive the reward of the righteous; and whoever gives even a cup of cold water to one of these little ones in the name of a disciple — truly I tell you, none of these will lose their reward.

Matthew 10:40–42

Reflection Questions

◆ Throughout the Old Testament, the people of God are regularly admonished to care for orphans and widows, the powerless in the ancient society. The verses from Psalm 68 are one example of this message. Orphans are certainly among the powerless of our society. Who else are our "orphans" of today? How are children powerless in our society and culture?

◆ Consider together the biblical quotes above and the quote from James Carroll. Note his title: "Our Homes, God's House." As parents, what is our calling and ministry to children and youths? As Christians? As equals with children and youths in the eyes of God?

◆ Although some commentaries suggest that "little ones" in the quote from Matthew refers to a group broader than children, the reference is clearly to the vulnerable ones in society and children are in that group. How do we give "even a cup of cold water" to children and youths? Especially to the most vulnerable children and youths in our community and world?

◆ Read the passage from Matthew several times. Instead of "little ones" substitute the names of groups of vulnerable children, such as infants born of drug-using mothers, children living in poverty, children who are homeless, youths who cannot read, and girls who are pregnant. What is the "cold water" that you can offer to each of these groups? This exercise can be used as a meditative exercise by substituting the names of vulnerable children you know for "little ones."

Vulnerable Children and Families

More and more we hear stories about a rapidly increasing population of vulnerable children and families and a severely overburdened child welfare system charged with meeting their needs. Here are just a few of the disturbing facts:

◆ An estimated 2.9 million children were reported abused or neglected in 1992, about triple the number reported in 1980.

◆ An average of three children a day died of some form of maltreatment in 1992. About half of these children were younger than one at their time of death.

◆ Every year, nearly 1 million infants start life at a disadvantage because their mothers did not receive early prenatal care.

◆ By the year 2000, an estimated 80,000 to 125,000 children will have lost a mother to AIDS.

◆ Families with children are the fastest growing population among the homeless, accounting for about one-third of the homeless population in the U.S. At least 100,000 children are homeless each night.

◆ In 1991, more than one in five children were poor. Each year in the U.S., an estimated 10,000 children die from poverty's effects.

◆ Every three hours a child is murdered. More than 400,000 students were victims of violent crime at school between 1988 and 1990.

Any one or two of these trends would strain the resources of the child welfare system. Together, these trends are overwhelming the system's capacity to respond. In June 1992, an estimated 442,000 children were living apart from their families in the care of the child welfare system — a 68 percent increase from a decade earlier.

A System on Overload

Increasing reports of child abuse and neglect are forcing child welfare agencies to devote more and more resources to investigation and intake. As a result, preventive efforts to support and improve family functioning have not increased to meet the need. Nor has an adequate supply of foster family care been developed. Some children who enter care simply are dumped in emergency shelters where they don't have even basic protection, let alone good care.

It is particularly troubling that infants and very young children are entering state care at greater rates and with more complex problems than ever before. In a group of states — California, Illinois, Michigan, New York, and Texas — one of five first admissions to care in

1988–1992 was a child younger than one. These children tend to remain in care longer than older children.

The need for good foster homes becomes more urgent every day. But the sad reality in many states is that the supply is dwindling, partly because children entering care are increasingly troubled and have very special needs, partly because of increasing pressures on parents to work outside the home, and partly because reimbursement to foster families has fallen far behind the costs of adequately supporting a child. In some communities foster parents are paid less each week for caring for a child than a kennel operator receives for boarding a dog.

The abandoned infants who linger in hospital wards as "boarder babies" are among the most heartbreaking evidence of the foster care system's inadequacy. These babies — some of whom have never been out of doors in their entire first year of life — are medically ready for discharge, but there are no foster families to care for them.

The child welfare system also suffers from a terrible shortage of trained, qualified child welfare workers to look out for vulnerable children. Low salaries, inadequate training and supports, and high rates of staff turnover and burnout weaken the system's effectiveness. Huge caseloads and crushing responsibilities make it impossible for child welfare workers to support families adequately where children are at risk, or to keep close check on children in out-of-home placements.

Needed: New Responses

There always will be a need for family foster care and residential treatment facilities for children who have very specialized treatment needs or whose families cannot care for them. To make sure there are enough good foster homes and treatment facilities for the children who really need them, the experts argue, our child welfare system must not overuse out-of-home placement. These experts insist that a child should be separated from his or her family only after other interventions have been exhausted and only when it is clear that the child cannot otherwise be protected. But a new emphasis on keeping families together must be accompanied by a new kind of help that protects children's safety at the same time it improves family functioning. This help may never turn vulnerable families into model families, say the experts, but it can enable many families to function adequately, nurture and protect their children, and remain intact.

One kind of special support for families — generally the most intensive — is called "family preservation services." In this program, a child at imminent risk of being removed from the family is left in the home if the family agrees to participate and the child can be protected adequately. A trained professional or team of professionals with a small caseload of two to four families is available on a 24-hour-a-day basis for up to three months. The staff spends time with the family in the home, concentrates on active, practical aid in solving the family's immediate problems, gives on-the-spot instruction in and help with parenting, and assists the family in linking up with other family support systems in the community. The highly intensive but short-term intervention is aimed at involving the entire family, supporting the family's own goals, and building on the family's strengths in order to increase its ability to cope.

Many communities also are developing less crisis-oriented programs to strengthen families' abilities to care for their children before problems intensify. These "family support programs" generally are based on the assumptions that a child's development is related to the strength and health of the parent-child relationship; that most parents want and are able to help their children grow into healthy, capable adults; and that all families need help at some time, but not all families need the same kind or intensity of support.

Like family preservation, family support programs focus on families' strengths and help them supplement their own resources with community resources offered by employers, churches, and community organizations. Most programs rely on voluntary participation and try to reach families as early as possible. Often the programs are housed in accessible neighborhood drop-in centers, and may include a home visiting component. Many programs offer comprehensive services, meaning they treat the family's needs as an interrelated whole and try to provide a wide range of assistance that may include parenting education and parent support groups, cooperative child care, assistance in obtaining health care and job training, special supports for young parents, and hotlines for child abuse prevention.

Beginning in 1994, the federal Family Preservation and Support Services Program started providing states and communities new opportunities to help strengthen families and make the delivery of services more responsive.

An Agenda for Change

Ideally, every community should have a range of adequately staffed and funded services for vulnerable families. The available services must begin with preventive programs to strengthen family functioning and improve families' abilities to nurture their children. For families in crisis, the continuum should provide intensive family preservation services that treat the whole family's needs and preserve the family unit whenever possible. There must be a variety of quality options for caring for children outside of their homes when that is necessary. And finally, for children in care who cannot be reunited with their families, there should be vigorous efforts to find permanent adoptive families.

Churches and other community organizations can play an important role in making sure their communities realize the full potential of the new federal reforms. Churches can organize their own family support programs or "adopt" ongoing programs that need assistance. Churches also can enrich the experience of foster children through a variety of efforts and can help provide new permanent families and foster families for children by recruiting adoptive and foster parents.

At another level, churches also can become voices for change in the child welfare system. Churches should advocate for public policies and programs supporting family services that reduce the need for unnecessary out-of-home placements, as well as to improve the system for children who must be removed from their homes.

What Can You Do To Improve Services for Vulnerable Children and Families?

Educate Yourself and Others

◆ Find out how your state is using new federal funds from the Family Preservation and Support Services Program. Make sure community leaders and families are involved in developing these new initiatives.

◆ April is Child Abuse Prevention Month. Sponsor a special program to educate your congregation about child abuse and other domestic violence and steps that can be taken to prevent it and to assist families where abuse has occurred. Consider dedi-

cating a Sunday sermon each April to the theme of preventing child abuse and neglect.

◆ Thanksgiving week each year is National Foster Care and Adoption Week. Earlier in November, sponsor a special program about the needs of foster children in your community, about the need for adoptive families and what the congregation can do to help. Check on local events being planned to celebrate Foster Care and Adoption Week so they can become more involved.

◆ Have your youth group prepare a directory of family resource and support programs in your community and learn how these programs can benefit from your congregation's support.

- Join with other religious congregations and community groups in sponsoring a one-day conference on successful programs in your community and state for serving high-risk children and families. Make a special effort to include programs that can benefit from volunteer contributions.

- Write to the national headquarters of your denomination and ask for information on programs for high-risk children and families that are operated by congregations in other communities.

Get Involved

Supporting Families and Preventing Child Abuse and Neglect

- Sponsor parenting education programs for members of your congregation and others in your community. Conduct separate sessions for parents of young children, elementary school children, and teenagers. You may want to cosponsor these sessions with schools in the area served by your church.

- Have your congregation adopt a family in need of assistance and offer that family ongoing assistance and support. Assist the family with its basic needs, such as employment, food, and housing, but also arrange for children in your congregation to serve as peer companions for children in the family.

- Encourage senior citizens in your congregation to volunteer for the Foster Grandparent Program if there is a chapter in your community. If not, establish a program whereby you team senior citizens with teen parents in your congregation to offer them ongoing counsel and support. The senior citizens involved in the program may want to sponsor a "Mother's Morning Out" program one day a week, when parents can bring their children to the church for a couple of hours while the parents engage in specially organized activities.

- Adopt a social worker in your community's public department of children and family services and help support that worker by responding to the unmet needs of the children and families he or she is serving. The worker may ask for basic supplies, such as food, clothing, bedding, or health care supplies; for financial assistance to get the family through a crisis; or for help with home repairs, transportation, child care, or other services.

- Join with other churches to establish a family resource center that can offer parents and children a variety of services and supports.

- Encourage members of your congregation to serve as respite care parents for children who are in foster care and whose foster parents need temporary relief from their full-time responsibilities. Although this might be done on an informal basis, there may be a special training program in your community for respite care providers, especially for those caring for children with special needs.

- A growing number of communities are establishing various systems staffed by volunteers to ensure that children in foster care get the attention they need in the court process and are reviewed periodically and not allowed to drift endlessly with no attention to reuniting them with their birth families or moving them toward adoption. If your community has a Court Appointed Special Advocate program or a Citizen Foster Care Review Board, urge members of your congregation to volunteer their services.

- Consider establishing a place at your church where birth parents can visit in comfortable surroundings with their children who are in foster care. Senior citizens could be available to assist local social workers with transportation for both the foster children and their birth parents. Together with teens from the youth group, they also might provide on-site child care.

Finding Adoptive Families for Children

- Encourage members of your congregation to consider adopting children with special needs, particularly children who have various mental, emotional, or physical disabilities, who are older, who are members of minority groups, or who are part of a sibling group. Offer to cooperate with outreach activities being conducted by adoption agencies in your community. Incorporate a flyer in the bulletin, sponsor an informational meeting, or let adoption agencies have a recruitment stand in the lobby after your service. If a "One Church, One Child" program is operating in your community, participate in that.

- Establish a Permanent Families Now fund for a local adoption agency that places children with special needs. These dollars can be used by the agency to waive fees for families approved to adopt special-needs children, or to assist with other nonrecurring costs that create barriers to permanence for these children.

- Adopt a crisis nursery in your community, and offer members of the staff the support they need. Such support may include material items, financial assistance, or help from volunteers. For example, senior citizens in your congregation may set up a transportation network to enable parents to visit their children on a regular basis. Or you may want to hold a baby shower several times a year to collect clothes and other items that the nursery supplies to parents in need.

- Sponsor a post-adoption support group for families who have adopted children with special needs. Sponsorship might involve making space available for monthly meetings, offering clerical support for the group's regular communications, offering child care assistance for parents who are attending the meetings, or providing a portion of the salary of the group facilitator.

Assisting Children in Foster Care

- Designate four Sundays a year as Foster Care Sunday and ask members of your congregation to bring in certain supplies or make financial contributions to assist children in foster care in your community. Contact social workers at your local department of children and family services or the foster parent association in your community to determine the greatest needs at the time.

- Establish a tutoring and peer mentoring program for children who are in foster care in your community.

- Establish a scholarship fund to support participation by children who are in foster care in various extracurricular programs or summer activities in your community.

- Make arrangements with one of your denomination's colleges to provide a full tuition scholarship each year to a child in foster care from your community. Find a host family in your congregation, preferably a graduate of that school, who will offer the student ongoing emotional support throughout the school year.

- Many of the young people "aging out" of foster care at 18 or 19 have no family or friends to whom they can return. Ask for volunteers from your young adults group who are willing to serve as community sponsors for these young people. Your public agency may have a formal program of this sort, or your congregation may want to team up with a private agency that has children in its care.

- Encourage members of your congregation to consider becoming foster parents. Give foster parents who are in your church the opportunity to share their experiences with others. Set up a network of families who are available to offer assistance to the foster families when emergencies arise.

Support Policy Improvements

- Join with other child advocates to ensure that your state is using its Family Preservation and Support Services Program funds to expand services for vulnerable children and families. Set a goal of implementing these programs on a statewide basis.

- Push your state officials to examine trends in numbers and costs of children in out-of-home care in your state. Urge them to look not only at increases in children in the care of the child welfare system, but at the juvenile justice and mental health systems as well, as children in the three systems often have very similar needs. Data of this sort can be very useful in making the case for greater investment in family support and family preservation services and community based programs. Useful studies already have been done in California (*10 Reasons to Invest in the Families of California*, County Welfare Directors Association of California, Chief Probation Officers Association of California, and California Mental Health Directors Association, 1990) and Missouri (*Where's My Home? A Study of Missouri's Children in Out-of-Home Placement*, Citizens for Missouri's Children, 1989).

- Support legislative initiatives designed to expand and improve income supports, health care, child care, and education for low-income children and families, and those designed to create comprehensive services and support for homeless families with children and families with serious substance abuse problems. These initiatives are critical steps to enabling families to offer better care and support for their children.

Vulnerable Children and Families Information Resources Worksheet

Social worker from a local agency: _____

Speaker: yes ❑ no ❑   Send materials: yes ❑ no ❑   Site visit: yes ❑ no ❑

Ask about: needs of children and families served, barriers to serving families, successful prevention and treatment programs, help needed.

Comments/information: _____

_____

_____

_____

Area congregation with family support program: _____

_____

Speaker: yes ❑ no ❑   Send materials: yes ❑ no ❑   Site visit: yes ❑ no ❑

Ask about: program, how established, needs of children and families served, resources contributed by congregation, help needed.

Comments/information: _____

_____

_____

_____

Area foster care/adoption agency: _____

Speaker: yes ❑ no ❑   Send materials: yes ❑ no ❑   Site visit: yes ❑ no ❑

Ask about: special needs of children served, number of children awaiting foster or adoptive families, barriers to placement, help needed, if current foster parents can speak to the group.

Comments/information: _____

_____

_____

_____

State child welfare agency: _____

Speaker: yes ☐ no ☐   Send materials: yes ☐ no ☐

Ask about: trends in abuse and neglect reports and out-of-home placements, special needs of children, barriers to meeting those needs, successful prevention and treatment programs, family preservation service initiatives, help needed.

Comments/information: _____

_____

_____

Statewide or citywide child advocacy group (look under Children or Social Services in the yellow pages of the telephone book):

_____

Speaker: yes ☐ no ☐   Send materials: yes ☐ no ☐

Ask about: its policy or legislative agendas for vulnerable children, new programs and policies that need support, those it hopes to change, barriers to service that need attention, collaboration with other groups, help needed, membership.

Comments/information: _____

_____

_____

Children's Defense Fund, Child Welfare Division, 25 E Street, N.W., Washington, DC 20001, (202) 628-8787.

Send materials: yes ☐ no ☐

Ask about: current policy or legislative agendas, innovative policies and programs, help needed.

Comments/information: _____

_____

_____

Child Welfare League of America, 440 First Street, N.W., Suite 310, Washington, DC 20001, (202) 638-2952.

Send materials: yes ☐ no ☐

Ask about: current policy or legislative agendas, innovative policies and programs, help needed.

Comments/information: _____

_____

_____

ঽ

Homelessness and Housing

Why are times not kept by the Almighty,
 and why do those who know him never see his
 days?
The wicked remove landmarks;
 they seize flocks and pasture them.
They drive away the donkey of the orphan;
 they take the widow's ox for a pledge.
They thrust the needy off the road;
 the poor of the earth all hide themselves.
Like wild asses in the desert
 they go out to their toil,
 scavenging in the wasteland
 for food for their young.
They reap in a field not their own
 and they glean in the vineyard of the wicked.
They lie all night naked, without clothing,
 and have no covering in the cold.
They are wet with the rain of the mountains,
 and cling to the rock for want of shelter.
There are those who snatch the orphan child from the
 breast,
 and take as a pledge the infant of the poor.
They go about naked, without clothing;
 though hungry, they carry the sheaves;
between their terraces, they press out oil;
 they tread the wine presses, but suffer thirst.

Job 24:1–11

Children and families represent the single fastest growing population today among America's homeless.
Every day 100,000 American children are homeless.

National Academy of Sciences

And she gave birth to her firstborn son and wrapped
him in bands of cloth, and laid him in a manger,
because there was no place for them in the inn.

Luke 2:7

Truly I tell you, just as you did it to one of the least of
these who are members of my family, you did it to me.

Matthew 25:40

Reflection Questions

♦ Read the verse from Luke. Had you ever thought about Jesus as a homeless child before? How does identifying the baby Jesus with homeless people change the picture in your mind as you read this verse?

♦ Read Matthew 25:34–46. Who were "the least of these" in Jesus' time? Who are they today? Why is it difficult to respond to the needs of people who are homeless?

♦ Think about the homeless people you see in your community or on the streets of a nearby city. Read Job 24:1–11. How do you connect people who are homeless in our society with this passage? What images of children and families who are homeless might you create in the style of the passage from Job?

♦ The Israelites often were admonished by the proph-ets to care for the widows and orphans, those who often were homeless. How do church people today honor that admonition?

♦ Who pays the highest price for homelessness? What are the costs now and in the future? What are some of the basic needs of children that go unmet when they are homeless?

♦ What does it mean to be hospitable today? When might we be entertaining angels unaware?

♦ Think for a moment about Christ's compassion — Christ's suffering with, and for, others. Do we tend to feel compassion when encountering a person who is homeless, or do we push our thoughts and feelings away from that close form of identification? What do you think it would be like to be homeless? As a parent with young children, where would you seek help in your community?

Homelessness and Housing

Ray is a round-faced boy of 10 who seldom smiles. Until a year ago he and his mother, Jenny, lived in an apartment in San Jose, California. When Jenny, a self-employed auto mechanic, became disabled and was unable to pay the rent, Jenny and Ray were evicted. "We had to sleep by the freeway in the bushes," Ray explains solemnly. "We had a tent."

Now Ray and Jenny live in a shelter for homeless families. When he is asked about his hopes for the future, Ray says he would like to stay in one place and have a friend to play with. He ends his response by saying, "...if I ever get there."

"What do you mean?" the interviewer asks.

"Like I say," says Ray in a flat voice, "tomorrow may never come."

Every night an estimated 100,000 children in the U.S. go to sleep homeless, worrying about what tomorrow will bring. Wondering if tomorrow will come at all.

Homeless families with children are the fastest-growing segment of the homeless population. Our mental pictures of people who are homeless have not caught up with that reality. Homelessness is not confined to single men, substance abusers, and the mentally ill. The 1980s produced a rate of homelessness among families far greater than at any time since the Great Depression.

Estimates of the total homeless population range from 250,000 to 3 million. Homeless families with children make up at least one-third of the total. In Kansas City, Philadelphia, Phoenix, San Antonio, and Trenton (New Jersey), homeless families make up at least half of the homeless population. Children in homeless families are spending periods of their crucial childhood years living in cars, in campgrounds, or in crowded, unsanitary, and unsafe public shelters. Many of these children don't eat regularly and don't go to school. They have almost nothing to call their own except anxiety, weariness, and unfilled longings.

Three-year-old Denise lived such a life. For a number of months she spent her nights with her mother, Barbara, and five-year-old brother, James, in a cubicle in a school gym that was used as a homeless shelter in an East Coast city. Denise was awakened every morning at 5:30 when a staff member pounded on the side of their cubicle. At 7:00 a.m. a bus took Denise and her family across town to the welfare hotel where they waited for breakfast. After breakfast, the family boarded another bus to take James to a Head Start program. Most days, Denise was tired and cranky because the shelter closed during the day and there was no place for her to take the nap she needed. In the afternoon there was another bus ride to pick up James, dinner at the welfare hotel, and a final bus ride back to the gym.

How has it happened that so many children in America are growing up without a place to call home?

The Low-Income Housing Squeeze

During the 1980s more and more families were caught in the squeeze between high housing costs and inadequate family incomes. Homeownership, the traditional route to long-term housing security for American families, is increasingly out of reach. In 1991 only one-third of young families (headed by a parent younger than 30) were homeowners, down from almost half in 1980. More and more families that rent homes or apartments find rent taking a bigger bite out of their budgets as well.

Affordable housing for low-income families has been vanishing rapidly in recent years largely because of drastic Reagan-era budget cuts in federal housing programs. The federal government is responsible for several programs that support the construction of new affordable housing, provide low-rent public housing, and give poor families rent subsidies that can be used to cover rents in the private market. During the 1980s, federal funding for these programs was cut by 80 percent in real dollars. As of 1991 only one in three poor households was getting any help with its housing costs from the government.

The withdrawal of government help in the 1980s resulted in a severe shortage of affordable housing units. By the late 1980s, the federal government had virtually stopped building public housing. Moreover, it did not maintain the existing stock. More than 100,000 units of public housing cannot be lived in without some renovation, but little federal money has been available for repairs.

The loss of public housing units has increased the demand for other low-cost housing and contributed to the general inflation in rents. Between 1973 and 1987, for example, the median rent in the U.S. rose more than 30 times as fast as median income, making it very difficult for low-income families to find affordable housing.

While rents have been rising, so has the number of poor and near-poor families needing low-cost housing. Between 1980 and 1991 the number of poor families with children increased from about 4.8 million to 6.2 million, a 28 percent rise. Families headed by single women or parents younger than 30 are especially likely to be poor and to be homeless. Single-parent families make up about two-thirds of all homeless families.

The recession that began in 1990 only added to the damage done in the 1980s, as more workers lost their jobs or took pay cuts and states cut back on crucial support services. Even as the economy recovers, that alone will not pull our children and families back to financial security. The 1970s and 1980s showed that of

DEVELOPING A STUDY INTO ACTION PROGRAM

all the children who fall into poverty during a recession, only a fraction are pulled back out during the economic growth period following. Without specific actions to support families, therefore, countless children will remain poor and in danger of homelessness even if their country enjoys economic growth.

Families Forced To Spend Too Much

Housing experts say that generally no more than 30 percent of a family's gross income should be spent to pay the rent or mortgage and the utility bills. Yet poor and low-income families find it increasingly difficult to find housing in that price range. In 1991, 2.7 million families spent at least half their income on rent.

This huge deficit in the supply of low-cost housing forces millions of low-income families to use dangerously large portions of their incomes for housing. And then the only housing they are able to secure often is decrepit, unsafe, or unsanitary. No matter how carefully they budget, these families are just one crisis away from homelessness. They have no cushion. A single medical emergency or short-term job loss can deplete their financial resources — including rent money — and push them over the edge into homelessness.

How Housing Problems Hurt Children

Children who are homeless or live in substandard housing suffer a number of health, developmental, and educational risks. One of the most common and devastating housing-related problems among children is lead poisoning, which can cause lasting developmental and health problems and in extreme cases, convulsions, comas, mental retardation, even death. Nationwide, an estimated 12 million children younger than seven live in homes that contain lead paint, and 3 million to 4 million children have unsafe levels of lead in their blood.

Many homeless children fall behind academically because they don't go to school regularly. Children whose families move from place to place never get a chance to settle into one school. Despite recent federal legislation requiring schools to remove barriers such as rigid residency requirements that keep children out of school, the National Center on Homelessness and Poverty reported in 1989 that schools in three-fifths of the states it studied still refused to admit homeless children without proof of residency.

When homeless children do go to school they have many strikes against them. Without a quiet place to read or do their homework they find it hard to keep up with their class. They have trouble concentrating because they come to school tired and hungry. Teachers report that some homeless students fall asleep at their desks.

Finally, many poorly housed or homeless children are separated unnecessarily from family members. In 62 percent of the cases surveyed by the U.S. Conference of Mayors in 1992, families that had lost their homes sometimes had to break up to find shelter because many shelters accept women and children, but not men. Some families lose their children to foster care because they cannot provide adequate housing.

An Agenda for Change

Churches and informal community networks can provide critical help for homeless children and families. For example, they can provide short-term loans and emergency food, offer decent temporary shelter, or assist with child care and transportation as parents struggle to work and look for housing. Church organizations can help link homeless families to adequate health care and other social services. And churches can mobilize the community to provide people who are homeless with specialized services that are not available elsewhere, such as help with job and housing searches.

As necessary as these efforts are, they will never solve the root problem, however. Families are homeless because there is a huge shortage of permanent low-cost housing. More than anything else, homeless families need housing they can afford. The private sector can and should make significant contributions toward alleviating the low-cost housing shortage. But the private sector cannot solve the problem by itself. Some churches, often together with other nonprofit organizations, have played important roles in establishing affordable housing for low-income families, and expanded efforts are needed. Even so, a major responsibility lies with the government.

Since the Depression some poor families have received housing assistance through publicly subsidized rental housing, but government assistance to low-income renters has fallen far short of government assistance in the form of tax deductions to homeowners, who are primarily middle- and upper-income people. For example, the federal government spent $18 billion on housing assistance for low-income families in 1990 while forgoing $78 billion in tax revenues by giving significant tax breaks to homeowners.

The federal and state governments must invest more money in effective programs for building and rehabilitating affordable housing. As concerned citizens, we must tell our elected officials that we support programs to increase the stock of decent affordable housing.

What Can You Do about the Needs of Children and Families Who Are Homeless or Have Inadequate Housing?

Educate Yourself and Others

- Read articles in newspapers and denominational publications about homelessness and inadequate housing.

- Invite local housing advocates — and homeless people themselves — to speak to your congregation.

- Include basic facts about homelessness locally and nationally in your church newsletter or a worship bulletin insert.

- Develop programs for children and youths to raise their awareness of housing problems and to make them more sensitive to the needs of homeless children. Many children who are homeless avoid school because they are treated cruelly by other children. You can help children be more understanding.

- Learn about efforts in your community to help families with their housing costs and to prevent homelessness in other ways.

Get Involved in Meeting the Need

- Volunteer at a shelter for homeless families. Help clean or paint the shelter, prepare meals, or plan and participate in activities for the children and adults.

- Ask your congregation to support a shelter for homeless families by providing volunteers, clothing, bedding, food, or money.

- Hold a special worship service or church concert in a shelter for families who are unable to go to church.

- Create an emergency fund. Contributions can provide one-time grants or no-interest loans to help families pay security deposits, back rent, or utility payments. Grants or loans of this type can keep families from losing their homes or help homeless families secure housing.

- Assist a homeless family or a family on the brink of homelessness. You may want to provide assistance directly to a family known by your pastor. You also can work through a religious or public social service agency. Families may need help with child care, job leads, finding a place to live, or furniture. They may simply need to have someone in their lives who cares. This kind of support and assistance can prevent homelessness and help homeless families regain stability in permanent housing.

- Develop respite care programs for families living in homeless shelters. Include homeless children and youths in existing child care, religious education, and other ministries of your congregation. Recruit members of the congregation to provide child care and recreation for homeless children while their parents interview for jobs, attend worship, or seek permanent housing.

- Help develop housing for low-income families. Many congregations have joined with nonprofit organizations and local governments to construct and rehabilitate low-income housing. Your congregation actually can be the developer and builder or can provide financial and personnel support to other groups, such as Habitat for Humanity International, (912) 924-6935.

Advocate for Homeless Children and Families

- Tell local, state, and federal officials about the homeless families in your area. Urge them to make housing assistance available to all who need help and a priority for government funds. Also urge them to improve employment and income policies so low-income families will be able to afford decent and safe housing.

- Develop a program you can take to community groups to enlist their help in providing adequate housing in your area.

- Join with others to sponsor a Child Watch tour that invites business and religious leaders, public officials, and members of the press to go on guided visits of public and private agencies concerned with homeless children and families. For more information about Child Watch, contact CDF, (202) 628-8787.

- Find out if homeless children are getting the health care and education services to which they are entitled. If not, find out why, and advocate for changes.

What Young People Can Do To Help Homeless Children

Always treat homeless children the way you would want to be treated. It is very hard and sometimes very embarrassing to be homeless. Try to imagine what it would be like. Talk about it with your classmates.

- What would you do after school?

- How would it feel not to sleep in your own bed?

- Which of your things (clothes, toys, books) would you choose if you could only keep what you could carry yourself?

- What would it be like to eat all your meals in a cafeteria or soup kitchen and not be able to choose your favorite foods?

- What would it be like to have to miss a lot of school or change schools many times?

Ask your parents or teachers to help you find community organizations or churches that are helping homeless people. Here are some things you, your classmates, and your family can do to help such organizations:

- You can work in a soup kitchen, serving food to children and adults. Homeless people often don't get enough to eat, and soup kitchens offer them free meals.

- You can help a church or other group collect money to help people pay their rent so they will not be forced out of their homes. Sometimes just a little bit of money can help people keep their homes.

- Collect clothes that you and other people in your family do not wear anymore. Give them to a shelter. Many homeless children and adults lose clothing when they become homeless and often do not have the money to replace it.

- Ask someone who works with homeless children and adults to talk to your class about these families and the problems they face.

- Ask a person who works with homeless children and adults about ways you can help them.

- Write letters to the mayor and city council in your town, or to the governor and the state legislature, or to national politicians, including the president, your senators, and representatives, and ask them what they are doing to help homeless people.

Homelessness and Housing Information Resources Worksheet

Local family shelter: _____

Speaker: yes ☐ no ☐   Send materials: yes ☐ no ☐   Site visit: yes ☐ no ☐

Ask about: type of shelter, number served, number on waiting list, number of those served who are children, needs, resources.

Comments/information: _____

_____

_____

_____

Area church with program to serve homeless children and families: _____

Speaker: yes ☐ no ☐   Send materials: yes ☐ no ☐   Site visit: yes ☐ no ☐

Ask about: process to establish program, how it works, problems, needs, number served and the trend over time, costs.

Comments/information: _____

_____

_____

_____

Local housing authority: _____

Speaker: yes ☐ no ☐   Send materials: yes ☐ no ☐

Ask about: number of subsidized housing units; policy on affordable housing development, number on waiting list; policy on emergency shelters, number on waiting list.

Comments/information: _____

_____

_____

_____

(Copy and use this as a hand-out)

State or local agency for homelessness assistance: _____

Speaker: yes ❑ no ❑   Send materials: yes ❑ no ❑

Ask about: policy on homelessness, shelters; prevention programs, services.

Comments/information: _____

_____

_____

Statewide housing/homeless advocacy group (look for Habitat for Humanity chapter, or Low-Income Housing Coalition or Coalition for the Homeless in the telephone book):

_____

Speaker: yes ❑ no ❑   Send materials: yes ❑ no ❑

Ask about: membership, action agenda.

Comments/information: _____

_____

_____

Children's Defense Fund, 25 E Street, N.W., Washington, DC 20001, (202) 628-8787.

Send materials: yes ❑ no ❑

Ask about: current agenda, legislative items, and desired actions relating to housing and homelessness.

Comments/information: _____

_____

_____

Interagency Council on the Homeless, 451 7th Street, S.W., Room 7274, Washington, DC 20410, (202) 708-1480.

Send materials: yes ❑ no ❑

Ask about: current policy and programs to assist homeless children and families, including information on access to health and education resources for homeless children, homelessness prevention programs, income support, statistics and trends over time for number of homeless children and families.

Express concern/interest in: supporting policies and programs that prevent homelessness and help homeless people.

Comments/information: _____

_____

_____

(Copy and use this as a hand-out)

Maternal and Child Health

Thus says the Lord:
A voice is heard in Ramah,
    lamentation and bitter weeping.
Rachel is weeping for her children,
    she refuses to be comforted for her children,
    because they are no more.

Jeremiah 31:15

Each year, nearly 40,000 babies in the United States die before their first birthday. Another 400,000 develop a chronic or disabling condition. . . . Infant death and disability are not intractable problems. This country has the knowledge necessary to save 10,000 additional infant lives each year and to prevent an untold number of disabilities among infants. To do that, we as a nation must apply what we know about illness prevention and health promotion and ensure that the women at greatest risk of having an unhealthy baby have access to high-quality primary health and social services.

Report of the White House Task Force
on Infant Mortality, 1989

There is no finer investment for any community than putting milk into babies.

Sir Winston Churchill

Suddenly a leader of the synagogue came in and knelt before [Jesus], saying, "My daughter has just died; but come and lay your hand on her, and she will live." And Jesus got up and followed him, with his disciples. . . . When Jesus got to the leader's house and saw the flute players and the crowd making a commotion, he said, "Go away; for the girl is not dead but sleeping." And they laughed at him. But when the crowd had been put outside, he went in and took her by the hand, and the girl got up. And the report of this spread throughout that district.

Matthew 9:18–19, 23–26

Reflection Questions

- The passage from Jeremiah refers to Rachel, the mother of Joseph and Benjamin, who is lamenting their exile. The verse introduces the promise of the restoration of the kingdoms and the return from exile. This verse is also quoted in Matthew (2:18) to depict unrelieved grief. Which setting fits our world? What is the grief we have for the health of children? What is the promise or hope in the future?

- How do you interpret the last two lines of the poem by Gabriela Mistral found in Section I on page 23? What does the poet mean by "The child's name is 'Today'"? Why is investing in the health of pregnant women, infants, and children such an urgent concern?

- The passage from Matthew is one of a few stories in the Gospels that include children in an obvious way. It is significant because a child is healed. In the middle of this gospel story is the healing of a woman. This, too, is significant, for Jesus has taken special notice of these two of the powerless in Jewish society. How might you connect this story with a national concern for maternal and child health?

- As a society, what is our responsibility when children die of preventable causes? How would you characterize the moral cost to our society? How does this problem affect your life or that of your family?

Maternal and Child Health

When Tammy of Denton County, Texas, became pregnant, she couldn't get prenatal care. She had little money, no health insurance, and no physician. She tried to get prenatal care in a local hospital, but could not meet the rigid financial requirements for the indigent program. Twenty-six weeks into her pregnancy, she was taken to the emergency room with severe pregnancy-related high blood pressure, a condition that could have been controlled with proper prenatal care. Doctors had to perform a caesarean-section because her blood pressure couldn't be stabilized. The baby, born premature and in dangerous health, was transferred to a neonatal intensive care unit. He lived for 15 days.

The United States is one of the richest nations and perhaps the most medically advanced nation in the world. Yet by some measures this country is still underdeveloped when it comes to keeping our children healthy. In 1991, for every 1,000 babies born alive in the United States, nine died before their first birthday, giving us an infant mortality rate that ranks twenty-second in the world, behind nations such as Spain, Singapore, and Hong Kong. A Black infant born in the United States is less likely to survive until his or her first birthday than babies born in 39 other countries, including Jamaica and Costa Rica. Each year more than 35,000 infants die before age one.

These are shocking facts, for the United States spends more money per capita on health care than any other country. Every month we hear about new breakthroughs in medical research, new miracle drugs, and new surgical procedures. We assume that children in the U.S. get the best health care modern medicine can provide, but this may be true only for children covered by health insurance.

More than 8 million children in the U.S. — one in seven — had no health insurance of any kind in 1991. In addition, more than 14 million women in their prime childbearing years either were completely uninsured or were uninsured for maternity care. For these children and women, even the most basic health care can be out of reach.

The biggest reason for so many uninsured people in the United States is that the employer-based insurance system, the backbone of U.S. health care financing, is breaking down. Employer-based insurance has never been a good guarantee of adequate health care for all children, and in recent years it has become even less reliable. With health care costs shooting out of control, fewer and fewer employers are providing health benefits. In the past decade, the proportion of medium-size and large employers paying the full cost of family health care coverage has shrunk by one-third. That and labor market changes have resulted in more and more people working for employers who do not offer health benefits or do not pay the cost of their workers' family health coverage. Unable to buy insurance themselves, many families go without coverage.

Although the federal and state governments, through Medicaid, have picked up a large portion of children and pregnant women without employer-based insurance, Medicaid is far from filling the gap entirely. Medicaid works basically like insurance, paying the health care bills of welfare and low-income families. But the program's stringent eligibility rules and other shortcomings often make coverage fleeting. Moreover, although Medicaid provides vital relief to many of the poorest Americans, it does not reach the near-poor and middle-income families most affected by the collapse of employer-based insurance.

Families without Medicaid or private health insurance must rely on public hospitals and a patchwork system of public health clinics that is underfunded and understaffed to meet these families' needs. Many rural and inner-city areas do not have any public health clinics at all, or not have enough to serve the population. More than 43 million Americans, half of whom are children and women of childbearing age, live in such "medically underserved" communities. For these families, getting a routine prenatal care checkup, getting their children vaccinated, or getting a sick child to a doctor may be next to impossible even if they could afford it because there are simply too few doctors and clinics around.

The amount and quality of health care an American child receives has very little to do with what is necessary to keep him or her healthy. It has almost everything to do with the child's family income, whether he or she happens to live near a public health clinic, and the state's eligibility requirements for Medicaid.

Poor Health Begins before Birth...

The health problems of poor children often originate before birth because many low-income mothers can't afford adequate prenatal care. Women who don't see a doctor regularly while they are pregnant are more likely to have infants born at low birthweight — weighing less than 5.5 pounds. If they live, these tiny babies are likely to suffer from serious problems such as mental retardation, cerebral palsy, and vision and learning disabilities. But many don't live. In fact, low birthweight is the leading cause of infant mortality in this country. It is associated with nearly 60 percent of all infant deaths.

...and Continues through Childhood

One good indication of how well a nation is protecting the health of its toddlers and preschool children is to look at immunization rates. China immunizes 99 percent of its people against measles. By this measure, the United States clearly is failing, for during the first half of the 1980s immunization rates for preschoolers immunized began to drop. The latest studies show that fewer than 60 percent of two-year-olds are fully immunized.

The consequences of such low immunization rates are frightening, and in many cases deadly. Ten years ago the United States was on the verge of eradicating measles, but the drop in immunization rates among preschool children has caused a new measles epidemic. Between 1989 and 1991, 55,000 Americans, mostly preschoolers, contracted measles. At least 130 people died and 8,000 were hospitalized. What's more, medical experts warn that unless the nation improves its immunization rate, other childhood diseases, such as mumps, pertussis and rubella, could erupt into full-blown epidemics as well.

Other measures also tell the story of inadequate health care for many poor children. Low-income children are more than three times as likely as other children never to have had a preventive health exam, and one in five never sees a doctor in the course of a year. Anemia, which slows physical development and makes it hard for children to pay attention in school, is three times more common in poor children than in other children. Hearing loss from untreated ear infections is also more common.

Health Care Is a Good Investment

Many argue that because of the nation's huge budget deficit, the United States cannot afford to put more resources into health care. This argument is tragically shortsighted. Ensuring that all children and pregnant women have adequate good health care is not only morally imperative, it makes good economic sense. Indeed we must systematically address the health care problem if we have any hope of bringing down the deficit. Encouragingly, all the recent attention to national health care reform is a sign that more and more people — of all political persuasions — are recognizing that as a nation we no longer can afford not to invest in maternal and child health care.

Here's why:

First, the cost of emergency care and rehabilitation is far greater than the cost of prevention. Every $1 invested to immunize a child saves $10 in later medical treatment for illness or disability. Similarly, maternity care for pregnant women not only saves lives but saves the nation money down the road. Tammy and her baby's hospital bills, for example, came to $124,000. For less than $2,000 in prenatal care, that expense — not to mention the baby's life — might have been spared.

Second, there are many hidden costs associated with poor health. Unhealthy children have a hard time learning, and learning problems often lead to

delinquency, dropping out of school, and unemployment. Our nation loses a great deal of potential talent, productive work, and tax dollars as a result of the diminished productivity of adults who were physically or educationally disabled by preventable causes during childhood.

An Agenda for Change

Despite heightened interest in the U.S. in reforming the health care system, the nation has a long way to go before all American children and pregnant women truly can get the basic health care they need, regardless of income. No child or pregnant woman should be without an accessible doctor, clinic, or health insurance. As the nation works to put in place a new health care financing and delivery system, it is critical to keep children's needs firmly in mind and make sure they remain at the forefront of debates and negotiations.

A Good System for Children

If universal insurance coverage is to be phased in over time, children and pregnant women must be covered first. In addition, children need a health care system that:

♦ Provides comprehensive benefits for children and pregnant women. Medicaid's Early and Periodic Screening, Diagnosis, and Treatment (EPSDT) program serves as a guide. The benefits covered in any new system should include at least those covered in EPSDT, namely, the full range of basic preventive and primary care, from maternity care and family planning to vision, dental, and hearing care to in- and out-patient hospital services and lab tests.

♦ Ensures that children's coverage continues uninterrupted and remains affordable even if their parents lose or change jobs. Eligibility requirements and application procedures must be kept simple, and cost-sharing for services must be prohibited.

♦ Has hospitals, clinics, doctors, and nurses in all communities, and transportation help in rural areas, so that health care is easy to reach for families no matter where they live. The nation must devote funds to develop and sustain high quality primary care programs, school health, and other special services. It also must bolster the National Health Service Corps, a federal program that assures a better supply of doctors and other health workers in medically underserved communities.

♦ Has medical and administrative personnel who understand the socioeconomic aspects of health issues and are responsive to special community needs, including bilingual staff, staff trained to work with families with low levels of literacy, and staff trained to serve persons with disabilities. Doctors, nurses, administrators, and support workers must be committed to being health educators and take the time to make sure patients understand the prescribed treatment and how it relates to their complaints.

Immunization

An indispensable component of any health care system is an effective national childhood immunization program. Recent work at the federal level on immunization has been a major step forward. But state and local governments and community groups also have an important role: that of making sure national immunization policies are implemented as they were intended. States and communities must understand the key elements of a complete immunization system and work to make them a part of the primary care system in their local areas.

The three most important elements are:

- Universal vaccine purchase and distribution, which provides vaccines free of charge to public and private health providers. This system saves states millions of dollars in vaccine costs and keeps children from being turned away from immunizations because their families can't afford the vaccine.

- A national immunization registry. The registry follows the vaccination status of individual children, sends reminder notices to families for their children's shots, and identifies communities with low immunization rates for outreach and public education.

- Public health service delivery and outreach. In many communities, overcrowded clinics and inadequate clinic hours prevent children from getting their vaccinations on time. Communities must open clinics on weekends and evenings, hire nurses, and place services in more convenient locations. Outreach workers also are needed to educate families on the importance of their children getting shots on time.

Nutrition

In addition to universal health care and immunization, all children and pregnant women must have complete nutrition, the cornerstone of good health. For families too poor to buy all the food they need, the federal government has a highly successful nutrition program called the Special Supplemental Food Program for Women, Infants, and Children (WIC). WIC gives families vouchers they can use to buy extra food. It also offers valuable health and nutrition advice and helps link families up with prenatal care. And like many other preventive programs, WIC is cost effective: each $1 spent through WIC to provide nutrition and support services to a pregnant woman saves $3 in the first year of a child's life by reducing prematurity and low birthweight.

Despite its effectiveness, WIC only has funds to serve about half of the eligible population. In virtually every state, WIC has a waiting list of families who need food supplements. Federal funding for WIC should be raised to serve all poor and nutritionally at-risk women, infants, and children who apply. As well, every state should follow the example of the approximately one dozen states that use their funds to supplement federal WIC dollars and that use their purchasing power to secure competitive bids and reduce infant formula prices.

People in churches must make sure that elected officials and community leaders know they support policies and programs that ensure basic health care for all infants, children, and pregnant women. In addition, we can offer various kinds of assistance to help community clinics and health care programs do a better job of serving low-income families.

What Can You Do To Meet the Needs for Maternal and Child Health Care?

Educate Yourself and Others

◆ Invite a representative from your city or county health department, WIC program, or a community health clinic to speak to your congregation or committee about the health needs of pregnant women and children in your area.

◆ Write a letter to the editor of your local newspaper about the unmet health needs of women and children in your area and encourage strong local action.

◆ Create a chart that shows the health services available to people at various economic levels of your community. Display it in your church building. Distribute copies of it to other congregations and community groups.

Get Involved in the Community

◆ Organize volunteers to transport pregnant women and parents and children to and from local health clinics that provide prenatal and pediatric care. Work with clinics to advertise the availability of the free transportation and to schedule it at appropriate times.

◆ Set up and staff a play area in a health clinic or WIC program office for children waiting with family members.

◆ Donate congregational space for prenatal care classes. Encourage women from the congregation to take part in staffing or attending the courses.

◆ Give a community baby shower to educate pregnant women about the need for prenatal care and to provide them with baby clothing and other necessary items.

◆ Adopt a health clinic — much like the "adopt a school" program — and provide financial support, volunteers, and help with community relations.

◆ Work with local, public, and religious-affiliated hospitals to develop arrangements that will enable pregnant women who lack health insurance to get hospital care for their deliveries.

◆ Donate congregational space for immunization clinics. Weekend and evening clinics can help working families have access to services. Encourage congregation members to take part in staffing these clinics.

◆ Volunteer time to accompany public health nurses or social workers. Members of congregations, especially those located in inner-city areas, could assist public health staff making home visits to pregnant women and parents.

Advocate for Adequate Maternal and Child Health Care

◆ Educate yourself and others through forums and other community meetings about how health care reform will positively affect maternal and child health.

◆ Help generate business and corporate support for community groups working to improve the health of infants and children.

◆ Join a local or state coalition of groups and individuals that seeks to improve the health status of children and pregnant women by removing financial barriers to care, increasing access to health services, and educating the public about available health services.

◆ Organize health care professionals within your own congregation or help area congregations take a more visible and active role in educating, volunteering, and advocating on behalf of at-risk pregnant women, infants, and children.

◆ Help educate policy makers at the federal, state, and local levels. Write to elected officials, outlining your concerns and advocating for preventive, cost-effective investments in the health of today's children.

◆ Help educate community leaders and policy makers by organizing visits to public clinics, hospital neonatal intensive care units, and WIC program sites.

Maternal and Child Health
Information Resources Worksheet

Local health clinic/neighborhood health center (ask for the medical director or head of clinical staff):

_____

Speaker: yes ❑ no ❑   Send materials: yes ❑ no ❑   Site visit: yes ❑ no ❑

Ask about: number of uninsured children and pregnant women, most critical health problems, types of maternal and child health care services offered (e.g., prenatal care, preventive health care, services for children with special health needs), whether women and children are able to enroll in Medicaid on-site, and need for volunteer assistance.

Comments/information: _____

_____

_____

_____

Local public, community, or children's hospital (ask for chief of obstetrics or pediatrics):

_____

Speaker: yes ❑ no ❑   Send materials: yes ❑ no ❑   Site visit: yes ❑ no ❑

Ask about: proportion of children and pregnant women admitted who are uninsured, whether other facilities for the uninsured are available, and types of preventable conditions that hospitalized children have.

Comments/information: _____

_____

_____

_____

City/county health department (ask for agency head's office): _____

Speaker: yes ❑ no ❑   Send materials: yes ❑ no ❑

Ask about: county/city statistics for uninsured children, infant mortality, proportion of low-birthweight babies, childhood immunization, WIC funding and enrollment.

Comments/information: _____

_____

_____

_____

(Copy and use this as a hand-out)

State maternal and child health (MCH) agency (contact state agency head, who is located in the state health department):

_____

Speaker: yes ❑ no ❑   Send materials: yes ❑ no ❑

Ask about: statewide statistics on infant mortality and low birthweight; immunization; proportion of children with disabilities; proportion of children who are uninsured; WIC funding and proportion of eligible women, infants, and children served.

Comments/information: _____

_____

_____

State Medicaid agency (ask for director's office, usually part of state welfare or health agency):

_____

Speaker: yes ❑ no ❑   Send materials: yes ❑ no ❑

Ask about: whether all pregnant women and infants with incomes below 185 percent of poverty level are covered; proportion of children under age 6 who receive Medicaid's Early and Periodic Screening, Diagnosis, and Treatment (EPSDT) program benefits, proportion of children ages 6 to 20 who receive EPSDT benefits; whether women and children can enroll in Medicaid at area health clinics and neighborhood health centers; proportion of state pediatricians who treat Medicaid patients; and proportion of obstetricians who treat Medicaid patients.

Comments/information: _____

_____

_____

Statewide health advocacy organization (call CDF Health Division, state MCH agency, or state legal services program for contact suggestions):

_____

Speaker: yes ❑ no ❑   Send materials: yes ❑ no ❑

Ask about: major issues on which the organization works and any available reports and statistics.

Comments/information: _____

_____

Children's Defense Fund, Health Division, 25 E Street, N.W., Washington, DC 20001, (202) 628-8787.

Send materials: yes ❑ no ❑

Ask about: current agenda, legislative items, and desired actions.

Comments/information: _____

_____

Youth Development and Teen Pregnancy Prevention

But now hear, O Jacob my servant,
   Israel whom I have chosen!
Thus says the Lord who made you,
   who formed you in the womb and will help you;
Do not fear, O Jacob my servant,
   Jeshurun whom I have chosen.
For I will pour water on the thirsty land,
   and streams on the dry ground.
I will pour my spirit upon your descendants,
   and my blessing on your offspring.
They shall spring up like a green tamarisk,
   like willows by flowing streams.

Isaiah 44:1–4

May our sons in their youth
   be like plants full grown,
our daughters like corner pillars,
   cut for the building of a palace.

Psalm 144:12

Let no one despise your youth, but set the believers an example in speech and conduct, in love, in faith, in purity. Until I arrive, give attention to the public reading of scripture, to exhorting, to teaching. Do not neglect the gift that is in you.

1 Timothy 4:12–14a

The United States' teen pregnancy rate is twice as high as that of other industrialized countries. Before the age of 20, two in five American girls get pregnant and one in five American girls bears a child.

Children's Defense Fund analysis

Children almost never do what we say but almost always do what we do.

James Baldwin

Reflection Questions

◆ What is the prevalent attitude toward young people in these biblical quotes? How is that attitude manifested in your congregation? How is it ignored?

◆ As you think about the teenagers in your congregation and community, what words or images come to your mind? How many of your congregation's youths do you know by name?

◆ If you were writing a psalm of praise to God for young people, what would you say? What images would you use to express what you hope for the young people?

◆ What kind of an environment, or what supports, do the sons and daughters of our nation need to flourish "like plants full grown" and to be as solid and stable as "corner pillars of a palace"? What kind of education, job preparation, and information on issues related to sexuality and family life do they need?

From Adolescence to Adulthood

What kind of future do we want for the teenagers we love? We want them to be well-educated, to have jobs they enjoy and incomes that will support a home and a family. We want them to become nurturing parents and citizens who contribute to their community.

We work hard to provide the material, emotional, and spiritual resources for our teenagers to achieve. But there are far too many teenagers who are not receiving the support and guidance they need to make a successful transition from adolescence to adulthood. Many make risky choices, shortsighted judgments, and test limits. The consequences of these choices are far more serious now than ever before, ranging from single parenthood and prolonged poverty to AIDS to death by gunshot.

Thirty years ago, a teenager who dropped out of school generally could find a job and look forward to earning enough eventually to support a family. Today, a high school dropout has only one chance in three of even finding a full-time job. Until the past decade, unprotected sex might lead to pregnancy, but it was not likely to lead to death. By March 1991, however, more than 34,000 young people in their twenties had been diagnosed with AIDS. The lag time between HIV infection and the onset of AIDS suggests that many were infected with the fatal disease as teens. And while AIDS was the sixth leading cause of death among 15- to 24-year-olds in 1989, experts fear that teenagers' feelings of invulnerability are causing many of them to ignore the risks of unprotected sex.

Early pregnancy and parenthood are both symptoms and causes of an adolescence that offers few positive options for the future. So are drug and alcohol abuse, crime, school dropout, low academic achievement, and unemployment. The prevalence of these outcomes tells us that families, churches, schools, and other community groups are falling short in preparing our most vulnerable teenagers for healthy, productive lives as workers, citizens, and parents. Consider these facts:

♦ About one-quarter, or 7 million, of U.S. youngsters between the ages of 10 and 17 are at serious risk of school failure, substance abuse, and teen pregnancy and parenthood, according to the Carnegie Council on Adolescent Development.

♦ After declining since the early 1970s, the teen birth rate started to rise in 1987. In 1991, there were 62.1 births per 1,000 girls ages 15 to 19 — the highest rate since 1973.

♦ In 1990 almost one-quarter of surveyed 12- to 17-year-olds and more than half of 18- to 25-year-olds reported having used drugs other than alcohol and tobacco.

♦ In 1990 more than 14 percent of 18- and 19-year-olds had not graduated from high school and were not in school.

♦ In 1991 nearly one in five teenagers actively looking for work could not find a job.

As the proportion of young people in the U.S. population drops, we cannot afford to let our teenagers be sidetracked from a productive adulthood. In 1950, 17 people were working to support each retired person; in 1992 there were only three workers for every retiree. By 2030 the number of senior citizens will equal the number of teens and young adults. If even a small portion of these young people reach adulthood unhealthy, unskilled, or alienated, the nation will be dangerously short of the energy and creativity necessary to maintain its standard of living.

The Causes of Too-Early Parenthood

According to social scientists, school failure, adolescent crime, drug and alcohol abuse, and teenage pregnancy are caused by such conditions as premature birth or low birthweight, poor health, family stress, inadequate schools, and the lack of close relationships with loving adults. The children most likely to face such risks are those who grow up in poverty. School-age children and young adults are more likely to live in poor families now than in the late 1960s. A total of 3.5 million 12- to 17-year-olds were living in poverty in 1990.

Poor children are less likely to receive key building blocks of early development such as adequate nutrition, good medical care, and a safe, stimulating environment. Children who are ill, undernourished, or undernurtured often are less alert, less curious, and interact less effectively with their environment than do other children. They also are more likely to live with parents who themselves did poorly in school, dropped out, and lack job skills.

Girls who grow up craving love, who have little sense of self-worth and no dreams for the future, are likely to feel they have nothing to offer but their bodies and not much to lose if they get pregnant. Carrying a baby, to some girls, represents the one thing they can do to get a sense of achievement. Says one young mother, "It's the one time in my life I really felt like I'm somebody, like I'm doing something. People come around and expect me to feel ashamed of myself, but instead I feel proud of myself, like I can at least make a baby."

Disadvantaged boys may be particularly likely to view the initiation of sexual activity as the marker of adulthood. Low-income youths generally lack the family expectations and life scripts that point to other benchmarks of progress toward adulthood. Without motivation for delaying sexual activity, disadvantaged teenage boys are likely to have a considerable stake in sexual activity and the ability to become a parent.

The Disastrous Consequences of Too-Early Parenthood

Even if many teenagers have not learned the wisdom of avoiding too-early parenthood, the disastrous consequences are apparent:

- In a high-tech economy, the lack of a high school education is an increasingly serious barrier to economic self-sufficiency. Yet half of all young women who give birth before age 18 do not obtain a high school diploma by their mid-twenties.

- Without higher education, many older teenagers and young adults cannot find jobs that offer a future and pay a living wage. Male high school dropouts between the ages of 20 and 24 earned on average $8,349 in 1990; young female dropouts earned a shockingly low $3,109.

- Two incomes are increasingly necessary to maintain a young family above the poverty line, but most teen mothers raise their children alone. Almost two-thirds of all births to teens are to unmarried girls, compared with less than one-third in 1970.

Early childbearing jeopardizes the future of both parents and children. But it is not merely a personal issue. The vicious cycle of too-early parenthood and poverty repeating themselves in the next generation deprives the nation of educated, productive workers, so it has serious implications for the nation's economic future.

What Teenagers Need to Prevent Pregnancy: Positive Life Options

The good news is that we know a great deal about what works for young people. One effective program is the Multi-Service Family Life and Sex Education program of the New York Children's Aid Society. While reducing teen pregnancy is a primary goal, the program tackles much more, offering seven parallel but separate services for teens and their parents. Counseling, academic help, sports activities, self-expression, employment experience, and health services, as well as family life and sex education, are part of the five-day-a-week program, run almost entirely by professional staff.

The sex education course, offered separately to teens and their parents, includes not only sexual anatomy and reproduction, AIDS education, and information about contraception, but discussions of gender and family roles, body image, and values. The program serves about 300 young people and 110 adults at three separate sites in Harlem's mostly Black and Latino central, east, and west communities.

Co-Director Michael Carrera says perseverance and long-term commitment are keys to success when working with vulnerable teens. The youths in his program participate for at least five years, constantly interacting with staff members who provide consistent nurturing and role modeling. Every participant is guaranteed admission to Hunter College upon completing high school, and financial aid is available. In June 1992 a young woman who was one of the program's original participants in 1985 graduated from Hunter.

The Children's Aid Society program demonstrates that high-risk adolescents can work toward a promising future if they receive early, intensive, comprehensive, personalized help. No one foundation, social service program, school system, or community group can provide the full range of supports that disadvantaged students need. But working together, communities and schools can offer a comprehensive web of support, with the family at the center, that ensures the following opportunities for all teens:

- A first-rate education and strong basic skills (see education chapter for recommendations).

- A range of nonacademic opportunities for success such as recreation programs, hobbies, and other activities that integrate teens into the community and build confidence, self-esteem, and a sense of cultural belonging.

- Links to caring adults who provide positive role models and friendship.

- Family life education and help with life planning that offer realistic alternatives to self-destructive and dangerous behaviors.

- Comprehensive adolescent health services that address teens' developing sexuality and emotional vulnerabilities, and offer counseling about the consequences of too-early sexual activity and parenthood.

- Economic opportunity that sustains a decent standard of living such as school-to-work programs that lead to meaningful employment for those who do not go on to postsecondary education.

- Violence prevention curricula and peer mediation training that give teens the understanding and skills they need to resolve conflicts nonviolently.

It is important to begin offering youngsters these life-enhancing experiences during early adolescence, before they drift onto the paths where pregnancy and parenthood, drug use, and dropping out of school "just happen." Fears that increased information and accessible contraceptive services will increase sexual activity among teens are not supported by the evidence. In a Baltimore demonstration program, the proportion of girls who became sexually active by age 14 went down by 40 percent after a teen health clinic was established, and the median age at which girls began sexual activity was delayed by seven months.

The difference between what works for girls and for boys poses a significant obstacle to efforts to help teens delay sexual activity. Since young men generally are not as interested as young women in sexuality-specific services and programs, motivating boys to prevent pregnancy requires innovative approaches that integrate sex education into other activities. These approaches include:

- Taking the message and the service to the places and programs where young men congregate.

- Adding a sex education component to programs and services that attract young men, such as employment, recreation, and athletic programs.

- Making sure that programs and services are offered by adults with whom teenage boys can identify and in surroundings in which they feel comfortable.

The supports, experiences, and opportunities we would want for our own teenagers are exactly what we must give all teenagers. We must be advocates in our communities and our states for public policies and programs that provide teenagers with the services they need to become happy, productive adults. But even more, we must contribute our own time and efforts to church and community programs that give teenagers a real stake in their own futures.

What Can You Do To Heighten Opportunities for Youths?

Educate Yourself and Others

- Talk with young people in your neighborhood or congregation to hear what they need and want. Arrange intergenerational activities for young people and adults to meet and get to know one another.

- Do the youths of your congregation feel they can draw on the church for confidential guidance and support? How can you convey its availability?

- Survey the counseling resources for young people in your community. How does your congregation support them?

- Create a bulletin board of youth-serving agencies and services, including information and referral to accessible and affordable health facilities, counseling, and academic and vocational training sites.

Get Involved in the Needs of Young People

- Offer communication workshops for parents and teens, programs on alcohol and other drugs, and peer group or intergenerational discussions on human sexuality and teen pregnancy issues.

- Talk with adult education or fellowship group members about being mentors to young people in the community. Check with local schools to see if such a program is in place, or contact the Big Brothers and Big Sisters organization in your area.

- With the youth group, set up an employment service for teens to do odd jobs for people in the congregation and community. This can help them develop good work habits as well as earn money.

- Develop a community service project run by disadvantaged teens to encourage their sense of having something to give.

- Acknowledge the achievements of the young people in your congregation when they receive awards, or scholarships, are graduated, or enter new schools.

- Set up a scholarship fund to help young people go to college or training institutions.

- Work with community organizations to create systems of support for pregnant and parenting teens.

- Volunteer to help area schools or youth programs.

- Make your church available after school and in the evenings for structured recreational activities for youths, and for tutorial and special enrichment programs. Help transport young people to cultural events and recreational activities.

Advocate for Young People in Your Community

- Write to elected officials informing them of the needs you have discovered. Urge them to recommend a course of action.

- Help young people advocate for themselves. Hold a voter registration project in cooperation with the high school student council. Use a real voting machine to familiarize teens with the actual process.

- Ask the program chairpersons of professional, business, or service groups to schedule at least one meeting in the coming year to focus on ways the members can help young people who are at risk.

- Work with the local high school to offer a school-to-work program through which professionals from your congregation offer internships to students, particularly those at risk.

Youth Development and Teen Pregnancy Prevention Information Resources Worksheet

Local program serving teens (look under Youth Programs or Community Organizations in the telephone book; local branch of the United Way, Boys and Girls Clubs, YMCA, or YWCA; or self-help programs within the poor community such as welfare rights organizations or tenant councils):

_____

Speaker: yes ❏ no ❏   Send materials: yes ❏ no ❏   Site visit: yes ❏ no ❏

Ask about: most critical teen problems (e.g., running away, pregnancy, dropping out), services provided, who is the population being served, resources and needs, gaps in local services.

Comments/information: _____

_____

_____

Area church with outreach program to teens: _____

Speaker: yes ❏ no ❏   Send materials: yes ❏ no ❏   Site visit: yes ❏ no ❏

Ask about: how program meets needs, how established, resources, needs, services provided, population served.

Comments/information: _____

_____

_____

Local social service agency serving teens (look in the telephone book under Social Services or Family Services, and in government section under those categories in addition to Health and Recreation Departments):

_____

Speaker: yes ❏ no ❏   Send materials: yes ❏ no ❏

Ask about: most critical problems facing area teens, most successful programs, goals for program or policy changes, and gaps in local services.

Comments/information: _____

_____

_____

(Copy and use this as a hand-out)

State-level agency for adolescent policies and programs (start by calling the governor's office and state health department):

_____

Speaker: yes ❏ no ❏   Send materials: yes ❏ no ❏

Ask about: most critical problems facing teens in your state, trends in population in need and in population served, most successful programs and policies, program or policy areas needing improvement.

Comments/information: _____

_____

_____

Statewide advocacy group (ask the above contacts or the Children's Defense Fund):

_____

Speaker: yes ❏ no ❏   Send materials: yes ❏ no ❏

Ask about: relevant statistics regarding teens in your state (e.g., dropout rate, teen pregnancy rate); legislative and administrative agenda and desired actions; membership information.

Comments/information: _____

_____

_____

Children's Defense Fund, 25 E Street, N.W., Washington, DC 20001, (202) 628-8787.

Send materials: yes ❏ no ❏

Ask about: Current legislative items, desired actions, relevant statistics regarding teens in your state, successful program models, and research reports.

Comments/information: _____

_____

The Alan Guttmacher Institute, 360 Park Avenue, New York, NY 10003, (212) 254-5656.
Ask about: policies it supports, model programs, publications, and other sources of information.

Association of Junior Leagues, Inc., 825 Third Avenue, 27th Floor, New York, NY 10022, (212) 355-4380.
Ask about: their school-based pregnancy prevention Teen Outreach Program (TOP).

Center for Population Options, 1012 14th Street, N.W., Washington, DC 20005, (202) 347-5700.
Ask about: policies it supports; model programs; periodicals, fact sheets, and other publications related to adolescent pregnancy and prevention.

National Organization on Adolescent Pregnancy and Parenting, P.O. Box 2365, Reston, VA 22090, (703) 435-2365.
Ask about: its national membership-based network, resources, newsletter.

Family Income

Give justice to the weak and the orphan; maintain the right of the lowly and the destitute. Rescue the weak and the needy; deliver them from the hand of the wicked.

Psalm 82:3–4

If there is among you anyone in need, a member of your community in any of your towns within the land that the Lord your God is giving you, do not be hard-hearted or tight-fisted toward your needy neighbor. You should rather open your hand, willingly lending enough to meet the need, whatever it may be. Be careful that you do not entertain a mean thought, thinking, "The seventh year, the year of remission, is near," and therefore view your needy neighbor with hostility and give nothing; your neighbor might cry to the Lord against you, and you would incur guilt. Give liberally and be ungrudging when you do so, for on this account the Lord your God will bless you in all your work and in all that you undertake. Since there will never cease to be some in need on the earth, I therefore command you, "Open your hand to the poor and needy neighbor in your land."

Deuteronomy 15:7–11

He said also to the one who had invited him, "When you give a luncheon or a dinner, do not invite your friends or your brothers or your relatives or rich neighbors, in case they may invite you in return, and you would be repaid. But when you give a banquet, invite the poor, the crippled, the lame, and the blind. And you will be blessed, because they cannot repay you, and you will be repaid at the resurrection of the "righteous."

Luke 14:12–14

Reflection Questions

◆ Why is the psalm in the imperative? What is our moral responsibility to respond to those in need? Why might it be important to consider "rescuing" needy children and families within the context of giving *justice* and maintaining *rights*?

◆ How is "a member of your community" defined in the passage from Deuteronomy? Who do you consider members of your community? How do you feel people of faith are called to respond to poor children and their families? Why is it important that the land was given by God? Why would we incur guilt in the sight of God if we failed to help our neighbors in need?

◆ Reflect on the passage from Luke. What would be a modern equivalent to giving a "banquet"? What do people who are poor, crippled, lame, and blind have in common with each other? What do they have in common with children? With families that are in need?

Family Income

On a television news program, a young husband and wife talked about their lives. Both work, neither has health insurance, and they are struggling to support themselves and their two children on a combined income of $1,200 a month — just over what the federal government considers the poverty level. Another working mother on the same program summed up her experience of raising a family in the U.S. today: "When my parents got married I'm sure they had the same American dream just like we have now, but I think it was a little easier for them to see that dream than it'll be for us."

For the past two decades in the U.S., the economic position of families with children has been slipping. Families have been squeezed from all sides by rising prices, increasingly inadequate wages, and the erosion of public assistance and other "safety net" programs.

At the same time, more families today are headed by mothers only. These families are more likely to be poor, because there is no second wage earner, and often no child support from the absent parent, and because women generally still make less money than men.

It is not just one-parent, poorly educated, or somehow troubled families — those we traditionally associate with poverty — that have been hurt, however. A sizable and growing portion of middle-income and two-parent families have been affected as well. Trying to stay afloat, parents are working more hours and have less time to spend with their children. Families worry more about making ends meet and have become increasingly pessimistic that their children will make it when they leave home to build a life of their own. Gary Domstraud, 54, the president of a small technology firm in Minnesota, said in a focus group study conducted by the Twin Cities' *Star Tribune* newspaper in 1992, "I look at my children and it scares the living daylights out of me what their future's going to be."

Rise in Child Poverty

The most devastating consequence of the economic crisis among America's families has been the dramatic rise in child poverty during the 1980s. According to the federal government's official definition, in 1993 a family of three was considered poor if its total annual income was less than $10,860. For a family of four, the poverty threshold was $13,924, and so on. Using the official definition, poverty rates are alarming. In 1991 more than one in five American children was poor. Among children younger than six, one in every four was poor. The total number of poor children reached 14.3 million, 4.7 million more than in 1979. Many experts say these numbers do not accurately reflect today's cost of living, and that even families making more than the official poverty thresholds often have a hard time surviving.

By far the hardest hit of American families during the past two decades have been young families, those headed by parents younger than 30. The median income of young families with children plummeted by one-third from 1973 to 1990, after adjusting for inflation. As a result, fully 40 percent of children in young families were poor in 1990, twice the proportion in 1973. Poverty among young families is especially disturbing because most children spend part of their earliest and most developmentally vulnerable years in a young family. If their families are unable to provide the security, care, and material necessities so important to childhood development, their future — and the nation's — may be seriously jeopardized.

The consequences of child poverty are well documented. From the womb to young adulthood, poor children are at higher risk of setbacks in health, development, and education. These problems are likely to follow them through life, working against their attempts to become self-reliant, productive citizens. For some children, poverty is deadly. Each year an estimated 10,000 American children die from poverty's effects. For many more, poverty leads to inadequate health care, hunger, family stress, inability to concentrate in the classroom, and school dropout.

An Economic Recovery Alone Is Not Enough

The recession that began in 1991, coming on the heels of a decade of hard times for children, only worsened their plight. But even as the nation heads into economic recovery, that alone will not be enough to reverse the effects of the recession and pull children back to secure ground.

In the past, large numbers of children escaped poverty during economic growth periods. Since the 1970s, however, not only have recessions hurt children more, but economic recoveries have helped them less. Between 1979 and 1983, 3.5 million children became poor because of back-to-back recessions, but fewer than 40 percent of that number were rescued from 1983 to 1989, when the economy grew. If these patterns repeat themselves in the 1990s, by the year 2000 the United States will have almost 15 million poor children. Reversing the tide of poverty will require more than general economic growth. It will take church, society, and government working together to launch specific, strong efforts that attack the root causes of poverty.

We Can Eliminate Child Poverty

Contrary to what some people think, there is nothing inevitable about child poverty. The United States has the knowledge and more than enough resources to make sure no child is poor — if it chooses to do so. History tells us that poverty can be fought and beaten by the right combination of policy choices and strong economic growth. For example, the U.S. government's commitment to improve Social Security and the Supplemental Security Income program has cut the poverty rate among the elderly in the U.S. by nearly two-thirds since 1967. And in the 1960s, when a strong economy was coupled with concerted government action to fight poverty, the U.S. cut child poverty rates in half.

Other countries' experiences offer further evidence that the war against poverty can be won. The U.S. child poverty rate is more than double those of Canada, Germany, Norway, Sweden, Switzerland, and the United Kingdom. A key reason, economists say, is that these countries are more likely to provide the financial assistance to lift families with children out of poverty.

An Agenda for Action

No nation can afford to throw away the next generation of young people — young people who will be tomorrow's workers, parents, and citizens — by letting so many of them grow up in deprivation. We cannot afford to tell more and more parents that working hard is not enough to support a family. For our own self-interest and for the future of our children, we must make sure that every family has the secure economic foundation it needs to provide children a good start in life.

First, we must make work pay and ensure that families that work are not poor.

- As part of this "make work pay" effort, the U.S. minimum wage should be raised substantially to make up for inflation. During the past decade the cost of living has climbed, but the federal minimum wage has not been adjusted enough to keep up. As a result, in 1993 earnings from full-time, year-round work at the minimum wage ($4.25 an hour) still left a family of three well below the poverty line.

- We should make sure the Earned Income Credit (EIC), a federal tax credit for low-income working families with children, provides meaningful assistance to larger families that typically suffer the most severe poverty. The EIC helps make work pay by allowing the working poor to combine their earnings with the tax credit to lift their families out of poverty. Local governments should conduct public outreach and education to inform low-income families and their employers about the EIC. Employers can ensure that employees eligible for advance payments of the EIC receive them as part of their regular paychecks.

- Families on AFDC (the nation's chief cash assistance program for low-income families with children) should be given the help they need to earn their way out of poverty. The federal government should strengthen education and training opportunities for AFDC recipients, particularly by increasing funding for the Job Opportunities and Basic Skills (JOBS) program. At the same time, states should improve their efforts to provide the matching funds needed to receive the full allotment of federal JOBS funds. Equally important, the federal government should eliminate unreasonable asset limitations and other rules that in effect are disincentives for families to work and build savings.

Second, we must ensure that every child has the support of two parents.

- The U.S. government should establish a national child support assurance system that includes strict federal enforcement of absent parents' child support obligations, and, as a last resort, provides an assured minimum level of support in cases where absent parents' payments are inadequate or uncollected.

- As an interim step, we must ensure that states pursue child support aggressively. States can strengthen their child support enforcement by allocating more resources to child support enforcement and by improving procedures for locating absent parents, establishing paternity, getting child support orders, and collecting payments. States also can create child support assurance demonstration projects to guide the development of national efforts.

Third, we must build a stronger economic foundation for families that protects children from poverty and assures that they have the basic necessities of life.

- As the National Commission on Children and members of Congress of both parties have proposed, the United States should establish a refundable children's tax credit — a per-child amount of assistance for all families regardless of income or employment status. Families would receive this amount as a reduction in their taxes or as a payment if they have no tax liability. The credit would ease the financial burdens of raising children and provide a stable economic base for families, especially young families just getting started, without the stigma and other pitfalls of welfare. The United States is one of the few major industrialized countries that does not have a universal child assistance of this sort.

- State unemployment insurance eligibility rules should be reformed so that more low-wage and part-time workers can qualify for benefits. On several occasions in the early 1990s, the federal government responded to the high jobless rates of the recession by allowing people to receive unemployment benefits for a longer period of time. But that change did not help the millions of jobless workers and families who do not meet the strict eligibility requirements.

- Even with a stronger unemployment insurance system, some families will need a safety net during periods of prolonged joblessness or family crisis. AFDC, the joint federal-state program intended for this, is not doing the job. Benefit levels, which differ from state to state, were never adequate, and have become intolerably low in the past 20 years as states cut deeply into their AFDC budgets. Between 1970 and 1992 the median monthly state AFDC grant for a family of three dropped from $652, or 71 percent of the poverty line, to $372, or only 41 percent of the poverty line. AFDC benefits must be raised to levels that more adequately meet the costs of raising a family. In addition, arbitrary time limits on eligibility and rules that bar two-parent families from AFDC should be removed.

What Can You Do To Help Ensure Families Have Adequate Income?

Educate Yourself and Others

◆ Read and share newspaper articles about child poverty and family income issues. Include basic facts or short articles about family income in your church worship bulletin or newsletter.

◆ Invite a local child advocate to speak — and a family who lives in poverty.

◆ Write a letter to the editor. Or talk with the staff of the local newspaper and suggest a story on child poverty and family income issues in the community.

◆ Find out what AFDC benefit levels are in your state. As an exercise for an adult or youth group, try to make a realistic family budget on an AFDC-level income. Do the same for a poverty-level income. Discuss your budget shortfalls. What emergency help would you need to provide for your family's basic necessities? What long-term help might help your family become economically stable? Assign members of the group to find out if such help is available in your community. Also find out how much the buying power of your state's AFDC benefit has declined in the last five, 10 or 20 years because of failures to adjust it regularly for inflation.

Get Involved in Efforts That Help

◆ Find out about food banks and other emergency family assistance in your community. Ask if they need fund raisers, food drives, or volunteer workers. Have your congregation create an emergency fund or food bank of its own to help families get through times of crisis.

◆ Inform eligible families in your congregation and community about the Earned Income Credit (EIC), a federal tax credit worth up to $2,000 or more for low-income working families with children. To learn how you can help publicize the EIC and to receive outreach posters and other materials, contact the Center on Budget and Policy Priorities, 777 N. Capitol Street, N.E., Suite 705, Washington, DC 20002, (202) 408-1080.

◆ Talk with local nonprofit agencies that provide job training about how to help unemployed or underemployed families in your congregation and community find jobs. Arrange transportation and child care to allow parents to go to interviews, attend education and job training, and keep their jobs. (See the Child Care and Head Start chapter, pages 62–69, for what your congregation can do to help meet families' ongoing child care needs.)

◆ Find out if local schools serve breakfast to low-income students in the morning. Or have your church start a summer feeding program to stop students from going hungry during summertime. For information on promoting the federal school breakfast and summer feeding programs in your community, contact the Food Research and Action Center, 1875 Connecticut Ave., N.W., Suite 540, Washington, DC 20009, (202) 986-2200.

◆ Find out how well your local child support agency is helping welfare families (and nonwelfare families who ask for help) with child support enforcement services, including working with hospitals to establish paternity for newborns at the time of birth.

Advocate for Stronger Family Income Supports

◆ Urge your senators and representative in Congress to enact legislation that boosts family economic security. Emphasize creating national child support assurance and a refundable children's tax credit.

◆ Convince your state legislators to support important family income support measures at the state level, such as raising the state minimum wage above the inadequate federal level; improving state child support enforcement procedures; and restoring the value of AFDC to make up lost ground.

◆ Remind your state legislators of ways to help low-income families get through short-term crises, such as divorce or the threat of eviction. Find out if your state has a policy (called "expedited processing") to cut red tape for families who need to get onto AFDC quickly because of a crisis, or if it offers joint federal-state Emergency Assistance benefits (available no more than once per year for up to 30 days for needy families with children). If not, encourage state officials to do so. For information, call your state income maintenance agency or the benefits attorney at your local legal services office.

◆ Tell your state legislators to support efforts to help low-income families find and keep well-paying jobs. Find out if the state is drawing down all available federal funds for the Job Opportunities and Basic Skills program, which provides families on AFDC with education, training, employment, transitional health and child care, and related services. Encourage state officials to do so. For information or help in understanding the issues, call your state income maintenance agency.

Family Income Information Resources Worksheet

State income maintenance or child support agency: _____

Speaker: yes ❏ no ❏   Send materials: yes ❏ no ❏   Site visit: yes ❏ no ❏

Ask about: trends in children served, successful education, employment and training programs, child support enforcement programs, administrative barriers to expanding such efforts.

Comments/information: _____

_____

_____

_____

Area congregation with program to support low-income families and children: _____

Speaker: yes ❏ no ❏   Send materials: yes ❏ no ❏   Site visit: yes ❏ no ❏

Ask about: program and how established, needs of children and families served, resources contributed by congregation, help needed.

Comments/information: _____

_____

_____

_____

Area job training center or community college: _____

Speaker: yes ❏ no ❏   Send materials: yes ❏ no ❏   Site visit: yes ❏ no ❏

Ask about: needs of low-income families, available services in the community, number of jobs available to employ families at adequate wages.

Comments/information: _____

_____

_____

_____

(Copy and use this as a hand-out)

The benefits attorney from a local legal aid agency for the poor: _____

Speaker: yes ☐ no ☐   Send materials: yes ☐ no ☐   Site visit: yes ☐ no ☐

Ask about: adequacy of public assistance benefits, who receives benefits, who may need but not receive benefits, services needed to move families off AFDC and out of poverty.

Comments/information: _____

_____

_____

Statewide or citywide child advocacy group (look under Children or Social Services in the yellow pages of the phone book):

_____

Speaker: yes ☐ no ☐   Send materials: yes ☐ no ☐

Ask about: policy or legislative agendas for low-income children, new programs and policies that need support, programs and policies that need change, barriers to service that need attention, collaboration with other groups, help needed, membership.

Comments/information: _____

_____

_____

Children's Defense Fund, Family Support Division, 25 E Street, N.W., Washington, DC 20001, (202) 628-8787.

Send materials: yes ☐ no ☐

Ask about: current policy or legislative agendas, innovative policies and programs, help needed.

Comments/information: _____

_____

_____

Center on Budget and Policy Priorities, 440 First Street, N.W., Suite 310, Washington, DC 20001, (202) 638-2952.

Send materials: yes ☐ no ☐

Ask about: current policy or legislative income support agendas, innovative policies and programs on welfare reform or welfare-to-work, help needed.

Comments/information: _____

_____

_____

(Copy and use this as a hand-out)

Children of Every Nation

PHOTO BY PAMELA HASEGAWA

How To Use This Section

This section was especially prepared by Betty Jane Bailey on behalf of Friendship Press and is designed to help you know more about children beyond the borders of your church, your community, and your nation. While the picture may seem very different from that in North America, in fact there are many children in parts of the U.S. and Canada facing similar issues. This material is not meant to suggest that one situation is more important than another, but rather to emphasize the broader nature of global children's issues.

The material that follows can be used for congregational study and action on international issues alone, or it can be used to enhance and expand your study of any of the domestic issues raised previously. Some suggestions are given on how to globalize your use of **Section III, Chapter 1: A Four-Part Format for a Study into Action Program.**

> ## Children around the World
>
> - 250,000 children die each week from diseases that are, for the most part, preventable.
>
> - 30 million children are homeless.
>
> - 7 million children are refugees.
>
> - uncounted and uncountable millions work long hours instead of attending school and playing with friends.
>
> - hundreds of thousands work as virtual slaves to pay off debts incurred by their families.
>
> - thousands work as prostitutes, losing their childhood and often their very lives for the pleasure of adults.

Expanding the Borders of Our Minds

[God] executes justice for the orphan and the widow, and...loves the strangers, providing them food and clothing. You shall also love the stranger, for you were strangers in the land of Egypt.

Deuteronomy 10:18–19

One of the scribes came near and heard them disputing with one another, and seeing that he answered them well, he asked him, "Which commandment is the first of all?" Jesus answered, "The first is, 'Hear O Israel: the Lord our God, the Lord is one; you shall love the Lord your God with all your heart and with all your soul, and with all your mind, and with all your strength.' The second is this, 'You shall love your neighbor as yourself.' There is no other commandment greater than these."

Mark 12:28–31

We...stand on the edge of a new era of concern for the silent and invisible tragedy that poverty inflicts on today's children and on tomorrow's world. Whether the world will enter decisively into that new age depends on the pressure that is brought to bear by politicians, press, public, and professional services in all nations.

State of the World's Children 1993

Reflection Questions

◆ How are strangers treated in your congregation? What happens when people of different ethnic or racial backgrounds try to find room in your congregation? Is it easier to accept the stranger who is far away or the one nearby?

◆ What is the meaning of "stranger" in the Christian faith? What gets in the way of our love for children who are "strangers"?

◆ Jesus, in the parable we often call "The Good Samaritan" (Luke 10:30–37), opens up the word "neighbor" to include those beyond our own group. How might this apply to our concern for children? What is the relationship between "stranger" and "neighbor" in the two Scripture passages above?

Children of Every Nation

In the previous chapters we have focused on the situation of children in the United States. We have seen that despite the wealth of the North American economies, the democratic structure of our political systems, and even the good intentions of our people, children in North America too often lack the basic necessities for a healthy, happy, and productive life.

What about children in the rest of the world? It can come as no surprise that in many places around the globe the scourges of poverty, war, famine, disease, and ethnic hatreds wreak their most destructive effects on children. In societies with poor economic development, children are additionally victimized by being employed inappropriately as they and their families struggle to survive.

A false dichotomy separates what we do about children in our own country and children of other nations. North American economies and policies have a major effect on world economies and policies. Economic and military decisions that we make affect not only "our" children but children around the world. A country paying more in interest on its debt than it receives in aid, or struggling to meet the requirements of an IMF structural adjustment program, or purchasing the military hardware necessitated by armed conflict, has few resources to devote to its children.

To help your congregation begin making connections between "we" and "they," here are some suggestions on how to adapt the lesson plan in **Section III, Chapter 1,** to a more global approach to children's issues.

Expanding the Borders of Our Minds

Week 1: Include material from this section on an issue of interest, or research others (see resources listed on page 156). Since a site visit to another country may not be possible, find up-to-date pictures of children from other cultures for your bulletin board or display area. Photographs may be available from the national agency of your denomination which deals with world mission and service.

Week 2: Invite as a speaker someone who has firsthand experience with the situation of children in another part of the world. If you cannot find church workers, missionaries, or development experts, talk with people in your community who have traveled. Whether their trip was for business or pleasure, they will have observations to share.

Week 3: Include information on national church resolutions that deal with the world's children as well as projects sponsored by your denomination or subgroups such as women's organizations. Invite speakers from governmental or nongovernmental agencies to explain what they are doing (or not doing), so that you can clarify where your congregation might be effective in advocacy or action.

Week 4: Include both global and local action or advocacy on your agenda. For example, if you are going to help develop a child care center, consider contacting a child care program in another part of the world. We can learn from their experience in managing with few resources or under adverse conditions!

Denominational offices, or community agencies with overseas connections, can put you in touch with projects around the world with which to build a partnership. These connections help us recognize that human, financial and physical resources are available in many places. Remember, a partnership is a more appropriate approach than one in which "we" send and "they" receive.

Children and War

We have in Nicaragua around 12,000 people who are fatherless because of the war. We have many children who have been shot in the war, who are legless or armless because of the war. And this is the question we ask everyone: What has a child done so that he is fatherless, what has he done so that he has no leg?

> Ajax Delgado, Secretary General of the Asociación de Niños Sandinistas (as quoted in *Broken Promise* by Annie Allsebrook and Anthony Swift)

Since World War II there have been 150 military conflicts, almost all of them in developing countries. Millions of children already living on the edge of poverty have had their conditions worsened by these conflicts.

War is always going on somewhere in the world and civilians are right in the midst of the fighting. Children are recruited as soldiers. Their small stature and agility make them ideal spies and runners for the armed forces even when they do not carry guns. After the fighting has ended, they may be sent out into fields planted with landmines. Even if they survive a war, the exposure to violence and accompanying traumas wreak havoc on their psyches. Children may be separated temporarily or permanently from their families and communities.

With or without their families, millions of children wind up in refugee camps where there is little provision for children's needs beyond basic food, shelter, and health care. Primary education may be available but secondary education often is lacking. There are no playgrounds or activities for young children, nor after-school activities for those lucky enough to go to school. With the community broken, cultural values and traditions disappear. Refugee camps often function in a quasi-lawless state in which children find themselves powerless. Children who have lived for long periods of time in refugee camps are ill prepared for life outside.

For millions of children, the only world they know is one where gunfire and explosions, death, injury, separation are commonplace. In 40 of the wars in the past ten years children have taken an active part.

Broken Promise

Homelessness and Housing

Too many children live in camps, shelters, institutions, temporary foster care, and other settings that aren't "home." But a significant number, especially among the poor, lose all or most of their family ties and end up fending for themselves on the streets of major cities. We call them "street children."

Children become street children for many reasons. In Romania in the 1980s, thousands of children were placed in institutions for a variety of physical or mental disabilities or because their parents could not care for them. These institutions were often little more than prisons, and when the Ceausescu dictatorship fell in 1989, hundreds of children simply ran away from them. Many have no idea where their relatives are and live in train stations and abandoned buildings in Bucharest and other cities.

In several Latin American countries, poor children from urban *barrios* and rural villages go into the streets seeking work in order to survive. Thousands earn essential income for their families, working alongside siblings and parents. These children are known as "children in the street." But if they lose their families, they become "children of the streets." For these children, home is the street, and bed is a doorstep or patch of dirt under a bridge.

Street children often commit desperate and illegal acts in their struggle to stay alive. Many steal, rob, or prostitute themselves. City dwellers often view them as a menace. Recently, in Brazil and Guatemala the police and quasi-official death squads have engaged in campaigns to rid the cities of street children by intimidating, beating, and even killing them.

Children's natural resilience has led them to band together for protection, with older children caring for younger ones. Many of these children aspire to a better life and regular jobs. Survival remains a day-to-day affair, though, and insecurity is a street child's constant companion.

Some success stories:

♦ In Nairobi, Kenya, the Undugu Society links working street children with trades people. It combines apprenticeship with business management training to encourage boys to start their own businesses.

♦ In Khartoum, Sudan, street children are employed as bicycle messengers.

♦ In the Philippines, street children are employed to clean soft drink bottles.

Breaking the cycle of poverty for families is the crucial key to the future of these children and the next generation.

Child Prostitution

Katia, a child from Brazil, tells her story:

My family's got a house and a bit of land, but I've been living on the streets since I was seven, the year after my mother died. I worked as a servant in a family's house, but then a friend told me to come to the city.

I got by in the city, picking up men, though I had to put up with them hitting me. What really makes me angry is the way that these machos beat you up all the time. It makes you want to kill them. That's why I don't live with a guy. I just sell my body to them from time to time.

From *Brazil: War on Children* by Gilberto Dimenstein, New York; Monthly Review Press, 1991, as quoted in *Children at Risk — Child Exploitation*, National Council of Churches, Office on Global Education

Child prostitution is a very profitable industry.

♦ Prostitution training centers have been set up in Argentina for children ages eight to 10.

- The number of child prostitutes in Manila has doubled since 1987.

- A flourishing $5 billion sex industry, primarily in Asia, caters to tourists from Europe, North America, and Asia.

- Several countries host sex tours arranged by travel agencies.

These children are innocent pawns. Trusting of adults, often their own parents, they are tricked or sold into prostitution with the promise of jobs, education or a better life. Poor, uneducated and from rural areas, they are totally overwhelmed by the urban setting of most brothels where many end up or in the street where a woman's body belongs to everyone. They are trapped with no skills, often hampered by a language barrier and have no comprehension of their rights or where to turn for help. And the working life of a street girl is short indeed. It's no wonder that little children are induced into the trade to provide a "fresher product" or a virgin to allay the fears of clients that they might contract HIV/AIDS.

Ending Child Prostitution in Asian Tourism...Starts in the USA: A Guide to Action, ECPAT

The United Nations Convention on the Rights of the Child forbids child sexual exploitation in both sexual activity and in pornography. Religious groups in Asia and in other parts of the world are working to end child prostitution, but increasing poverty among street children makes them ever more vulnerable to profiteering agents of the sex tourism industry.

Child Health

Each day, 35,000 children under the age of five die in the developing world. Every week, a quarter of a million children lose their lives. Countless others hang on to the edge of life, their poor growth and health limiting the development of their full God-given potential.

Under-five mortality is more than just a measure of survival. It is also the best single guide to the quality of life for the far greater number of children who survive.

The Progress of Nations 1993

Maria del Carmen Paja, a mother from a rural area in South America, has lost two young children — one from a respiratory infection and the other from measles.

"For the baby boy, I tried to get help," Maria said. "But as I was carrying him for help, he just died in my arms. My daughter was older. I had got used to playing with her, being with her. It's difficult...It's sad to remember those times with my children. She was all right when she went to bed. By midnight she was sick. She died as day broke. I am not alone. It's happened to a lot of women."

In Maria's village there is a trained health worker now, and deaths from such diseases can be nearly eliminated. Almost 60 percent of child deaths around the world are caused by pneumonia, measles, and diarrhea, all of which can be prevented and treated by proven low-cost means.

Pneumonia — the Greatest Killer

Pneumonia and other respiratory diseases account for more than a quarter of all illnesses and deaths among children of the developing world. Pneumonia claims 3.5 million young lives each year. Children from poor families or those without access to doctors and hospitals often do not get antibiotics, yet the dosage of antibiotics necessary to control bacterial pneumonia costs a mere 25 cents.

In villages everywhere, parents are now learning to identify the first danger signs of pneumonia. Community health workers are being trained to diagnose pneumonia, prescribe on-the-spot antibiotics, and ensure that the small proportion of children in critical condition are rushed to the nearest hospital. More than 60 developing countries are trying this simple strategy to reduce deaths from pneumonia by at least one-third in this decade.

Immunizations: Demonstrating the Possible

A goal set in the 1980s, to immunize 80 percent of the world's children, was achieved. According to UNICEF, almost 2 million children who would have been crippled by polio if they had not been vaccinated are now walking, running, and playing normally. Deaths from measles were reduced from approximately 2.5 million a year in 1980 to under 900,000 in 1990. Nonfatal attacks of the disease, which can lead to malnutrition, pneumonia, diarrhea, vitamin A loss, blindness, and deafness, were reduced from 75 million a year to 25 million a year.

These amazing gains were the result of a massive campaign by UNICEF, the World Health Organization, various national health services, and thousands of nongovernmental organizations, including schools, churches, mosques, and temples.

The work goes on to reach the 20 percent of children who are not yet immunized, and to sustain the high levels of immunization in the future. Despite the successful campaign, 1.7 million children still die each year from vaccine-preventable diseases.

Diarrheal Diseases: A Life-Saving Solution

Ten years ago, diarrheal disease was the biggest killer of the world's children; two-thirds of those deaths were caused by dehydration. Today, diarrheal disease has dropped to second place; approximately 1 million lives are saved each year by a cheap and simple method of prevention and treatment called Oral Re-

hydration Therapy (ORT). One family in three now knows about this technique, which uses a lifesaving, carefully balanced solution of sugar, salt, potassium, baking soda, and water that costs a mere 10 cents per dose.

However, a majority of the developing world's families do not know about this technique, and dehydration still causes over 1.5 million needless deaths a year. The remaining deaths are caused by dysentery and persistent diarrhea, which normally require antibiotic treatment in addition to ORT.

Continued efforts to combat the deadly disease must include campaigns for clean water, safe sanitation, and education of parents about handwashing and other simple habits that prevent diarrhea. The challenge is to close the gap between what can be done and what is being done.

Education

Primary education for the world's children is a case of good news and bad news. According to the United Nations Children's Fund (UNICEF) publication, *The Progress of Nations*, the proportion of the developing world's children enrolled in primary school rose from 48 percent in 1960 to 78 percent in 1990 — an enormous achievement considering that the actual number of children almost doubled in that same period.

The bad news is that primary education is in crisis. Under pressure from debt, falling raw material prices, and military spending, governments in every part of the world are cutting education expenditures. Dropout rates (including those in some areas of the U.S.) are as high as 50 percent between grades 1 and 5. In some places, the incidental costs of school (books, supplies, uniforms, food), may be too high for a family. In others, people believe that girls do not need to go to school; they are needed at home. In still other places, education does not lead to jobs. Many governments spend the bulk of education money on secondary and higher education, to the neglect of basic education.

A Success Story

The Bangladesh Rural Advancement Committee (BRAC), a nongovernmental organization, has opened more than 10,000 schools, mainly for children of the poor and landless, in the past eight years. For $15 per pupil the BRAC schools provide three years of basic education, including literacy, numeracy, and social studies. Then their pupils move on to the government schools.

Central to BRAC's success are the twin ideas of para-teachers and community involvement. In

BRAC schools, parents are involved in putting up classrooms, selecting educated members of the community to be teachers, discussing matters of syllabus and timetable, and achieving a better fit between school and the realities of children's lives and expectations. Para-teachers, recruited locally from among the educated and the "good-with-young-children," can be quickly trained in today's methods of stimulating eagerness to learn in the very young. More qualified teachers can then be freed for more advanced work in literacy and numeracy.

The Progress of Nations, 1993, UNICEF

Unfortunately, the program reaches less than 2 percent of the primary-school-age population of Bangladesh.

Obviously, there are more international children's issues than could possibly be covered in the space of this book. Some other subjects you might wish to explore are:

- ◆ The role of gender
- ◆ Refugee children
- ◆ Intercountry adoption
- ◆ Sexual abuse of children by tourists
- ◆ Racism and classism
- ◆ Child care and preschool programs
- ◆ Youth development
- ◆ Teen pregnancy and parenting
- ◆ Child sponsorship programs
- ◆ AIDS orphans
- ◆ Maternal health
- ◆ Infant formula vs. breast-feeding

An Agenda for Change

Convention on the Rights of the Child

On November 20, 1989, the United Nations General Assembly adopted the Convention on the Rights of the Child, a "Magna Carta" or "Bill of Rights" for children. Sixty-one countries signed the convention on January 26, 1990. It became international law on September 1, 1990, after 20 nations ratified or acceded to it. As of January 1994, 155 nations had ratified the convention and another 15 had signed it. All of the nations in NATO and the Organization of American States have signed or ratified the convention — except for the United States. (An update may be obtained by calling (202) 547-7946, the Washington office of the U.S. Committee for UNICEF.)

In its 54 articles, the convention recognizes the special vulnerability of children.

> Under the convention, *survival* rights include such factors as adequate living standards and access to medical services. *Development* rights include education, access to information, play and leisure, cultural activities, and the right to freedom of thought, conscience, and religion. *Protection* embraces all the above and also covers all forms of exploitation and cruelty, arbitrary separation from family, and abuses in the criminal justice system. *Participation* rights include the freedom to express opinions and to have a say in matters affecting one's own life, as well as the right to play an active role in society at large. The chief underlying principle of the convention is that the best interests of the child shall always be a major consideration.

Nations that have ratified the convention are expected to report regularly to the Committee on the Rights of the Child. They qualify for aid by UN bodies, particularly UNICEF, and nongovernmental agencies. The convention has given all countries a framework with which to monitor and implement children's rights. A Plan of Action was developed during the 1990 World Summit for Children.

World Summit for Children

In 1990, heads of state and ministers from 159 countries met at the United Nations in New York for the World Summit for Children. They adopted a declaration and plan of action that includes goals for the year 2000 and steps to reach these goals. Using the theme "First Call for Children," the leaders committed themselves to providing an estimated $20 billion a year throughout the 1990s to achieve these goals. (Today's estimates have raised the funding needs to $25 billion per year.) Each nation agreed to develop a 10-year plan of action. In 1995, high-level government representatives will meet again to review the summit goals.

Promises made by world leaders at the Summit include the following:

- Reduce child deaths by one-third, or 70 per 1,000 births, by the year 2000, whichever is the greater reduction. (Now, every day, 35,000 children under the age of five die from preventable malnutrition and diseases.) Steps toward achieving that goal include low-cost primary health care, such as immunization and antibiotics, which could cut these deaths significantly.

- Cut maternal death rates in half by the end of the decade. (Every year, an estimated 500,000 women die of complications during pregnancy and childbirth, leaving 1 million children motherless.) Steps toward that goal include promotion of birth spacing, prenatal care, and the assistance of trained birth attendants, which can reduce these maternal deaths at a very low cost.

- Cut severe and moderate malnutrition among children under five in half by the year 2000. (That still leaves more than one child in three in the developing world suffering from malnutrition and unable to grow to full mental and physical potential.)

- Make access to safe drinking water and sanitation universal by the end of the century. (More than one-third of all families in the rural areas of the developing world do not have access to clean water and one-half do not have safe sanitation.) Governments will provide the materials and advice needed to construct latrines and improve drinking water supplies.

- Assure universal access to basic education and completion of primary education by at least 80 percent of primary school-age children. (Now, 100 million children of primary school age are not in school; 60 percent of these are girls.) Steps toward achieving that goal include giving priority and funding to basic education, rather than secondary and higher education.

- Reduce the adult illiteracy rate to at least half of its 1990 level, with emphasis on female literacy, which contributes to increased family income and improved child health and survival. (There are approximately 960 million adults in the world who cannot read or write, two-thirds of whom are women.) Steps toward achieving this goal include providing adults with classes in basic reading and writing, with special attention given to basic education for women.

- Protect children living in especially difficult circumstances, particularly in situations of armed conflicts.

(Around the world, an estimated 80 million children are exploited in the work place and 30 million are left to fend for themselves on city streets. Millions more are the victims of war.)

Commitment to the world's children is not only a religious and moral imperative but an investment in our own future.

What Can You Do about the Needs of Children around the World?

Educate Yourself and Others

- Include information about the global concerns of children whenever you are studying local issues.

- Lift up these concerns in Bible study and worship settings. Worship services, weekly meditations, and service leaflets are available or can be adapted. See **Section VI, Chapter 4** for details.

- Invite someone to speak to your congregation about the needs of the world's children and ways the congregation can help. Such speakers might come from your denominational offices, a committee of your judicatory, one of the organizations listed in **Section VI, Chapter 3,** or a local affiliate. Even more effective might be a talk by a new immigrant from a developing nation.

- Devote a shelf in the church library to materials about children around the world. Feature one or more books or reports in your church newsletter. Invite congregation members to use these resources, and add others.

- Plan a special adult education program around the National Council of Churches campaign for U.S. ratification of the UN Convention on the Rights of the Child. A 48-page booklet is available (see page 156 for ordering information). Sign up interested people to work on the issue.

- Each year, obtain a copy of UNICEF's *State of the World's Children* report and plan a brief program to look at progress and needed action. Urge your local television and radio stations to cover the release of the report each year.

- Rent a copy of *341,* the video shown to the world leaders at the World Summit for Children, and arrange to show it to your congregation. Invite community members to attend as well. (See page 159 for ordering information.) Discuss possibilities for action.

- Use some of the curricula listed under International Issues in the resource section (page 156), in your Christian education program. Possibilities include *Children at Risk* for high school students and adults,

and *Children Hungering for Justice* for grades K through 12.

- If meeting times do not permit undertaking a full curriculum, distribute copies of the *Facts Have Faces* leaflets focusing on children, prepared by the Office of Global Education of the National Council of Churches.

Get Involved in the Community

- Invite members of other congregations in your community to join you in education and action programs. Make your plans ecumenical whenever possible.

- Offer to speak to other churches or service groups in your community about what you have learned about the world's children.

- Encourage your congregation to "adopt" or support a project in a developing country that is child- or family-based.

- Organize a fund raising activity to benefit an international children's organization or your denomination's hunger or child advocacy program.

- Participate in or sponsor a participant in the annual CROP Walk in your area. These walks are sponsored by Church World Service as a part of the community hunger appeal of the National Council of Churches and are held throughout the country. The money goes for direct hunger relief and development programs.

- Arrange for UNICEF greeting cards to be sold in your church and community. Remember that this doesn't have to happen just at Christmas, nor are pennies for UNICEF limited to Halloween. Join the National Observance of Children's Sabbaths, and devote the third weekend in October every year to proclaiming your commitment to respond to the crises that are overwhelming children.

Advocate for Children around the World

- Write a letter to your local newspaper or radio or television station, describing what you have learned about the needs of children around the world.

◆ Mobilize public opinion to press the United States to ratify the Convention on the Rights of the Child and see that the promises made at the World Summit for Children are fulfilled.

◆ Write a letter to the president of the United States urging him to sign the Convention on the Rights of the Child and send it to the Senate for ratification. Organize your congregation to write similar letters.

◆ Share what you have learned about children in developing countries in a meeting with your member of Congress or Parliament. Ask what she or he will do to address the problems.

◆ Write to your denominational office that advocates on international issues or one of the national organizations listed in the **Section VI, Chapter 3.** Find out how to get more information, how to subscribe to newsletters, and how to join.

Giving Voice
to the Voiceless

PHOTO BY SUSIE FITZHUGH

How To Use This Section

Speak out for those who cannot speak, for the rights of all the destitute. Speak out, judge righteously, defend the rights of the poor and needy.

Proverbs 31:8–9

Speaking out for fair public policies for children is a vital part of child advocacy. Such work is an appropriate and important extension of Christian worship and study as well. Scripture reveals a God who cares deeply for those who are without power. Faith is not meant to be compartmentalized or limited to Sunday worship, but rather to be lived and acted upon throughout all aspects of our lives. Advocating for public policies that benefit children and families — and giving them opportunities to speak for themselves — is one vital way that we can embody God's love for others.

This section of the book is designed to help you advocate for children in the political arena. **Chapter 1: Why Should We Raise Our Voices for Children?** contains reproducible material that makes a compelling case for why we should raise our voices, immediately, on behalf of children.

Chapter 2: What Will We Proclaim? suggests what goals, policies, and programs would make the greatest and most critical differences for children. Featured in this chapter is a call to action from Marian Wright Edelman.

Chapter 3: How Can We Make Our Voices Heard? details how you can make your voice heard and effective. You will find basic, step-by-step information to help you become a citizen advocate for children through communicating with political candidates, elected officials, and governmental staff.

If you are interested in developing your skills as a public policy advocate for children beyond the level covered in the book, refer to **Section VI: Resources to Help You Help Children.** Chapter 3 provides information about ecumenical networks, denominational public policy offices, and some national organizations that can provide you with information and put you in touch with others in the community who share your concerns. Chapter 4 lists a variety of publications and videos that may be helpful as you deepen your involvement.

CHAPTER 1

Why Should We Raise Our Voices for Children?

Speaking up for our own child or the child of a family we know and love is something we do, often without a second thought. But what about raising our voices for all children — many of whom we don't know and never will see — in the halls of local, state, and federal governments? What about building platforms and pulpits where children's voices can be heard? Why are we called to be public policy advocates for children?

The articles and fact sheets here present information that conveys the urgency of advocating for public policy changes on behalf of children. Use this material to educate yourself, and duplicate these materials to share with others as bulletin inserts, articles in your church newsletter, or handouts for educational programs and events. The facts about the state of children in the U.S. may surprise, and even shock, many. Use this new knowledge to motivate yourself and others into action to change public policies and improve the well-being of our nation's children.

Children and the Budget

The budget deficit is the most frequently heard political excuse for neglecting children. Our response is five-fold:

1. Children did not cause the deficit and hurting them more will not cure it.

2. Children and their families have sacrificed proportionately more than any other group — as much as $10 billion per year in the early 1980s deficit-reduction war (in which the Pentagon, the rich, and corporate America never were enlisted).

3. Investing in children now saves money later. To fail to prevent sickness, malnutrition, and early childhood deprivation is to perpetuate the very dependency cycle and high remediation costs so many currently decry.

4. Investing in children is feasible and increases our chances of success before problems get serious; we know how to do it and how to achieve positive results for relatively modest investments.

5. Children are dying unnecessarily right now from poverty — one every 53 minutes in the U.S., one every two seconds in the world. How can we dare not to save them if we believe God exists?

(Copy and use this as a bulletin insert)

One Day in the Lives of Children in the U.S.A.

17,373	women get pregnant.
2,781	of them are teenagers.
1,115	teenagers have abortions.
329	teenagers miscarry.
1,340	teenagers give birth.
636	babies are born to women who have had inadequate prenatal care.
801	babies are born at low birthweight (less than 5 pounds, 8 ounces).
145	babies are born at very low birthweight (less than 3 pounds, 4 ounces).
63	babies die before one month of life.
101	babies die before their first birthday.
27	children die from poverty.
3	children die from child abuse.
14	children die from guns.
30	children are wounded by guns.
135,000	children bring guns to school.
6	teenagers commit suicide.
8,400	teens become sexually active.
480	teenagers get syphilis or gonorrhea.
202	children are arrested for drug offenses.
340	children are arrested for drinking or drunken driving.
2,255	teenagers drop out of school.
7,945	children are reported abused or neglected.
1,234	children run away from home.
2,350	children are in adult jails.
3,325	children are born to unmarried women.
2,860	see their parents divorce.
100,000	children are homeless.

(Copy and use this as a bulletin insert)

WHY SHOULD WE RAISE OUR VOICES FOR CHILDREN?

The Reality of Child Poverty in America

Shamal died in New York City, when he was eight months old. Cause of death was poverty complicated by low birthweight, poor nutrition, homelessness, and viral infection. During his short life he never slept in an apartment or house; his family was always homeless. He had been in shelters, hospitals, hotels, and the welfare office. He and his mother sometimes rode the subway late at night. Robert Hayes of New York's Coalition for the Homeless said Shamal died because the infant didn't have the strength to resist the "system's abuse."

Baby C was born prematurely with lung disease. His parents lived in a car. His mother received no prenatal care and inadequate nutrition. The family lived on handouts from neighbors and hospital staff. Baby C died at seven months of age in a Michigan hospital. Five days later his mother gave birth prematurely in the car to another baby, who was delivered stillborn. The state paid for a double funeral.

Sally F and her husband have been separated from their three children for more than three months because they cannot find a place to live. After they lost their apartment because they could not afford the rent increase, the family lived in their car until the weather turned cold. Then, in desperation, the father secretly sheltered his children during the night at the warehouse where he worked, stopping when he feared that he would lose his job if discovered. Without a place to live, the parents finally put their children in the temporary care of the state welfare division, which placed them in separate foster homes. The children, still apart, are having increasing problems in school, and their parents have been unable to find an affordable apartment that will accept them and their children. The end of a family life, due to poverty.

(Copy and use this as a bulletin insert)

Questions and Answers about Children in the U.S.

1. How many U.S. children live in poverty?

2. How many children are homeless in the U.S. right now?

3. Are the majority of poor children White or Black?

4. Which of these countries has the highest infant mortality rate: Spain, Austria, Germany, Hong Kong, or the United States?

5. How many children in the United States die every day from the effects of poverty?

6. How many teenagers get pregnant every day?

7. How does the U.S. assure that all its children are immunized against childhood diseases?

8. What is the average welfare payment for a destitute family with children?

Answers

1. More than 14 million in 1992. 2. Approximately 100,000. 3. White, but minority children face a higher risk of being poor. 4. The United States. 5. 27. 6. 2,795. 7. It doesn't. In 1985, the last year national data were collected, fewer than 80 percent of America's two-year-olds were fully immunized against polio. The rate was lower than in 1980. 8. $4.44 per person per day.

(Copy and use this as a bulletin insert)

U.S. Children in the World

The majority of citizens cling to the notion that children growing up in the U.S. are the luckiest and most blessed children in the world. They simply refuse to believe that a wealthy nation is not competitive with other industrialized nations in caring for its children and preparing for its future. The truth is that the United States ranks among the highest nations in the world in per capita gross national product, but does not rank even in the top 10 in any of these measures that are crucial to children's health and well-being:

- One-year-olds in the U.S. have lower immunization rates against polio than one-year-olds in 14 other countries. According to UNICEF, polio immunization rates for minority babies in the United States rank behind the overall rates of 68 countries, including Botswana, Sri Lanka, Albania, Colombia, and Jamaica.

- The U.S. infant mortality rate in 1991 lagged behind that of 21 other nations. The Black infant mortality rate ranked fortieth compared with other countries' overall rates. A Black child born in inner-city Boston has less chance of surviving the first year than a child born in Cuba, Bulgaria, or Poland.

- In a study of eight industrialized nations (the United States, Switzerland, Sweden, Norway, Germany, Canada, England, and Australia), the U.S. had the highest child poverty rate. Children are the poorest Americans.

- The United States has the highest teen birth rates among six industrialized nations studied (including France, England and Wales, Canada, the Netherlands, and Sweden).

- The United States and South Africa are the only industrialized nations that fail to provide universal health coverage, child care, and parental leave for their children and parents.

- The United States invests a smaller portion of its gross national product (GNP) in child health than 18 other industrialized countries. It invests a smaller proportion of its gross domestic product in education than 13 other industrialized countries.

(Copy and use this as a bulletin insert)

CHAPTER 2

ᘒᕱ

What Will We Proclaim?

The problems that too many children face are very real, but they can be changed. Dedicated individuals, groups, and congregations — working in partnership — are creating remedies and solutions. The Bible is replete with the images and power of small things that achieve great ends when they are grounded in faith: a mustard seed, a jawbone, a stick, a slingshot, a widow's mite. Each and every one of us can make a difference in the lives of children, if we care enough to empower our compassion with skills, targeted action, and persistence.

In this chapter you will find a call to action from Marian Wright Edelman, the president and founder of the Children's Defense Fund, offering both encouragement and challenge.

A Call to Action

Take care that you do not despise one of these little ones.... It is not the will of your Father in heaven that one of these little ones should be lost.

Matthew 18:10a, 14

Every Sunday in the U.S., as we wake up, 100,000 children wake up homeless. Every 32 seconds, about the time it takes us to say the Lord's Prayer, a baby is born into poverty. Every 14 minutes, while we listen to the sermon or homily, a baby dies in the U.S. Every 59 seconds, while we "pass the peace," a baby is born to a teenage mother. And every 12 hours, before we go back to sleep each night, a preschooler is murdered.

Today, the tragic and unconscionable reality is that too many of our nation's children are being left behind. Too many don't have the education, health care, homes, strong communities, and family supports they need to develop their God-given potential.

I believe our nation is at a crossroads of great national opportunity and danger that we must seize now to protect our children, our ideals, and the future. We can succeed, but only if we mount a massive movement for children strong enough to convince a critical mass of the public and policy makers to share our belief that the growth of child poverty, drug abuse, violence, and family and neighborhood disintegration pose more of a threat to prosperity, security, competitiveness, and moral leadership in the new decade than any other enemy outside or inside our borders; and only if we can translate this awareness of child and family crises into real and sustained solutions, rather than symbolic, cosmetic, short-term, politically attractive responses that fail to address substantially the underlying causes of child poverty and misery and that continue to leave children behind.

Thanks to the work of child advocates, caring educators, citizens, and people of faith like you, significant progress for children has been made over the past two decades:

More Children Get a Healthy Start:

◆ Five hundred thousand more mothers now get the prenatal care they need to improve the chances of healthy births;

◆ One million more low-income children are eligible for basic health care, including preventive checkups.

More Children Get a Head Start:

◆ The effective Head Start program has been expanded to reach more children and efforts are under way to improve its quality;

◆ Hundreds of thousands of disabled children now get a free and appropriate public education, most in mainstream classes.

More Children Get a Fair Start:

◆ Tens of thousands of neglected, abused, and foster children have the right to decent care while placed outside their parents' home and to services to reunify the family if possible;

- Single parents have a greater capacity to secure child support payments from the parent who is not in the home; and

- Families with children are among the protected groups against whom it is prohibited to discriminate in the sale or rental of housing.

In addition, the recently passed Budget Reconciliation signed by President Clinton on August 10, 1993, recognized the importance of dealing with the human deficit as well as this country's budget deficit. The package included major gains for children and families ($25 billion over five years) in the areas of childhood immunizations, family preservation and support services, expansion of the Earned Income Credit, and improvements in the food stamp program.

But these significant gains, which are wonderful though long overdue, are not enough. Despite progress, more than 8 million children still lack any form of health insurance — public or private; only about one-third of eligible poor children are able to participate in the successful, comprehensive Head Start program, and our child poverty rate is worsening, rather than getting better, leaving more than 14 million children without the basics they need to survive and develop fully. Our overarching goal must be to eliminate child poverty in this decade — to Leave No Child Behind and ensure every child a Healthy Start, a Head Start, a Fair Start, and a Safe Start. *All* children need and deserve:

- A Healthy Start — basic health care for every child and pregnant woman.

- A Head Start — good quality preschool and child care to help them get ready for school, keep up in school, and prepare for the future.

- A Fair Start — jobs at decent wages, assured child support, and a refundable tax credit for families with children so that no child is homeless or hungry or so poor that she or he is left behind.

- A Safe Start — homes, neighborhoods, and schools that are free of violence.

If we all work together as we approach the new millennium, we can begin to rediscover the best within ourselves. I would like our children to read in the history books that in the 1990s the U.S. came to its senses. Child poverty was wiped out. The nation stopped clinging to its racial past and recognized that its future was as intertwined with the fate of its poor and minority children as with its privileged and White ones. And, through positive leadership, vision, hard work, and systematic investment in proven strategies, gaps separating minority and poor children from other young Americans were eliminated.

If we do this, the U.S. will face the twenty-first century with its ideals intact — showing the world through example that all God's children are precious and that we have heeded God's will that not even one of these little ones should be lost or left behind.

Marian Wright Edelman
President, Children's Defense Fund

CHAPTER 3

ॐ

How Can We Make Our Voices Heard?

Introduction

Exodus 5 is the Bible's first record of an advocacy visit. Moses and Aaron go to Pharaoh and ask him to let the Hebrew people take three days for a religious celebration. Pharaoh not only says "No," he orders the overseers "not to supply the people with the straw used in making bricks as they had done hitherto." They still must produce the same quota of bricks but also must spend time gathering the needed straw.

Understandably, the people, flogged, punished, and even more overworked, turn on Moses and Aaron. Moses and Aaron had failed as advocates. When they complain to God, God tells them, "Go [back] and tell Pharaoh king of Egypt to set the Israelites free to leave his country." God gave the advocates a commission to bring the Israelites out of Egypt.

Like Moses and Aaron, when we first venture into advocacy, we may feel inadequate. As with Moses and Aaron, God calls us to go to the powerful and ask for justice even though "political realities" would make our request seem outrageously naive. Like Moses and Aaron, though our advocacy is critically important, the outcome does not rest on our efforts alone.

Adapted from Concern into Action: An Advocacy Guide *for People of Faith,* INTERFAITH IMPACT, 1990, Preface

As citizens of the United States, our task as advocates is much less daunting and, in fact, is protected by the Constitution. In a democracy, we are encouraged to make our concerns known to our elected officials and to candidates for office.

This chapter provides the basic information you need to communicate with your members of Congress on issues affecting children and to make children a priority during the election process.

As Christians, we can use our gift of citizenship in ministry by advocating for those in our society with no power of their own — the children. As with Moses and Aaron, the outcome of our political advocacy on behalf of children does not rest on our efforts alone, but on God.

Communicating the Needs of Children to Your Members of Congress

Many people think children's issues are "above the political process." Children don't need lobbyists, people say. After all, they are our future. Members of Congress naturally take their needs into account on the House or Senate floor, just as they rush to kiss babies in their home districts.

Sadly, it doesn't work that way. When it comes to voting on laws, programs, and budgets, Congress often finds children the easiest people in America to ignore. Children don't vote, speak out, write letters, or make campaign contributions. As a result, many millions of American children do not have their basic survival needs met.

You are the key to your policymaker's political life. You elected your senators and representatives. Even if you did not personally vote for them, they care about pleasing you.

It's their job to listen to any constituent who takes the time to write or talk to them, and they do. They pay attention to their mail, and they often meet with constituents at their local and national offices.

Writing your first letter or making your first telephone call may seem intimidating. As with other new experiences or tasks, communicating with members of Congress feels more natural and easier the more you do it. All you need is a little practice! Fortunately, you don't have to do this alone. There are people and organizations eager to encourage, facilitate, and support your efforts. The purpose of the national public policy organizations and the denominational offices in Washington, DC, is to inform and mobilize concerned citizens. They can help you learn which issues Congress currently is considering, and what kind of contact from you will be most useful. In some cases, these organizations and offices can put you in touch with a local group. Refer to Chapter 3 of **Section VI: Resources to Help You Help Children** for more information about these organizations and the services they provide.

Make your voice heard on Capitol Hill. You can make a difference for our nation's children!

Sending a Letter to Congress

"Most people believe that writing to a member of Congress is like putting a drop in the bucket. 'I'm only one person,' they tell themselves, 'my letter isn't going to make a bit of difference.' But it does. You may think your representative is being flooded with hundreds of thousands of letters on the issue you care about. The truth is the average member of Congress typically receives fewer than 100 letters on any one issue. One letter out of 100 — your letter — can carry a lot of weight. Letter writing works.

"You don't need a secretary, a typewriter, or engraved stationery to write a good letter. The best letters, the ones members of Congress pay attention to, are written in your own words. Members of Congress do read their mail. They are interested in its contents. The mood and tenor of the daily mail from home is a recurring topic of conversation in chambers or in the dining rooms of the Capitol."

Excerpted from *You and Your Congressman*
by Rep. Morris Udall

When to Write

Write anytime you are concerned about an issue. Your letters are particularly important when an issue is timely, for example, when a vote is expected or there has been a lot of news coverage.

How to Write

- **Be brief.** Address only one issue. A letter need not be longer than four or five sentences.

- **Be specific.** If you are writing about specific legislation, include its bill number or title.

- **Write your own letter,** adapting a sample letter as appropriate. Form letters do not receive the same attention as individually written letters.

- **Be positive and constructive.** Try to say something complimentary in the first paragraph. It is just as important to thank members of Congress for voting the right way as to criticize them for voting the wrong way.

- **Say in your own words why the legislation matters** to you and to children. Clearly state your reason for supporting or opposing the bill or issue you are writing about.

- **If you have particular knowledge or expertise, describe it.** Relating the bill to local or state conditions is especially effective.

- If you wish, feel free to **include a copy of a report,** a newsletter story, or a local survey, to support your arguments. Don't presume that the legislator is aware of such information, even if you think it is common knowledge.

- Be sure to **sign your name legibly and include your address** so your representative or senator can respond.

Encourage Others to Write to Members of Congress

Effective as one letter is, 30 on the same issue are even better. Getting others to help send those letters is not as hard as it sounds. Make a party out of it. Take inexpensive writing paper and envelopes to your church, your service organization, your office — anywhere you gather with other people. Write the letters together. In 10 to 15 minutes you will end up with a considerable amount of mail.

Other Ways to Communicate Your Message

Mailgram

You can also send a 20-word (or less) Opiniongram to any member of Congress or the president for about $10.00. This is called a Public Opinion Message. Call Western Union at (800) 325-6000.

Telephoning the Staff of Members of Congress

When to Telephone

- Call when lead time on action is limited or when a vote is expected.

Where to Telephone

- Washington office: the Capitol Switchboard, (202) 224-3121, will connect you with the correct office.

- Local office: look up the number in your local telephone book under U.S. Government.

What to Say

- Always give your name and town when calling your legislator.

- When calling the Washington office, ask for the legislative aide who deals with the issue of concern to you.

- Be brief. When possible, know the title or bill number of the legislation and what you want your member of Congress to do.

How Can We Make Our Voices Heard?
Sample Letter

The Honorable _____   The Honorable _____
United States Senate   House of Representatives
Washington, DC 20510   Washington, DC 20515

Dear Senator _____:
    I am writing to urge you to support full funding for the Head Start program. Head Start is an investment that will make a difference in the lives of millions of children and families.
    This program not only helps children enter school ready to learn but also ensures that they receive necessary immunizations, regular health checkups, and nutritious meals. Equally impressive is the way Head Start reaches out to parents to help them become involved in their child's learning.
    I truly believe that an investment in Head Start is a sound investment in our nation's future. Please let me know that you will support full funding of Head Start.
    Sincerely,

(Your name)
(Your address, if not on letterhead)
(Your telephone number)

- -

How to address your envelope:

The Honorable _____   The Honorable _____
United States Senate   House of Representatives
Washington, DC 20510   Washington, DC 20515

(Copy and use this as a hand-out)

When to Call the Local Office

Call the local office when you wish to schedule an appointment to meet with your representative or senator. Members of Congress usually are back in their home districts on the days surrounding any federal holiday (such as Labor Day or President's Day) as well as during the month of August.

You may also call the local office to register your opinion on a pending vote in Congress if long distance charges are a barrier to calling Washington, DC.

Meeting with Your Legislators

The first time you meet with your senator or representative, you probably will have butterflies in your stomach. It would be unusual if you didn't. You should realize, however, that the best way to communicate with your legislator is to make a personal visit. You probably will enjoy the experience and he or she will appreciate the time you spent communicating your views.

How to Have an Effective Visit

- Decide on the issues you want to discuss.

- When making an appointment explain what issue you would like to discuss. If the legislator is unavailable, the aide who deals with your issue often will be knowledgeable and influential in helping to form the member's views.

- Study the legislator's voting record on a number of issues, using CDF's Nonpartisan Congressional Voting Record and other sources, so you can comment on something positive, if possible, and know if the particular issue is one on which the legislator tends to agree or disagree.

- If there is a bill that interests you, know its status and whether your legislator has taken a position on it.

- If possible, go with a person or group actively engaged in the issue you are addressing.

- Plan and organize your presentation, limiting yourself to five minutes. You can expand on the topic if you are given time.

- Tell of personal experiences you have had, if possible, to illustrate your point.

- If your legislator or aide disagrees or is noncommittal, don't threaten or argue after you have made your case because it is counterproductive. A better strategy is to plan another visit with others to show more community support for your position, to put together a bunch of letters from constituents, or to think of another tactic such as a letter to the editor. Persistence often pays. Even the most recalcitrant member of Congress can change. Remember the gospel story of the widow and the judge (Luke 18:1–8)!

- Follow up your visit with a letter thanking the legislator for the time spent listening to your concerns. Enclose any documentation you had agreed to provide to bolster your position, and briefly restate your views.

- If the legislator votes with your position on the issue, recognize that vote with a written "thank-you." Such recognition may influence his or her next vote on children's issues. It also lets your legislator know that you are watching closely.

- If the legislator votes against your position, write or call to express your disappointment, and urge reconsideration of the issue the next time it comes up for a vote.

A Word about Advocating in the Local Office

- Legislators feel that those who visit at the home office are often the "real voters," not the activists or tourists who troop to Washington. Take advantage of this to show that there are others in the community who feel as you do.

- Get to know at least one staff person in the local office. Local staff members often have a good sense of how the legislator feels, and even small talk can reveal useful pieces of information about the legislator's attitudes and voting patterns.

- Invite members of Congress to see successful programs for children in your community, such as a child care program, well-baby clinics, and a program for homeless children. This is a very effective way to show the importance of investing in children's needs.

What You Can Do During an Election Year To Help Make Children a Priority

1. Call the candidates' offices, ask for a copy of their children's agenda, and talk to or meet with the staff person handling children's issues. Deliver a message to the candidates about the importance of investing in children and provide them with information on children's needs.

2. Meet with your U.S. senators and representative to urge their support for legislation currently pending in Congress that would benefit children and families.

3. Organize a committee to sponsor a town meeting and invite your U.S. senators and representative, state legislators, and county commissioners or city council members to hear about the most pressing problems of children in your community and discuss state or local solutions designed to address the problems. Distribute materials on children's needs to all the participants. Be sure to invite persons who are experiencing the problems you want to discuss.

4. Raise visibility and generate discussion on children's issues in the election debates by sponsoring a nonpartisan Candidates' Forum to hear their positions on key issues affecting children. Attend rallies and meetings; question the candidates about children's issues.

5. Develop a Candidate Questionnaire to send to candidates for public office asking them to state their proposals for solving key problems affecting children. The questions need to be drafted carefully so as not to be partisan. Note also that there are legal limits on churches and other 501(c)(3) organizations on disseminating the answers to voters.

6. Arrange to take candidates, public officials, and other community leaders on visits to see firsthand the costs of our neglect of children — boarder babies, children in homeless shelters, teenagers in juvenile detention centers. Then show them church or other programs that are working successfully to address and prevent these problems. Be sure to invite members of the media to these visits. Contact the Children's Defense Fund and request a "Child View Kit" to help you do so.

7. If you are personally involved in a political party, work to get an Agenda for Children incorporated into the platform. If you work for a group, present children's issues to both major parties' platform committees.

8. Register to vote and organize nonpartisan voter registration campaigns in your community.

9. Visit editorial boards of your local newspapers or meet with representatives of the media to brief them on issues of importance to children in your community. Focus particularly on the status of children living in your state and whether your state invests enough in children. (Information is available from the Children's Defense Fund.)

The attention paid to issues and constituents' needs during election years provides a major opportunity to make great strides for children. Take leadership in local, state, and national activities.

Some Questions To Ask Candidates Running for State Offices

- What specific steps will you take to ensure that all young children are immunized fully?

- What steps would you support to ensure that all pregnant women have full access to prenatal care and that all children receive regular preventive health care and treatment?

- Do you support including funding in our state's budget to supplement federal funds for Head Start and the Special Supplemental Food Program for Women, Infants, and Children (WIC)?

- What should our state do to increase the availability of affordable, quality child care, preschool, and early childhood development programs?

- How would you reduce child abuse and strengthen and preserve families?

- What extra resources would you target to schools whose children need special assistance?

- How do you propose to reduce our state's dropout rate?

- What steps do you propose to reduce this state's high teenage pregnancy rate?

- What specific steps have you taken and will you take to reduce this state's large number of families with children that cannot find affordable housing?

- What will you do to reduce childhood poverty in this state?

Some Questions To Ask Candidates Running for the U.S. House and Senate

- What will you do to ensure that all young children are immunized fully?

- What steps would you support to ensure that all pregnant women have full access to prenatal care and that all children receive regular preventive health care and treatment?

- Do you support full funding for programs such as Head Start and the Special Supplemental Food Program for Women, Infants, and Children (WIC) so that they can serve every eligible child?

- How do you propose to improve the quality of schools serving poor and minority children, so that all American children can achieve the National Education Goals? What should be the federal role in ensuring that all children receive a first-rate education?

- How would you reduce child abuse, preserve and strengthen families, and avoid the unnecessary removal of children from their homes?

- What steps will you take to expand the supply of affordable housing for families with children?

- How do you propose to reduce childhood poverty in America? Will you work for a refundable tax credit that will benefit *all* families with children?

- How do you propose to assist America's economically squeezed young families?

- What will you do to ensure that health care reform guarantees comprehensive, continuous coverage for all U.S. children and families?

- What steps would you take to ensure that welfare reform embraces the goal of eliminating child poverty?

Resources To Help You Help Children

PHOTO BY SUSIE FITZHUGH

How To Use This Section

Some of the wonderful things you will discover as you take steps to serve children are the quality and number of individuals, organizations, and resource materials available to help you. Whether you look within your own congregation, in the community, or to state and national child advocacy organizations, you can find expertise, support, and current resources. Best of all, once you've made some connections, you'll find yourself part of a dynamic and growing network of child advocates and those who care for the well-being of our nation's children.

The purpose of this section is to share some of these resources with you. Keep them in mind as you and your congregation strengthen your ministries to and with children.

Chapter 1: Congregational Model Programs describes many programs housed in congregations or church-supported organizations that successfully meet the needs of children. Various models will give you an idea of how congregations that differ in location, size, and resources can make a concrete difference. In most instances a contact person and address are listed, in case you would like more information. We hope this chapter will stimulate your thinking on ways your particular congregation can best utilize its resources to benefit children.

Chapter 2: National Faith-Based Efforts for Children highlights some advocacy efforts by denominations that are members of the National Council of the Churches of Christ in the USA as well as the Southern Baptist Convention, the United States Cath-

olic Conference, and the Unitarian Universalist Service Committee. In recent years, the national denominations have devoted greater attention and resources to children's issues. This intensified focus on children has led to the formation of comprehensive and coordinated child advocacy campaigns and programs.

Chapter 3: Faith-Based Public Policy Offices and National Organizations lists the ecumenical and denominational public policy offices, ecumenical agencies and networks, and some national organizations that focus on children, public policy, poverty, or community organizing.

Your religious denomination may have an office based in Washington, DC, the staff of which can help you advocate to Congress. Such offices provide denominational members with a variety of programs and resources including legislative alerts, speakers, trainers, telephone consultations on issues, and assistance in setting up congressional visits.

In addition, quite a few national organizations provide information, resources, and technical assistance on programs and policies related to issues affecting children.

Chapter 4: Resources includes a selection of resources listed by topic. It is not meant to be comprehensive in scope or inclusive of all issues related to children. You will find a few entries under such categories as child advocacy, children and the church, maternal and child health, child care, education, youth development, international issues, homelessness and housing, and child welfare.

CHAPTER 1

Congregational Model Programs

Child Care

Congregations Concerned for Children
(A Metropolitan Ecumenical Program)

Congregations Concerned for Children (CCC) is a program of four councils of churches in Minnesota — the Greater Minneapolis, the St. Paul Area, the Arrowhead, and the Rochester Area. The purpose of the program is to direct the resources of religious congregations toward the needs of children living in poverty and pain. Replicated from a program in Dallas/Ft. Worth, CCC is based on the premise that people in religious congregations are most ready to respond to the needs of children. CCC's experience affirms that premise.

There are three components to the program:

Adult Education

CCC educates people in religious congregations on child poverty, child care, and child abuse through a volunteer speakers bureau. The program also offers periodic workshops and seminars to leaders in the religious community to give them the knowledge and the tools they need to encourage congregational action for children in need. CCC provides congregations with its own and CDF's worship materials for annual Children's Sabbaths, finding the worship service a powerful way to touch people with the reality of children's lives today.

Partnerships/Consultations

CCC develops partnerships between congregations and child care centers and other programs that serve children in need such as homeless shelters and child abuse programs. The congregations meet the pressing needs of the programs and the families by donating books, toys, playground equipment, clothing, bedding, and furniture. Congregation members also are active volunteers in the programs. The partnerships frequently give volunteers a first personal experience of the struggles of low-income families. Often this leads to political advocacy on behalf of children. Through their firsthand experience volunteers learn that the needs of children require the attention of both the public and private sectors.

CCC also assists congregations in developing their own child care and parent education programs. CCC has written materials for congregations that offer step-by-step instructions on how to develop a child care center. The program also has a publication for planning parent education programs in congregations.

Advocacy

CCC has a network of thousands of child advocates in congregations throughout the state. The advocates are kept informed on issues affecting children through the CCC newsletter and a child advocates letter. Motivated by their faith, these advocates call and write legislators on behalf of children's legislation, giving voice to the needs of children.

For more information, contact Carolyn Hendrixson, Congregations Concerned for Children, Greater Minneapolis Council of Churches, 122 West Franklin Avenue, Room 218, Minneapolis, MN 55404, (612) 870-3660.

Central Baptist Church's
23 Years of Care for Children

Twenty-three years ago, Central Baptist Church (Lexington, Kentucky) member Anita Privitt, a mother with young children and later one of the first chairs of the child care committee, was going back to school. She asked the church about beginning a child care program.

"We didn't know the amount of work involved or the regulations we would face to begin a program," she recalled. "It was work and it did create controversy within the church. Some thought the walls would get dirty, and it's true they have been painted many, many times. But we saw it as a mission and a service to meet the need of our members."

Director Betty Morrison says, "We have no advertising, yet we have a waiting list of around 100. We are licensed for 85 in child care and 25 in kindergarten, but because of the space, we serve only about 96 children. Although parents don't have to be Central members to work in the program or for their children to attend, we minister to many of our own.

"We also have a ministry with Central Baptist Hospital and the University of Kentucky Medical Center. We help when a parent is slated for surgery or for a long hospitalization by caring for the patient's children. Sometimes we have to cover the cost of the child care as a part of our commitment to ministry."

Judy Browning, a former kindergarten teacher, adds, "Churches have a responsibility to nurture children. A child care center is the greatest way to do that. It provides peace of mind to parents and security to children that they need. Many don't have a secure home life, and for them, this is it."

For more information, contact Helen Stumbo, Assistant Director, Central Baptist Church, 1644 Nicholasville Road, Lexington, KY 40503, (606) 278-5913.

Education

Adopt-a-School Program of the United Methodist Women Local Units

Every Monday, from 8 to 9 a.m., Chris Keels has breakfast with some of the children in the federally funded breakfast program at Baltimore's Elmer A. Henderson Elementary School. While they eat, the children chat with Keels about school and what is happening at home. Keels, in turn, tells the children about events in her own life.

Keels is a "Monday morning mentor" from the nearby Christ United Methodist church, which has "adopted" the Henderson School. Church volunteers planned to tutor children but learned that the school really needed volunteers to work with the children's behavior and to expose them to new experiences.

"By talking about our own lives, we try to show them that everyone has difficulties to overcome in life," says Keels. "We tell them that we work hard at our jobs and we expect them to work hard at their job — which is school. We continually say, 'We're counting on you to do your best.' "

The Monday morning mentor program is one of several activities started at the inner-city school as part of a six-year Campaign for Children co-sponsored by the United Methodist Women and the Children's Defense Fund.

The volunteers provide cultural excursions once a month to reward students for good behavior in the classroom. The women also initiated a creative dance program that has attracted both boys and girls, a Reading Partners project to help children with reading difficulties, and a neighborhood clean-up project for the whole community on Saturdays.

Principal Anne E. Larkins says the children are responding to the church women's nurturing presence in the school. When a child becomes disruptive in class, a teacher may call the child's volunteer reading partner or a Monday morning mentor and ask her to come to school. "Sometimes," says Keels, "the mentor just sits beside the child in the classroom to help him or her concentrate on school work. Then after school the two of them work on the particular problem."

That approach reduces the number of expulsions and keeps the children from falling behind academically, says Keels. The volunteer also takes the time to discover the underlying causes of the disruptive behavior. The interaction allows the church to identify families that need assistance from the church or other community organizations.

For more information, contact Laura Smith, United Methodist Women, 7359 Stout Hill Road, Sykesville, MD 21784.

Operation Getting It Together

This tutoring program in Sebastopol, California, teams at-risk students referred by the public schools with older youth outreach workers.

The tutors are paid a modest service allowance that covers the cost of transportation, recreation for the child being tutored, refreshments, and other minor items. Outreach workers who remain in the program for a full year are eligible for Community Service Scholarships of $300 per worker, and college students who serve in this capacity also can receive college credits for their work. Often the older youths or administrators of the program are called upon to intervene with or advocate for the child in school relationships, and sometimes with the courts, and to assist the child's family in this task. One measure of success: a high number of students who entered the program as children in need of help are now serving as youth outreach workers.

For more information, contact the Rev. Don Schilling, Operation Getting It Together, 500 North Main Street, Sebastopol, CA 95472, (707) 823-6967.

Vulnerable Children and Families

Covenant to Care

Adopt a Social Worker Ministry

Connecticut's Adopt a Social Worker Ministry provides a structured link between a local religious congregation and the abused and neglected children in the community. The local congregation covenants with a social worker who serves these children and their families. The unmet needs of the children and families (such as food, diapers, or bedding) are identified by the adopted social worker, who describes them to the congregation through a liaison member of the church.

Hundreds of children are helped each month through the ministry, which supports the work of social workers across the state. The ministry gives churches an opportunity to be involved in a valuable and heart-warming outreach mission. It stands as a tangible, growing voice saying that God's people care about poor, abused, and neglected children in their area.

Congregation members respond to the needs of these children through the wealth of caring and goods found among individual members. Good quality used items are shared with those in need. Volunteers from the congregation contribute their time to bake, sew, make simple home repairs, or deliver large items. Some congregations also have been able to provide financial assistance through this ministry to help families needing security deposits, health care, emergency food, or a mover to relocate furniture. Each congregation provides what it is able to and at any time may determine that it cannot meet an identified need.

Families for Children Program

The aim of the Families for Children Program (FFCP) is to support safe, caring, and nurturing environments that are conducive to the healthy development and well-being of Connecticut's foster children. The FFCP provides concrete resources to foster families, educates the public on issues of child abuse prevention and intervention, trains communities to support neglected children, and builds cooperation among human service providers.

For more information, contact Executive Director, Covenant To Care, Inc., 26 Wintonbury Avenue, Bloomfield, CT 06002, (203) 243-1806.

The First Baptist Church of Fresno, California

The First Baptist Church in Fresno, California, ministers to its community in many unique ways. Once a large community church, it now finds itself to be a suburban congregation with an inner-city ministry. Examples of First Baptist's outreach include:

- Every Tuesday there is a night preschool for children whose parents work in the evening.

- Through donations raised from the congregation, 130 children are fed each Tuesday night.

- The church has the largest library in the community. Members found that a lot of books were not returned, so they started a "toss books" box with books the children can keep.

- Because many children drown each year in the city canals, congregation members have opened their family pools and given swimming lessons to the children.

- The "Linking Project" with the Delmar Elementary School has resulted in two retired nurses covering for days when there is no paid nursing staff, the associate pastor teaching wrestling, and the purchasing of the cheerleaders' uniforms.

For more information, contact the Rev. Gordon Salsman, The First Baptist Church, 1400 Saginaw, Fresno, CA 93704, (209) 227-8476.

Homelessness and Housing

Martha's Table

Martha's Table, a program serving poor and homeless children and their families, demonstrates the effectiveness of partnerships between child-serving programs and the religious community in Washington, DC. Martha's Table is made possible by the service of nearly 9,000 volunteers in all programs representing a variety of ages and walks of life. It began 13 years ago as a soup kitchen for the homeless and since has expanded to include a variety of programs for poor and homeless children.

The Children's Program offers a variety of programs and activities for children ages five to 17. Children at Martha's Table come from poor homes in the surrounding neighborhood as well as from area shelters for homeless families.

The After-School Drop-in Center run by Martha's Table provides recreational activities for children every weekday from 3 to 5 p.m. About 85 children, of whom 40 percent are homeless, are served by the program each day.

The Tutoring Project serves more than 125 students, each with a personal volunteer tutor. Each student and volunteer team meets twice weekly. The Mother-

Toddler Program provides parenting education and literacy sessions, and helps mothers prepare toddlers for school, while the toddlers participate in enrichment activities.

The Summer Program offers recreational and educational activities and nutritious meals daily throughout the summer. The Teen Program is available each evening for adolescents, ages 12–17.

McKenna's Wagon is the mobile soup kitchen operated by Martha's Table. The wagon distributes 2,300 sandwiches, 65 gallons of soup, beverages, and desserts every day of the year. In the past few years the number of families and children seeking food from the wagon has increased drastically.

Congregations and people of faith supply food, contribute financial support, and provide volunteers as partners with Martha's Table.

For more information contact Veronica Parke, Executive Vice-President, Martha's Table, 2114 14th Street, N.W., Washington, DC 20009, (202) 328-6608.

Health

The Elizabeth Project

The Elizabeth Project, based on a biblical story about the friendship between Elizabeth and Mary, provides a means for the religious community to address the problem of children having children. Its purposes are to encourage self-care leading to the birth of a healthy baby and to discourage additional pregnancies until a more appropriate time in the young girl's life. The project pairs pregnant teens who are in need of love and support with compassionate women willing to offer themselves as partners for the journey through pregnancy and birth. They work together in a 12-week program that provides information on prenatal care, childbirth and parenting, with a strong emphasis on responsible decision-making and building self-esteem. Through videotapes, related discussion, group activities, and personal visits, a supportive relationship develops, one that usually continues beyond the birth of the baby and offers life-changing possibilities. The Elizabeth Project began as a United Methodist response to Virginia's high rate of infant mortality. It is now administered through the Virginia Council of Churches and has volunteers from a number of denominations. Referrals come through local health departments, social services, schools, and pastors. There are Elizabeth Projects established at fifteen sites across the Commonwealth, with a dozen more slated to begin in 1994. For additional information contact the Rev. Judith FaGalde Bennett, Virginia Council of Churches, 1214 W. Graham Road, Suite #3, Richmond, VA 23220-4019, (804) 321-3300.

Caring Program for Children

In 1984 two ministers from Pittsburgh, Pennsylvania, recognized the growing number of children without health care and decided to do something about it. They approached Blue Cross of Western Pennsylvania and its president about children whose health care needs were being postponed or neglected when working parents lost their jobs and could not find other work that provided health care benefits.

As a result, Blue Cross of Western Pennsylvania researched this issue, estimating that approximately 40,000 children from low-income families in western Pennsylvania lacked health care coverage and did not qualify for Medical Assistance.

In response to this need, Blue Cross of Western Pennsylvania together with Blue Shield created the Caring Program for Children. The program's benefits are designed to meet the basic health care needs of children, including preventive care, visits to the doctor when the child is sick, diagnostic testing, prescription drugs, vision, dental, hearing, emergency care, and out-patient surgery. The program is free to the children and their parents. Children are eligible from birth to age 19 if their family income is below the poverty line but above Medicaid guidelines. The cost per year is shared equally by Blue Cross/Blue Shield and a sponsor, such as a congregation, individual, or group. The cost to sponsor a child is less than $300 per year.

One mother said: "Through the Caring Program for Children and our church, which sponsored Justin, he didn't just get medical care, he got great medical care.... Justin had a dozen ear infections a year. With each infection his hearing was always in jeopardy. With the Caring Program, we could take him to our pediatrician. We didn't have to go from clinic to clinic, hospital to hospital, or doctor to doctor.

"Justin was taken to the pediatrician, who knows his problems and his history. His care was consistent. There was a point when we had to rush him to the hospital. Our pediatrician was there. He told us had we waited, Justin could have lost 90 percent of his hearing. That didn't happen, because we had the Caring Program for Children and the consistency of care. It was a godsend and a lifesaver."

With support from a grant from the U.S. Department of Health and Human Services (Maternal and Child Health Division), the Caring Program for Children is being replicated throughout the nation. Currently there are Caring Programs in 21 states.

The Caring Program for Children has served as

a model not only for other Caring Programs nationwide, but also as the prototype for a new legislated child health care program in Pennsylvania. "BlueCHIP of Pennsylvania," administered by the four Caring Foundations in the state, is designed to provide a comprehensive package of inpatient and outpatient benefits to eligible children who meet age and income guidelines, yet who cannot qualify for Medical Assistance. The program is designed primarily to serve the birth to six-year-old population and is offered either free or at a subsidized cost to qualifying families. BlueCHIP is funded by a state cigarette tax sufficient to support the cost of benefits for 32,000 statewide.

To find out more about the Caring Program for Children and BlueCHIP of Pennsylvania, contact Charles P. LaVallee, Executive Director, Western Pennsylvania Caring Foundation, 500 Wood Street, Suite 600, Pittsburgh, PA 15222, (412) 645-6200.

Baby Basics

Churches and synagogues of Guilford County, North Carolina, combined resources to sponsor a layette program called "Baby Basics" for young pregnant women in the community. Members of churches and synagogues donate baby supplies such as diapers, baby formula, bottles, and crib sheets that are stored and distributed by the health department as incentive items for pregnant women to receive prenatal care. Women's groups and youth groups tend to be the ones coordinating their church's participation in "Baby Basics."

For additional information on the Baby Basics Project contact: Jane Thomas, Southern Regional Project on Infant Mortality, 444 North Capitol Street, N.W., Suite 200, Washington DC 20001, (202) 624-5897.

Youth Development

Lincoln Action Program's Education Outreach

Education Outreach works under the auspices of the Justice and Peace Committee of the Nebraska Conference of the United Church of Christ, building on the conviction that access to an appropriate education is a justice issue for each community. The program combines homework assistance and tutoring with cultural enrichment and career mentoring for children from many racial and ethnic backgrounds. It receives support from the United Church of Christ churches in the area, the Hispanic and Native American Community Centers, and the University of Nebraska at Lincoln.

Concentration on enhancing self-esteem through cultural pride is a major part of the program, and there are frequent field trips that allow students to learn about their own cultural heritages.

Education Outreach lists among its goals the provision of academic tutoring, support counseling, an increased awareness of educational and career opportunities available to high-school graduates, and offering a multi-cultural world view to youths through workshops, speakers, and other programs. Transportation is provided for all program activities.

The program now reaches out to over 100 junior high and high school students and averages 50–75 volunteer tutors, employs two contract drivers, and has two full-time paid staff. In his mid-year report on the program, Dan Williams noted that "the public schools here in Lincoln are more solidly than ever behind the program; we have had only positive feedback from teachers and administrators. In addition, we have received significant funding support from state and local agencies and foundations on a scale which means the program will effectively move on into the future."

For additional information on the Lincoln Education Outreach contact: Holly Abels, Lincoln Action Program's Education Outreach, 2202 S. 11th Street, Lincoln, NE 68502, (402) 471-4515.

Flowers with Care Youth Services

Flowers with Care Youth Services in Astoria, New York, was founded in 1974 by Father James R. Harvey to train young ex-offenders for jobs in the floral industry. Since then, the emphasis has changed to provide more basic services to a broader population of youths at risk: school dropouts, teenage parents, abused, neglected, and abandoned young people, and young people with substance abuse problems, as well as youthful offenders.

Despite Father Harvey's death in 1992, Flowers with Care has continued operations. The goal of the program is to give each young person in the program a sense of hope for the future. To this end, Flowers with Care offers a full range of holistic services — GED classes, counseling (individual, family, and group), medical attention, hot meals, referral and advocacy assistance, computer training coupled with remedial education, recreation activities, and training in basic job skills.

Qualities necessary for successful adulthood are emphasized: respect for oneself and others, daily attendance and punctuality, initiative, and cooperation. Students meet regularly with a counselor. Each student has an individualized educational plan based on his or her abilities and goals.

More than 450 teenagers come to the program

each year, referred by schools, social-service agencies, and the legal system. Gratifyingly, a large number are referred by former clients.

For more information, contact: Paula Beltrone, Flowers with Care Youth Services, 23-40 Astoria Boulevard, Astoria, NY 11102, (718) 726-9790.

Unitarian Universalist Congregation of Atlanta – Fowler Elementary Project

The Unitarian Universalist Congregation of Atlanta (UUCA) is entering its second year of partnership with the Fowler Elementary School Project. Essential to the success of the program is the members' commitment to become involved first as tutors or mentors. They recognize, however, that people have different gifts to contribute. Volunteer forms are distributed and individuals are invited to share their experiences, talents, and interest. Individuals can act as tutors, mentors, or classroom aides, present programs on the arts, or write grant proposals.

The Very Important Reader Program has members of the Unitarian Universalist Congregation of Atlanta purchase books, go to the school, and personally read the books to the children before donating them to the classroom. Also, volunteers have recorded books onto cassette tapes for the school's tape library.

The 12-week Earthkeepers program for the fifth grade classes entered its second year. All fifth graders enjoy a week of earth education in a mountain setting led by two congregation members.

After an intensive year of planning, the Unitarian Universalist Congregation of Atlanta and Fowler Elementary School conducted a series of workshops and programs for parents on conflict management.

With their ongoing commitment to inspiring other congregations and communities to undertake similar partnerships, the UUCA has participated in numerous seminars and conferences, which has resulted in increased interest and involvement in the Atlanta area. Hundreds of UUCA members are involved with this partnership in some way. The children look forward to the visits and learn about themselves, their community, and how to be "partners" in building a better future through the programs.

For more information on the UUCA–Fowler Elementary Project contact: Nancy Bartlett, 122 Greenwood Circle, Decatur, GA 30030, (404) 378-7782.

෫ঌ

National Faith-Based Efforts
for Children

A Growing Religious Movement
for Children

The increase in child poverty, child abuse and neglect, homelessness, and inadequate health care and education has called the church to a renewal and strengthening of its witness on behalf of children, "the least of these." This commitment stems from the biblical call to exercise compassion in the world.

In coordination with the Children's Defense Fund, national religious denominations and organizations have sought to focus more attention and resources on children's needs and on the networking of policies and programs related to children. This partnership between the Children's Defense Fund and the religious community builds on each other's strengths so we can multiply our effectiveness in bringing about change for our nation's children.

In this context, major long-term ecumenical and Protestant denominational efforts have been developed to strengthen the community's response to the needs of children and families. As well, the United States Catholic Conference has developed a comprehensive campaign for children drawing on the wealth of Roman Catholic resources and tradition. While these long-term projects vary in their design and implementation, their goals are the same — to make a positive difference in children's lives. From the United Methodist Women's Campaign for Children to the Presbyterian Church (USA) Five-Year Child Advocacy Project, these efforts are built on the church's long tradition of ministry to children and the wealth of compassion, experience, and expertise derived from congregations.

This chapter is not comprehensive in scope. It focuses on the specific efforts of the mainline Protestant denominations, the Southern Baptist Convention, the Unitarian Universalist Service Committee, and the U.S. Catholic Conference.

Get in touch with your own denomination, even if it is not mentioned here, to discover what it might have to offer in the area of child advocacy and to find out how you can become a part of the growing national religious movement for children.

National Ecumenical Efforts
for Children

The National Council of the Churches
of Christ in the USA

The Committee on Justice for Children
and Their Families

The Committee on Justice for Children and Their Families of the National Council of the Churches of Christ in the USA (NCC) has advocated for the rights and well-being of children for 15 years. It evolved from the Child and Family Justice Project, begun by the NCC in 1977.

The committee seeks to:

♦ Nurture child advocates and educators by offering them leadership training, resources, and technical assistance;

♦ Lift up justice issues of children and families, especially those who live in poverty; and

◆ Coordinate and strengthen the ecumenical community's efforts to inform and empower churches to respond to the needs of children and their families.

Today, the committee's work is carried out from the NCC's Department of Ministries in Christian Education, through 30 denominational and agency representatives who meet regularly to share information, plan actions, and initiate policies to strengthen the church's voice as it addresses justice issues affecting children. This ecumenical partnership has initiated important projects such as the Ecumenical Child Care Network and the Ecumenical Child Health Project. It is developing bibliographical pamphlets for such ministries as child abuse prevention and children's health. For more information, contact Margery Freeman, 1119 Dauphine Street #5, New Orleans, LA 70116, (504) 522-9895.

The Ecumenical Child Health Project

As millions of American children suffer the impact of a growing national health crisis, congregations and child care providers have been called on to intervene and try to compensate for inadequate health services. Recognizing the growing and evolving role of churches in assuring health care for our nation's children, the NCC launched in 1989 the first national study of how congregations provide health services for children.

The Ecumenical Child Health Project, an outgrowth of the national survey, is a five-year initiative (1990–1994) designed to improve young children's health by:

◆ Identifying model health programs operated by or within churches, and disseminating information about those models to the national church community;

◆ Increasing church awareness of the scope, danger, and effects of poor child health and what can be done about it; and

◆ Providing a vehicle within the religious community to work for public policy changes to ensure good health care for all children.

The Ecumenical Child Health Project is a partnership of the National Council of Churches' Prophetic Justice Unit and the National Center for Children in Poverty. It is funded by the Robert Wood Johnson Foundation. For more information, contact the Rev. Sharon Keeling, National Council of Churches, 475 Riverside Drive, Room 572, New York, NY 10115, (212) 870-2664, or Karen Bell, National Center for Children in Poverty, 154 Haven Avenue, New York, NY 10032, (212) 927-8793.

The Commission on Family Ministries and Human Sexuality

The Commission on Family Ministries and Human Sexuality is the arm of the National Council of Churches for family and sexuality-related policy development, leader development, and resourcing. A commission of the NCC's Department on Ministries in Christian Education, it addresses such concerns as violence in families, strengthening families, and sexuality education. It has a project on Black family ministries. The full commission, which meets annually, includes Canadian church bodies and many churches in the U.S. that are not member communions of the NCC. A number of family-oriented, church-related agencies are affiliate members. For more information, contact Dr. Joe Leonard, Executive Director, 243 Lenoir Avenue, Wayne, PA 19087, (215) 688-0629.

The Ecumenical Child Care Network

The national Ecumenical Child Care Network (ECCN) is an interfaith organization of religious educators, child caregivers, pastors, and congregational leaders who advocate for high quality, equitable, and inclusive child care and education in our nation's churches, synagogues, and other houses of worship. The ECCN has more than 1,000 members and associate groups in 25 states. Through its publications, technical assistance, and training events, the ECCN reaches thousands of congregations and their weekday ministries with children and families.

The ECCN was founded in 1983 at the initiation of the NCC Child and Family Justice Working Group. A 1982 landmark study conducted by the NCC among its member communions dramatized the enormous scope of child care ministries sponsored by the religious community. Research revealed that for every child who attends Sunday school, there are eight children who enter the church on Monday for nurture, care, and education. Indeed, religious institutions care for 2 million to 3 million children each day, making them the largest provider of child care in the nation.

ECCN members receive a bimonthly newsletter that keeps them abreast of congregation-related innovative programs, policy trends, resources, and events. Publications include *Called to Act*, a primer on child care advocacy in our churches, *Helping Churches Mind the Children*, a guide for starting or expanding weekday programs for children, and *Partners in Family Child Care, Opportunities for Outreach*, a guide for religious congregations. The ECCN sponsors national and regional conferences and training events, often in cooperation with other national early childhood and child advocacy organizations.

The ECCN's National Council on Recognition offers congregational leaders and weekday educators training and technical assistance to strengthen their relationship so that they can work together more effectively to serve children in their weekday programs. ECCN "recognition" is awarded to exemplary programs that complete the ECCN self-study *Congregations and Child Care*.

The ECCN welcomes all inquiries from congregations and children's ministry leaders who seek support, resources, and assistance for their weekday programs for children. For more information, contact Margery Freeman, Director, 1119 Dauphine Street #5, New Orleans, LA 70116, (504) 522-9895. To join the ECCN or order ECCN publications, contact ECCN headquarters at 1580 N. Northwest Highway, Park Ridge, IL 60068-1456, (708) 298-1612.

National Denominational Initiatives for Children

African Methodist Episcopal Church

Members interested in working on behalf of children and youths are invited to contact Rosa M. Baxter, Connectional Director, Young People's Division of the Women's Missionary Society, 3194 Baxberry Court, Decatur, GA 30034-5102, (404) 284-7015.

American Baptist Churches

The general secretary, Daniel Weiss, of American Baptist Churches USA has formed a Task Force on the Prevention of Child Abuse and Neglect. The goals of this task force are as follows:

◆ To increase awareness within American Baptist Churches of the pervasiveness of the problem.

◆ To be a clearinghouse for resources such as books, curricula, videos, work of other denominations, workshops, and lists of the many resources available.

◆ To reach targeted audiences with programs that will bring about changes.

There was a "Prevention of Child Abuse and Neglect" booth at the 1993 Biennial to help persons become aware of the resources available and to collect data. This group will continue to meet through 1995.

For more information on the work of this task force, write to American Baptist Churches USA, Box 851, Valley Forge, PA 19482-0851.

The Christian Church (Disciples of Christ)

The Christian Church (Disciples of Christ) addresses the issues confronting children through several of its units in addition to its cooperation with various committees of the National Council of Churches and the Children's Defense Fund.

Within the Division of Homeland Ministries, the Center for Education and Mission concerns itself with legislative issues affecting the plight of children and advocates on their behalf. A newsletter, *For the Children*, is produced six times a year. It deals with the religious education of children as well as issues affecting their well-being and encourages local congregations to become active in advocating for children. In addition, the Center has developed its *Child Protection Packet* for congregations to use in the prevention and detection of child abuse.

The women of the Christian Church (Disciples of Christ), through Christian Women's Fellowship, will be doing an intensive study in 1994–95 of the needs of children and how those needs might best be met. The theme for their year is "Cherish the Children."

The Division of Overseas Ministry is actively participating in the attempt to overcome the global problem of child prostitution.

For more information, contact Jane Lawrence, Children's Ministries, Division of Homeland Ministries, P.O. Box 1986, Indianapolis, IN 46206, (317) 353-1499.

The Episcopal Church

The Children's Advocacy Committee

In our Baptismal Covenant we are called to strive for justice among all people, and respect the dignity of every human being. We must not forget the children of our society as we seek to fulfill our Baptismal Covenant as the People of the Resurrection.

The Most Rev. Edmond Browning
Presiding Bishop

The Children's Advocacy Committee (CAC) of the Episcopal Church was established by the General Convention in 1988. The committee affirms the Episcopal Church's commitment to all children and seeks to involve congregations in addressing the issues of child abuse, child care, child welfare, family support, education, and public policy.

CAC is made up of leaders and professionals whose ministries support and enhance the well-being of children. Members represent such disciplines as mental health, social welfare, disability concerns, education, health, and child welfare.

The mandate of the Children's Advocacy Committee is to:

- Strengthen and expand ministry to children, while building networks among Christian educators, social service agencies, and advocacy groups;

- Educate and train local and regional church staff and members to act on behalf of children;

- Develop an Episcopal children's advocacy network composed of congregational, diocesan, and church leaders at the national level; and

- Advocate for children by influencing federal and state legislation related to child care, child health, education, and child welfare.

Since its inception, the Children's Advocacy Committee members have been working to provide Episcopalians with the resources and support necessary to meet children's needs in their communities. It has conducted a survey of all congregations to prepare a directory of child care programs housed in an Episcopal church; published and distributed a brief report, *The Children's Advocate*; and made presentations at the Families 2000 Project, 1990, of the Episcopal Church.

Those interested in becoming involved in the work of the CAC are encouraged to write Betty Coats, Children's Advocacy Committee, Washington Office of the Episcopal Church, 110 Maryland Avenue, N.E., Washington, DC 20002, (202) 547-7300, or Howard K. Williams, Office of Children's Ministries, The Episcopal Church Center, 815 Second Avenue, New York, NY 10017, (212) 922-5264.

The Evangelical Lutheran Church in America

Women of the ELCA

In 1990 Women of the Evangelical Lutheran Church in America launched a major programmatic emphasis on women and children living in poverty. This emphasis, which will continue at least through 1996, involves education about the realities of poverty, service in partnership with those who are living in poverty, and advocacy for economic justice. The ELCA-sponsored educational events across the country have resulted in the development of a large network of women committed to working for change in those systems and structures that perpetuate poverty. For information on programs and resources, contact Doris Strieter, Women of the ELCA, 8765 W. Higgins Road, Chicago, IL 60631, (312) 380-2465.

DESCAR

The DESCAR (Dedicated Early Support for Children at Risk) project is composed of a group of passionately concerned persons, early childhood professionals, church leaders, and health professionals who are working together to make a difference for young children, especially those at risk. Their commitment is to develop strategies to motivate, empower, and enable congregations to nurture children in their total development as support for their spiritual lives. This project was developed through the Inter-Lutheran Cooperative Parish Projects Committee of the Lutheran Church Missouri Synod and the Evangelical Lutheran Church in America. For further information, contact Dr. Connie Leean, Evangelical Lutheran Church in America, 8765 W. Higgins Road, Chicago, IL 60631-4188.

The Presbyterian Church (USA)

Child Advocacy Project

For the promise is unto you and to your children.

Acts 2:39

God's promise for children is being thwarted by human sin. For millions of children, their God-given promise to be free, happy creative persons dwelling in loving human community has not been realized. The divine promise, left to human stewardship, has been emptied of its hopefulness and misery prevails.

Church and Society, 1977

Thus began the issue of *Church and Society* magazine entitled "On Being a Child." The document was the result of a consulting Committee on the Needs and Rights of Children created by the 186th General Assembly of the former United Presbyterian Church. Many years have passed since this document was first published. Since that time, the Presbyterian Church (USA) was formed through the 1983 merger of the United Presbyterian Church in the United States of America and the Presbyterian Church in the United States. But a great many things have not changed, including the conditions for children. In fact, statistics tell us that the status of children in many key areas worsened in the 1980s and early 1990s.

Frustrated and deeply saddened by the status of children in the United States and the world, in 1988 staff members at the General Assembly level of the church developed a proposal to engage "the Presbyterian Church (USA), its governing bodies and its members in child advocacy to fulfill its baptismal commitments through education, service and networking." The proposal was submitted to the Presbyterian

Women's Birthday Offering, which recognized the critical need and responded by fully funding the project for 1990 through 1994.

The Child Advocacy Project (CAP) Committee was established to implement the project and included staff from three ministry units (Education and Congregational Nurture, Social Justice and Peacemaking, and Women's). The Expanded Child Advocacy Project Committee then was created to coordinate child advocacy efforts by including staff, elected committee members from the three ministry units, and representatives of grassroots child advocates and Presbyterian Women, as well as the CAP committee members.

The Child Advocacy Project's first task was to solicit ideas from Presbyterians and ecumenical child advocates from across the country, to find out what was happening in the local churches and what they needed to be more effective advocates for children. To accomplish this, a call for participants to a conference was made to the 16 synods (regional governing bodies). More than 130 people, representing every synod, gathered in Tampa, Florida, for reflection, education, and discussion, and are linked through the CAP.

Responding to suggestions made by conference participants, CAP supported the development of a network of child advocates. In 1992 the newly created Presbyterian Child Advocacy Network (PCAN) became a network of the Presbyterian Health, Education and Welfare Association (PHEWA) and elected a leadership team. Today, the network is growing and becoming an effective grassroots voice for children in church and in society.

Also as a result of input from conference participants, the CAP committee developed a comprehensive five-year plan. Forming partnerships with other ecumenical and secular child advocacy groups is a vital part of the work. The Children's Defense Fund, the Child and Family Justice Office of the National Council of Churches, the Ecumenical Child Care Network, and others have worked closely to support and develop the project.

ACTING NOW!

It is imperative that we act now to accelerate the pace and rate of change. For children there can be no further delay in providing optimum conditions for the fulfillment of human potential. The future of the child is now.... The church must continue... to support and undergird the efforts which would enable each child to become an inheritor of the kingdom.

Thelma Adair
General Moderator of the 188th General Assembly
Presbyterian Church (USA)

The Child Advocacy Project of the Presbyterian Church (USA) is seeking to provide faithful, effective advocacy for children. For more information about how you can become involved in the project, contact: Child Advocacy Project, Presbyterian Church (USA), 100 Witherspoon Street, Room 3011, Louisville, KY 40202-1396. For information on membership in the Presbyterian Child Advocacy Network, write to PCAN in care of PHEWA at the same address.

The Southern Baptist Convention

The Child Advocacy Network

In 1990, the Gheens Center for Christian Family Ministry, a center for research and education located at the Southern Baptist Theological Seminary in Louisville, Kentucky, convened the first meeting of the Southern Baptist Child Advocacy Network (CAN). CAN includes representatives from national Southern Baptist agencies, state Baptist child welfare agencies, seminary faculty, and staff members of local congregations. The staff of the Presbyterian Child Advocacy Project, the United Methodist Women's Campaign for Children, the Child and Family Justice Office of the National Council of Churches, and the Children's Defense Fund have served as key supportive consultants in CAN's development. CAN has defined child advocacy as:

- Prayer and Bible study concerning children's issues.

- Befriending and experiencing the world with children.

- Taking a pro-active role and pleading the case for children.

- Mobilizing resources and developing networks in behalf of children.

- Educating the church and community about the needs of children.

- Valuing, caring for, respecting, and celebrating children — and letting children speak.

- Programming for and in behalf of children.

In order to:

- Protect children.

- Help all children develop fully their God-given gifts.

- Integrate children into the life and worship of the church community.

CAN meets twice each year so that members can share and collaborate in their work and the work of their agencies and congregations as child advocates; inform one another about new developments and resources in child advocacy; and plan shared projects, such as major conferences. It serves as a network rather than a policy-making committee or organization; it encourages the development of child advocacy projects and emphases in the various agencies, congregations, and levels of organization in Baptist life.

CAN sponsored the development of the book *Precious in His Sight* (Birmingham: New Hope, 1993), an inspirational resource and guidebook for church groups and individual Christians who care about children and want to be their advocates. In addition, the Women's Missionary Union, an agency auxiliary to the Southern Baptist Convention, has made child advocacy a major focus in its work and has prepared a guide to use in teaching *Precious in His Sight* to church groups.

For information about the Southern Baptist Child Advocacy Network, contact Dr. Diana Garland, Dean of the Carver School of Church Social Work and Director of the Gheens Center for Christian Family Ministry, Southern Baptist Theological Seminary, 2825 Lexington Road, Louisville, KY 40280, (800) 626-5525 or (502) 897-4607.

Unitarian Universalist Service Committee

Focus on Children in the 1990s

Upon this gifted age, in its dark hour,
Falls from the sky a meteoric shower
Of facts...they lie unquestioned, uncombined
Wisdom enough to leech us of our ill
is daily spun, but there exists no loom
To weave it into fabric...

Edna St. Vincent Millay

Information about America's children abounds. One in five lives in poverty. One in six has no medical insurance. One in seven may not complete high school. Tens of thousands are homeless, their numbers increasing....The questions that such information raises about our society and our future demand response. Our challenge is to begin a process of inquiry and build a loom of understanding so that together we can, as the poet says, weave the facts into a fabric of wisdom — a fabric for action.

From *Promise the Children*, UUSC's study guide on the rights and needs of children

The Unitarian Universalist Service Committee (UUSC) is an independent, nonsectarian membership organization that promotes peace, justice, and freedom in the United States and around the world.

Because the UUSC is committed to seeking a better life for children in the United States, it has embarked on a program focused on the rights and needs of children, especially those in poverty. Over the next decade, the UUSC will build partnerships with Unitarian Universalists and their congregations to advocate for an enlightened government policy toward children. The agency will provide educational and policy resources and work with partner congregations to develop effective citizen education and action programs.

The UUSC monitors selected national legislation affecting children and provides constituents with "action alerts" outlining key bills pending in Congress. The alerts encourage members of congregations throughout the country to write or call their elected representatives, hold public forums or town meetings, or visit their representatives' offices.

The UUSC will assist partner congregations in working on behalf of children in their communities. Congregational projects will be tailored to local needs and to each congregation's readiness to mobilize for action.

It also provides constituents with educational materials including fact sheets, background reports, bibliographies, and issue analyses that examine the problems faced by children at risk. In its first year, the children's program concentrated on child care, Head Start, and the federal Special Supplemental Food Program for Women, Infants, and Children (WIC). In subsequent years the program will tackle issues such as education, homelessness, poverty, and discrimination.

For more information and to receive the UUSC's legislative action alerts, contact the Unitarian Universalist Service Committee, 130 Prospect Street, Cambridge, MA 02139-1813, (617) 868-6600.

The United Church of Christ

Who Speaks for the Children?

In September 1986 the Office for Church in Society of the United Church of Christ invited representatives of denominations, ecumenical agencies, child advocacy groups, and organizations helping low-income persons to join with them in a national ecumenical effort called Who Speaks for the Children? A National Planning Committee on Children in Poverty was formed to develop and implement an ecumenical effort to support public policies at all levels of government that benefit children and families, especially those in need, and to include the grassroots participation of low-income families.

The Who Speaks for the Children? campaign began with regional hearings on child poverty in five cities around the country, to focus local attention on the needs of children, recommend solutions, and mobilize local support. From the fall of 1987 to the winter of 1988, more than 1,000 poor children, mothers, families, and their representatives (such as community organizations, advocacy groups, and social service providers) participated. State legislators, social service providers, city administrators, low-income mothers, and others shared their stories about child and family poverty and recommended ways to address the problem. The local

RESOURCES TO HELP YOU HELP CHILDREN

planning team in Iowa produced a 20-minute video of the hearings.

The culminating event for the regional hearings was the National Consultation on Children in Poverty, which was held in Washington, DC, in February 1988. A focal point was testimony presented to members of the House Select Committee on Children, Youth and Families by a few of the regional hearing coordinators and participants.

Ongoing work within the United Church of Christ on issues affecting children is extensive and multifaceted. Public policy advocacy on such issues as child care, health care reform, welfare, and housing is coordinated through the Office for Church in Society. The Board for Homeland Ministries carries out programmatic work on a wide range of issues, including public education, health care, and housing. A bi-annual Children and the Church conference aims at strengthening ministries within the UCC. President Paul Sherry is leading a process to strengthen and refocus the commitment of the UCC to ministries with children within the church and for justice and empowerment within the society.

For more information about public policies affecting children and families, contact Patrick Conover, The United Church of Christ, Office for Church in Society, 110 Maryland Avenue N.E., Washington, DC 20002, (202) 543-1517. For information on programmatic child advocacy efforts, contact Faith Adams Johnson, Secretary for Human Development Programs and Concerns, Board for Homeland Ministries, United Church of Christ, 700 Prospect Avenue East, Cleveland, OH 44115-1100, (216) 736-3282.

The United Methodist Church

Women's Division

For more than 100 years United Methodist Women and predecessor groups of women organized for mission have been strong advocates for the rights and needs of children. This powerful legacy continues through the new Policy Statement of the Women's Division: "Ministries with Women and Ministries with Children and Youth: A Gift for the Whole Church," approved in March 1993. It states in part, "Until children have strong advocates in the general population, we will champion their cause. Our call is for the whole of church and society to share the urgency of this concern."

From 1988 to 1993, the Women's Division, in cooperation with the Children's Defense Fund, carried out its Campaign for Children. Nearly 10,000 local units of United Methodist Women made commitments to make a difference in the lives of children through worship, education, community service, and legislative action.

In October 1993, the Women's Division voted to continue the Campaign for Children with Phase II for 1994–99, entitled "Making the World Safe for Children and Youth in the Twenty-first Century." Phase II includes the following strategies:

- Call United Methodist Women to celebrate their accomplishments in the Campaign for Children during their annual meetings in 1994 or 1995;

- Emphasize the need to move commitments toward greater involvement and direct actions for advocacy;

- Place greater focus on the needs of youths, including issues of violence, teen pregnancy, and empowerment to become full participants in society;

- Expand concepts of mission by making connections between the local and global needs of children, through consciousness-raising and action on issues of children around the world;

- Vigorously support public policy legislation with intensive action for:

  1. **Funding:** Expansion of Head Start programs and the Special Supplemental Food Program for Women, Infants, and Children (WIC);

  2. **Health care reform:** Comprehensive health coverage for all Americans, especially pregnant women and children;

  3. **Welfare reform:** National child support legislation and additional legislation designed to assure education and training opportunities for welfare recipients and the availability of quality child care for children of low-income parents participating in education or training or at work;

  4. **Violence prevention:** Legislation for gun control and additional legislation designed to prevent violence;

  5. **Changes in the law:** Changes that assure that a person working full-time at the lowest wages can earn an income above the poverty level and support her or his family, including increases in the minimum wage and further expansion of the earned income tax credit.

- Expand the Child Watch Visitation pilot project with the Children's Defense Fund and evaluate for further development.

- Refer the implementation of the "Campaign for Children–Phase II" to the four Conference Mission Coordinators to develop programs of study and action related to the needs of children and youths;

- Encourage conferences, districts, and local units of United Methodist Women to actively promote the programs of UNICEF;

- Develop resource materials to interpret Phase II of the campaign.

For more information contact Kolya Braun, Executive Secretary for Children, Youth and Family Advocacy, Women's Division, Room 1502, 475 Riverside Drive, New York, NY 10115, (212) 870-3766.

Coordinator of Children's Ministries

The Coordinator of Children's Ministries in each annual conference and local church is responsible for designing a comprehensive approach to children's ministries, including helping the church take seriously the needs of children, planning effectively to meet those needs, expanding the ministry of the church with children, increasing the number of options for children within the church, and reaching out into the community to participate with others for the good of children.

For more information, contact the Office of Children's Ministries, General Board of Discipleship, P.O. Box 840, Nashville, TN 37202-0840, (615) 340-7171.

The United States Catholic Conference

A Catholic Campaign for Children and Families

In November 1991, the Catholic bishops of the United States issued a statement that called for renewed attention to children and families in our homes, our parishes, our communities, our nation, and our world. "Putting Children and Families First: A Challenge for Our Church, Nation, and World" urges Catholics and others to engage in "a spiritual and social reawakening to the moral and human cost of neglecting our children and our families."

Shortly after the statement was released, the bishops' Children's Initiative began to take off, moving from a well-received statement on children and families to a growing campaign for children and families. Across the country bishops launched their own diocesan efforts. Legislative networks focused on children's needs, educational efforts were initiated, and a variety of programs were launched to serve poor children and vulnerable families. Building on the church's extensive history of serving children and families, the Catholic Campaign for Children and Families has brought together a wide range of Church ministries, including those involved in liturgy, religious education, family life, social ministry, pro-life, and others.

Diocesan and Parish Resources

In August 1992, the *Parish Resource Manual for the Catholic Campaign for Children and Families* was sent to every Catholic parish in the U.S. This 88-page manual is designed to provide practical suggestions for integrating the Campaign for Children and Families into ongoing parish programs. It includes ideas and tools for parish religious education programs, parochial school programs, liturgy, preaching, family support programs, and social ministry. A condensed Spanish version was sent to all U.S. parishes with Spanish Masses. Additionally, a video recently was produced titled *I Am Only a Child*, which outlines the themes of the Campaign through compelling visual images. It too is available in English and Spanish. Other Campaign resources include a summary of diocesan initiatives and a camera-ready one-page brochure.

Public Policy Campaign

While some argue that the needs of children and families are best met by promoting better values and personal responsibility, others argue that we need better "family-friendly" and child-centered policies. The position of the Campaign is that we need both better values and better policies. In the pastoral statement *Putting Children and Families First,* the U.S. bishops said, "No government can love a child and no policy can substitute for a family's care, but clearly families can be helped or hurt in their irreplaceable roles. Government can either support or undermine families as they cope with the moral, social, and economic stresses of caring for children." They call on all Catholics to "become a persistent, informed, and committed voice for children and families."

Currently, the Catholic Campaign for Children and Families is focusing on four priority public policy areas: (1) Economic Help for Families, (2) Health Care, (3) Reshaping Foreign Aid, and (4) Peacemaking/Peacekeeping. These and other policy areas that support families and children will be the focus of the Catholic Campaign for Children and Families in the months and years to come.

For more information, contact Joan Rosenhauer, Outreach Director of the USCC Department of Social Development and World Peace, United States Catholic Conference, 3211 Fourth Street, N.E., Washington, DC 20017, (202) 541-3195.

≈

Faith-Based Public Policy Offices and National Organizations

Ecumenical Organizations

CAMPAIGN TO END CHILD PROSTITUTION IN ASIAN TOURISM (ECPAT)

U.S. Office:
475 Riverside Drive, Room 621
New York, NY 10015
(212) 870-2427

Canada Office:
11 Madison Avenue
Toronto, Ontario
Canada

CHURCHES' CENTER FOR THEOLOGY AND PUBLIC POLICY
4500 Massachusetts Avenue, N.W.
Washington, DC 20016
(202) 885-8648

CHURCH WOMEN UNITED

Washington Office:
110 Maryland Avenue, N.E.
Washington, DC 20002
(202) 544-8747

New York Office:
475 Riverside Drive, Room 812
New York, NY 10115-0050
(212) 870-2347

ECUMENICAL CHILD CARE NETWORK
1580 N. Northwest Highway
Park Ridge, IL 60068-1456
(708) 298-1612

INTERFAITH IMPACT FOR JUSTICE & PEACE
100 Maryland Avenue, N.E.
Washington, DC 20002
(202) 543-2800

THE CONGRESS OF NATIONAL BLACK CHURCHES
600 New Hampshire Avenue, N.W., Suite 650
Washington, DC 20037-7403
(202) 371-1091

THE NATIONAL COUNCIL OF THE CHURCHES OF CHRIST IN THE USA

Washington Office:
110 Maryland Avenue, N.E.
Washington, DC 20002
(202) 544-2350

New York Office:
475 Riverside Drive, Room 880
New York, NY 10115
(212) 870-2360

WORLD CONFERENCE ON RELIGION AND PEACE
777 United Nations Plaza
New York, NY 10017
(212) 687-2163

Regional Ecumenical Networks

A number of regional ecumenical networks sponsor programs for children or advocate on children's issues. These include:

CHRISTIAN CONFERENCE OF CONNECTICUT
60 Lorraine Street
Hartford, CT 06103
(203) 236-4281

CHURCH COUNCIL OF GREATER SEATTLE
4759 15th Avenue, N.E.
Seattle, WA 98105
(206) 525-1213

COLORADO COUNCIL OF CHURCHES
1234 Bannock Street
Denver, CO 80204-3631
(303) 825-4910

COUNCIL OF CHURCHES OF GREATER BRIDGEPORT
126 Washington Avenue
Bridgeport, CT 06604
(203) 334-1121

GREATER DALLAS COMMUNITY OF CHURCHES
2800 Swiss Avenue
Dallas, TX 75204
(214) 824-8680

GREATER MINNEAPOLIS COUNCIL OF CHURCHES
122 West Franklin Avenue, Room 218
Minneapolis, MN 55404
(612) 870-3660, ext. 125

NEW MEXICO COUNCIL OF CHURCHES
124 Hermosa, S.E.
Albuquerque, NM 87108-2610
(505) 255-1509

ST. PAUL AREA COUNCIL OF CHURCHES
1671 Summit Avenue
St. Paul, MN 55105
(612) 646-8805

VIRGINIA COUNCIL OF CHURCHES
1214 West Graham Road
Richmond, VA 23220
(804) 321-3300

Denominational Public Policy Offices

AMERICAN BAPTIST CHURCHES, USA
Office of Governmental Relations
110 Maryland Avenue, N.E., Suite 511
Washington, DC 20002
(202) 544-3400

CHRISTIAN CHURCH (DISCIPLES OF CHRIST)
Center for Education and Mission
222 S. Downey Avenue
Indianapolis, IN 46206
(317) 353-1491, ext. 374

CHURCH OF THE BRETHREN
110 Maryland Avenue, N.E., Box 50
Washington, DC 20002
(202) 546-3202

THE EPISCOPAL CHURCH

Washington Office:
110 Maryland Avenue, N.E.
Washington, DC 20002
(202) 547-7300; (800) 228-0515

Episcopal Church Public Policy Network
Public Ministries Cluster
The Episcopal Church Center
815 Second Avenue
New York, NY 10017
(212) 867-8400; (800) 334-7626

EVANGELICAL LUTHERAN CHURCH IN AMERICA
Office for Governmental Affairs
122 C Street, N.W., Suite 300
Washington, DC 20001
(202) 783-7507

FRIENDS COMMITTEE ON NATIONAL LEGISLATION (FCNL)
245 Second Street, N.E.
Washington, DC 20002
(202) 547-6000

JESUIT SOCIAL MINISTRIES, NATIONAL OFFICE
1424 16th Street, N.W., #300
Washington, DC 20036
(202) 462-7008

NETWORK: A NATIONAL CATHOLIC SOCIAL JUSTICE LOBBY
806 Rhode Island Avenue, N.E.
Washington, DC 20018
(202) 526-4070

PRESBYTERIAN CHURCH (USA)
110 Maryland Avenue, N.E., Box 52
Washington, DC 20002
(202) 543-1126

UNITARIAN UNIVERSALIST ASSOCIATION OF CONGREGATIONS (UUA)
100 Maryland Avenue, N.E., #106
Washington, DC 20002
(202) 547-0254

UNITARIAN UNIVERSALIST SERVICE COMMITTEE
2000 P Street, N.W., Suite 515
Washington, DC 20036
(202) 387-4587

UNITED CHURCH OF CHRIST (UCC)
Office for Church in Society
110 Maryland Avenue, N.E.
Washington, DC 20002
(202) 543-1517

UNITED METHODIST CHURCH

General Board of Church and Society
100 Maryland Avenue, N.E.
Washington, DC 20002
(202) 488-5660

General Board of Global Ministries
Women's Division
475 Riverside Drive, Room 1502
New York, NY 10115
(212) 870-3766

General Board of Discipleship
Division of Educational Ministries
P.O. Box 840
Nashville, TN 37212-0840
(615) 340-7171

National Organizations

AMERICAN ACADEMY OF PEDIATRICS
601 13th Street, N.W., Suite 400 North
Washington, DC 20004
(202) 347-8600

AMNESTY INTERNATIONAL USA
National Campaign Office
655 Sutter Street, Suite 406
San Francisco, CA 94102
(415) 441-2114

BREAD FOR THE WORLD
1100 Wayne Avenue
Silver Spring, MD 20910
(301) 608-2400

CENTER ON BUDGET AND POLICY PRIORITIES
777 North Capitol Street, N.E., Suite 705
Washington, DC 20002
(202) 408-1080

CHILD WELFARE LEAGUE OF AMERICA
440 First Street, N.W., Suite 310
Washington, DC 20001
(202) 638-2952

CHILDREN'S DEFENSE FUND
25 E Street, N.W.
Washington, DC 20001
(202) 628-8787

COALITION ON HUMAN NEEDS
1000 Wisconsin Avenue, N.W.
Washington, DC 20007
(202) 342-0726

DEFENSE FOR CHILDREN INTERNATIONAL (USA)
21 South 13th Street
Philadelphia, PA 19107
(215) 569-8850

FOOD RESEARCH AND ACTION CENTER (FRAC)
1875 Connecticut Avenue, N.W., Suite 540
Washington, DC 20009
(202) 986-2200

HABITAT FOR HUMANITY INTERNATIONAL
121 Habitat Street
Americus, GA 31709
(912) 924-6935

THE MIDWEST ACADEMY
225 West Ohio Street, Suite 250
Chicago, IL 60610
(312) 645-6010

NATIONAL ASSOCIATION FOR THE EDUCATION OF YOUNG CHILDREN
1509 16th Street, N.W.
Washington, DC 20036
(202) 232-8777

NATIONAL BLACK CHILD DEVELOPMENT INSTITUTE
1463 Rhode Island Avenue, N.W.
Washington, DC 20005 (202) 387-1281

NATIONAL COALITION FOR THE HOMELESS
1612 K Street, N.W., Suite 204
Washington, DC 20006
(202) 265-2371

NATIONAL COUNCIL OF LA RAZA
810 First Street, N.E.
Washington, DC 20002-4205
(202) 289-1380

NATIONAL LOW INCOME HOUSING COALITION
1012 14th Street, N.W., #1500
Washington, DC 20005
(202) 662-1530

NORTH AMERICA COORDINATING CENTER FOR RESPONSIBLE TOURISM
P.O. Box 827
San Anselmo, CA 94979
(415) 258-6594

U.S. COMMITTEE FOR UNICEF

Washington Office:
110 Maryland Avenue, N.E., Room 304
Washington, DC 20002
(202) 547-7946

New York Office:
333 East 38th Street
New York, NY 10016
(212) 922-2646

Resources

Addresses and telephone numbers are provided for resources that may not be available in a library. Otherwise, contact the publishers directly for more information.

Child Advocacy

Bobo, Kimberley. *Lives Matter: A Handbook for Christian Organizing.* 1986. Sheed and Ward, 115 E. Armour Blvd., P.O. Box 414292, Kansas City, MO 64141-0281.

Children's Defense Fund. *An Advocate's Guide to Fund Raising.* Washington, DC: CDF, 1990.

Children's Defense Fund. *An Advocate's Guide to the Media.* Washington, DC: CDF, 1990.

Children's Defense Fund. *An Advocate's Guide to Using Data.* Washington, DC: CDF, 1990.

Edelman, Marian Wright. *The Measure of Our Success: A Letter to My Children and Yours.* Boston: Beacon Press, 1992.

Fernandez, Happy Craven. *The Child Advocacy Handbook.* New York: The Pilgrim Press, 1980.

Garland, Diana R. *Precious in His Sight.* Birmingham, AL: New Hope, 1993.

Hatkoff, Amy, and Karen Kelly Klopp. *How to Save the Children.* Fireside/Simon and Schuster, 1992. Foreword by Marian Wright Edelman.

Kendall, Jackie, Steve Max, and Kimberley Bobo. *Organizing for Social Change: A Manual for Activists in the 1990s.* 1991. Seven Locks Press, P.O. Box 27, Cabin John, MD 20818. (301) 320-2130.

Unitarian Universalist Service Committee. *Promise the Children Guidebook.* 1990. Available from: UUSC, 130 Prospect Street, Cambridge, MA 02139-1813, (617) 868-6600.

United Methodist Women. *Campaign for Children Packet.* 1988. Available from: UMW's Campaign for Children, Service Center, 7820 Reading Road, Caller No. 1800, Cincinnati, OH 45222-1800.

United Voices for Children. *Handbook for the Child Advocate.* Available from United Voices for Children, 1580 N. Northwest Highway, Suite 111, Park Ridge, IL 60068.

Child Care

Evangelical Lutheran Church in America. *Congregations and Child Care.* An intensive self-study resource for congregations and early childhood education providers (child care or preschool) who want to evaluate and improve the quality of relationships between a church and its weekday early childhood program. For information about this resource, the self-study process, and its cost, contact Clarene Johnson, ELCA Early Childhood Resource Office, P.O. Box 99607, Tacoma, WA 98499.

Freeman, Margery, ed. *Called to Act: Stories of Child Care Advocacy in Our Churches.* 1986. Available from: Ecumenical Child Care Network, 1580 N. Northwest Highway, Park Ridge, IL 60068-1456, (708) 298-1612.

National Council of the Churches of Christ. *Helping Churches Mind the Children: A Guide for Church-Housed Child Care Programs.* Rev. ed. 1987. Available from: Ecumenical Child Care Network (see address above).

National Council of the Churches of Christ. *National Council of the Churches of Christ Policy Statement on Child Day Care.* 1984. Available from: Ecumenical Child Care Network (see address above).

Seaton, Kathleen Lull, and Linda L. Rothaar. *Early Childhood Ministry and Your Church: How to Start and Maintain an Early Childhood Center.* Minneapolis: Augsburg Fortress Press, 1991.

Steele, Dorothy M., ed. *Congregations and Child Care: A Self-Study for Churches and Synagogues and Their Early Childhood Programs.* 1990. Available from: Ecumenical Child Care Network (see address above).

Wessler, Martin, and Thomas Sauerman. *Caring for Children Before and After School.* Siebert Lutheran Foundation, 1986. Available from: ELCA, 333 South 12th Street, Minneapolis, MN 55404.

Child Welfare

Children's Defense Fund. *Helping Children by Strengthening Families: A Look at Family Support Programs.* Washington, DC, 1992.

Edna McConnell Clark Foundation. *Keeping Families Together: Facts on Family Preservation Services.* Information kit. Available from: Edna McConnell Clark Foundation, Communications Department, 250 Park Avenue, New York, NY 10177-0026, (212) 986-7050.

Exley, Helen, ed. *What It's Like to Be Me.* Written and illustrated entirely by disabled children. Watford, UK: Exley Publications Ltd., 1981. Available from Friendship Press, P.O. Box 37844, Cincinnati, OH 45222-0844.

MacDonald, Bonnie Glass. *Surely Heed Their Cry: A Guide for Prevention, Intervention and Healing.* Louisville, KY: Presbyterian Church (USA), 1993. Available from: Presbyterian Distribution Management Service, (800) 524-2612, DMS #257-93-010.

National Crime Prevention Council. *Mission Possible: Churches Supporting Fragile Families*. Washington, DC: 1990. For information, contact: Maria Nagorski, Director, Technical Assistance Center, NCPC, 1700 K Street, N.W., 2nd Floor, Washington, DC 20007, (202) 466-6272.

Children and the Church

Blazer, Doris A., ed. *Faith Development in Early Childhood*. Kansas City, MO: Sheed and Ward, 1989.

Children's Defense Fund. *Prophetic Voices: Black Preachers Speak on Behalf of Children*. Washington, DC, 1993.

Coles, Robert. *The Spiritual Life of Children*. Boston: Houghton Mifflin, 1990.

Evangelical Lutheran Church of America. *Our Children at Risk: Hope for Our Future Together* is a 12-session print resource that helps children, youths, and adults relate the themes of peace, justice, and care of creation to the various spheres of their daily life, congregation, and immediate and global communities. All ages explore together the issues that touch their lives, gain a greater awareness of the situations and problems children face, and work together to advocate for children locally and around the world. A leader guide is available (code #15-9009) for $6.95 from Augsburg Fortress Publishers, (800) 328-4648.

Glass, Dorlis Brown. *Children, Children: A Ministry without Boundaries*. Available from: General Board of Discipleship, United Methodist Church, P.O. Box 189, Nashville, TN 37202-0840, (615) 340-7285.

Heusser, D. B. and Phyllis. *Children as Partners in the Church*. Valley Forge, PA: Judson Press, 1985. Reprint with Foreword by Marian Wright Edelman, 1993.

Norton, Mary Jane Pierce. *Your Job as a Children's Coordinator*. Available from: General Board of Discipleship, United Methodist Church.

Sandell, Elizabeth J. *Including Children in Worship: A Planning Guide for Congregations*. Minneapolis: Augsburg Fortress Press, 1991.

Children and Poverty

Barrett, John M. *It's Hard Not to Worry: Stories for Children about Poverty*. New York: Friendship Press, 1988.

Brazelton, T. Berry. "Why Is America Failing Its Children?" *New York Times Magazine*, September 9, 1990.

Bread for the World. *Children, Let Us Love! Every Fifth Child in the U.S. Faces Hunger*. 1992. Available at $0.60 from either Reformed Church Press, (800) 688-7221, or Bread for the World, (202) 269-0200.

Children's Defense Fund. *Progress and Peril: Black Children in America*. A fact book and action primer. Washington, DC: CDF, 1993.

Children's Defense Fund. *Vanishing Dreams: The Economic Plight of America's Young Families*. Washington, DC: CDF, 1992.

Coles, Robert. *Children of Crisis*. Boston: Little, Brown & Co. Vol. 1, *A Study of Courage and Fear*, 1977. Vol. 2, *Migrants, Sharecroppers, Mountaineers*, 1973. Vol. 3, *The South Goes North*, 1973. Vol. 4, *Eskimos, Chicanos, Indians*. Vol. 5, *Privileged Ones: The Well-off and the Rich in America*, 1980.

Currie, Robin, and Debbie Tafton O'Neal. *Hunger Ideas for Children*. ELCA Distribution Service #67-3178. 1991. Free.

Evangelical Lutheran Church in America. *Women and Children Living in Poverty: A Report to the Evangelical Lutheran Church in America with Recommendations for Action*. Institute for Mission in the U.S.A., Trinity Lutheran Seminary, 2199 East Main Street, Columbus, OH 43209, 1989.

Kotlowitz, Alex. *There Are No Children Here: The Story of Two Boys Growing Up in the Other America*. New York: Anchor Books, 1991.

The New York Times. *Children of the Shadows*. 1993. Reprint of 10-part series on teenagers of inner cities available from The New York Times, Children of the Shadows Project, 229 West 43rd Street, New York, NY 10036.

Schorr, Lisbeth. *Within Our Reach: Breaking the Cycle of Disadvantage*. New York: Anchor Press, 1988.

Shames, Stephen. *Outside the Dream: Child Poverty in America* (Photodocumentary). Washington, DC: CDF and Aperture Foundation, 1991.

United Church of Christ. *Proceedings of the National Consultation on Children in Poverty*. 1988. Available from: Office for Church in Society, United Church of Christ, 700 Prospect Avenue East, Cleveland, OH 44115.

Education

Children's Defense Fund. *An Advocate's Guide to Improving Education*. Washington, DC: CDF, 1990.

Kozol, Jonathan. *Savage Inequalities: Children in America's Schools*. San Francisco: Harper Perennial, 1993.

United Church Board for Homeland Ministries. *Models of Service and Replicable Programs in Support of Public Education, 1988–1989*. Available from: Division of the American Missionary Association, UCBHM, 700 Prospect Avenue East, Cleveland, OH 44115.

Homelessness and Housing

Children's Defense Fund. *Your Family's Rights under the New Fair Housing Law* (Spanish/bilingual version available). Washington, DC: CDF, 1989.

Churches Conference on Shelter and Housing. *Building on Faith: Models of Church-Sponsored Affordable Housing Programs in the Washington, DC, Area*. 1989. Available from: CCSH, 1711 14th Street, N.W., Washington, DC 20009.

Evangelical Lutheran Church in America. *Hungry Times*, a magazine-format resource for middle-school youths focusing on hunger and homelessness, is available in multiples of 12 for $4.00. ELCA Distribution Service, (800) 328-4648, (code #69-4949).

Kroloff, Rabbi Charles A. *54 Ways You Can Help the Homeless*. Available from: Behrman House, Inc., 235 Watchung Avenue, West Orange, NJ 07052, (800) 221-2755. 1993.

Kozol, Jonathan. *Rachel and Her Children: Homeless Families in America*. New York: Fawcett Columbine, 1988.

McDaniel, James A., ed. *Homelessness and Affordable Housing: A Resource Book for Churches*. 1989. Available from: United Church Board for Homeland Ministries, United Church of Christ, 700 Prospect Avenue East, Cleveland, OH 44115.

National Alliance to End Homelessness. *Checklist for Success: Programs to Help the Hungry and Homeless*. Emergency Food and Shelter National Board, 601 North Fairfax Street, Suite 225, Alexandria, VA 22314-2007. Spring 1990.

How to Affect National Public Policy

Amidei, Nancy. *So You Want to Make a Difference.* OMB Watch, 1731 Connecticut Avenue, N.W., Washington, DC 20009, (202) 234-8494. $10.00

Children's Defense Fund. *The State of America's Children.* Washington, DC: CDF, annual publication.

Children's Defense Fund. *CDF Reports.* Washington, DC: CDF. Monthly newsletter.

Clarke, Tina. *Concern into Action: An Advocacy Guide for People of Faith.* 1990. Available from: INTERFAITH IMPACT, 100 Maryland Avenue, N.E., Washington, DC 20002, (202) 544-8636.

Unitarian Universalist Service Committee. *The Busy Person's Guide to Social Action.* Rev. ed. 1990. Available from: UUSC, 130 Prospect Street, Cambridge, MA 02139-1813, (617) 868-6600.

International Issues

Agnelli, Susanna. *Street Children: A Growing Urban Tragedy.* A Report for the Independent Commission on International Humanitarian Issues. 1986. London: George Weidenfeld & Nicolson Ltd., 91 Clapham High Street, London SW4 7TA, U.K.

Allsebrook, Annie, and Anthony Swift. *Broken Promise: The World of Endangered Children.* 1989. Hodder and Stoughton, Mill Road, Dunton Green, Sevenoaks, Kent TN13 2YA, U.K.

Barker, Gary, and Felicia Knaul. *Exploited Entrepreneurs: Street and Working Children in Developing Countries.* 1991. New York: CHILDHOPE-USA, Inc., 333 East 38th Street, New York, NY 10016.

Campaign to End Child Prostitution in Asian Tourism (ECPAT). *Ending Child Prostitution in Asian Tourism . . . Starts in the USA: A Guide to Action.* 1993. Available from ECPAT, 475 Riverside Drive, New York, NY 10115.

Castelle, Kay. *In the Child's Best Interest: A Primer on the U.N. Convention on the Rights of the Child.* 1990. Available from Foster Parents Plan International, 804 Quaker Lane, East Greenwich, RI 02818; or Defense for Children International, 21 South 13th Street, Philadelphia, PA 19107.

Children's Defense Fund. *America's Children Falling Behind: The U.S. and the Convention on the Rights of the Child.* Washington, DC: CDF, 1992.

Cornia, Giovanni Andrea, and Sandor Sipos, eds. *Children and the Transition to the Market Economy: Safety Nets and Social Policies in Central and Eastern Europe.* New York: UNICEF, 1991.

Defence for Children International. *International Children's Rights Monitor.* The quarterly publication of Defence for Children International, P.O. Box 88, CH-1211 Geneva 20, Switzerland. (See page 153 for address of U.S. office.)

Defence for Children International. *Protecting Children's Rights in International Adoptions: Selected Documents on the Problem of Trafficking and Sale of Children.* 1989.

Foreign Policy Association, Inc. *Great Decisions,* 1993 Edition. Foreign Policy Association, Inc. 729 Seventh Avenue, New York, NY 10019, 1993.

Grant, James D. *The State of the World's Children 1993.* New York: United Nations Children's Fund/Oxford University Press. Available from U.S. Committee for UNICEF, 333 East 38th Street, New York, NY 10016.

National Council of Churches, Human Rights Office. *The Rights of the Child: The Challenge to U.S. Churches Continues toward U.S. Ratification of the UN's Convention on the Rights of the Child.* Available from World Community Office, Room 670, 475 Riverside Drive, New York, NY 10115.

National Council of Churches, Latin America and the Caribbean Office. *Children in Danger: Boys and Girls in Latin America and the Caribbean.* 1992. Available from Latin America and the Caribbean Office, Room 622, 475 Riverside Drive, New York, NY 10115.

National Council of Churches, Office on Global Education. *Children at Risk.* Three parts: (1) Street Children, (2) Armed Conflict, and (3) Child Exploitation. Available from Friendship Press, P.O. Box 37844, Cincinnati, OH 45222-0844.

National Council of Churches, Office on Global Education. *Children Hungering for Justice: Curriculum on Hunger and Children's Rights.* Available for Grades K–4, 5–8, and 9–12. Available from Friendship Press (see address above).

National Council of Churches, Office on Global Education. *Facts Have Faces: Children on the Streets* and *Children for Sale.* Available from Office on Global Education, 2115 North Charles Street, Baltimore, MD 21218-5755.

National Council of Churches, Office on Global Education. *Make a World of Difference: Creative Activities for Global Learning.* 1989. Available from Friendship Press (see address above).

Newman-Black, Marjorie, and Patricia Light, eds. *The Convention: Child Rights and UNICEF Experience at the Country Level.* 1991. Available from U.S. Committee for UNICEF (see address above).

Nurkse, Dennis, and Kay Castelle. *In the Spirit of Peace: A Global Introduction to Children's Rights.* 1990. Available from Defense for Children International-USA, 21 South 13th Street, Philadelphia, PA 19107.

O'Grady, Ron. *The Child and the Tourist: The Story behind the Escalation of Child Prostitution in Asia.* 1992. Available from The Campaign to End Child Prostitution in Asian Tourism (ECPAT), 475 Riverside Drive, New York, NY 10115.

Results Educational Fund, editors. *Keeping the Promise: On the Anniversary of World Summit for Children.* Washington, DC: Results, 1991.

Spies, Karen Bornemann. *Visiting in the Global Village.* Minneapolis: Augsburg Fortress Press, 1991. Vol. 1, #15-9678; vol. 2, #15-9679.

United Nations Children's Fund (UNICEF). *First Call for Children.* Quarterly publication available from U.S. Committee for UNICEF, 333 East 38th Street, New York, NY 10016.

United Nations Children's Fund (UNICEF). *The Progress of Nations 1993.* Available from U.S. Committee for UNICEF (see address above).

United Nations Children's Fund (UNICEF). *The State of the World's Children 1993.* Available from U.S. Committee for UNICEF (see address above).

United Nations Children's Fund (UNICEF). *The Convention on the Rights of the Child.* Available from U.S. Committee for UNICEF (see address above).

Vittachi, Anuradha. *Stolen Childhood: In Search of the Rights of the Child.* Cambridge, UK: Polity Press, in association with Basil Blackwell, Inc., Cambridge, MA, 1989.

Maternal and Child Health

Booth, Beverly E., comp. *Striving for Fullness of Life: The Church's Challenge in Health.* A Compilation of Health-Related Church Models, A Pilot Study. 1989. For information, contact: Carter Center of Emory University, 1 Copenhill, Atlanta, GA 30307, (404) 420-5151; or Wheat Ridge Foundation, 104 South Michigan Avenue, Chicago, IL 60603, (312) 263-1182.

Caring Program for Children. *Health Care for Children in Need.* Pamphlet. Contact: Charles P. LaVallee, Director, P.O. Box Caring, Pittsburgh, PA 15230, (412) 687-5437.

Children's Defense Fund. *The Health of America's Children.* Washington, DC: CDF, annual publication.

Worship Resources

Anderson, Yohann, ed. *Songs.* Available from: Songs and Creations, Inc., P.O. Box 7, San Anselmo, CA 94960.

Bread for the World. *Banquet of Praise: A Book of Worship Resources, Hymns and Songs in the Spirit of Justice, Peace and Food for All.* 1990.

Charbonnet, Barbara, and Sam Harris. *Seven-Day Devotional Guide Based on the Promises of the World Summit for Children.* Available from Results Educational Fund, 236 Massachusetts Avenue, N.E., Suite 300, Washington DC 20003 (202) 543-9340.

Children's Defense Fund. *National Observance of Children's Sabbaths Organizing Kit,* annual publication.

Congregations Concerned for Children. *Recognizing and Celebrating Children.* 1990. Available from: CCC, 122 W. Franklin Avenue, #218, Minneapolis, MN 55404, (612) 870-3660.

Huber, Jane Parker, ed. *Peacemaking through Worship.* Presbyterian Peacemaking Program, Social Justice and Peacemaking Ministry Unit, 100 Witherspoon Street, Louisville, KY 40202-1396.

Weems, Ann. *Reaching for Rainbows: Resources for Creative Worship.* Philadelphia, PA: Westminster Press, 1980.

Youth Development and Teen Pregnancy Prevention

Brendtro, Larry. *Reclaiming Youth at Risk: Our Hope for the Future.* 1990.

Children's Defense Fund. *The Adolescent and Young Adult Fact Book.* Washington, DC: CDF, 1991.

Cellman, Carol D., and Peggy L. Halsey. *Children and Youth in Jeopardy: A Mission Concern for United Methodists.* Rev. ed. 1990. Available from: Service Center, National Program Division, General Board of Global Ministries, United Methodist Church, 7820 Reading Road, Caller No. 1800, Cincinnati, OH 45222-1800.

Dryfoos, Joy G. *Adolescents at Risk: Prevalence and Prevention.* New York: Oxford University Press, 1990.

National Academy of Sciences. *Risking the Future: Adolescent Sexuality, Pregnancy, and Child Bearing.* 2 vols. Washington, DC: National Academy Press, 1986.

Youth Workers Network for Peace and Justice. *Youthpeace.* Quarterly publication. Available from: Institute for Peace and Justice, 4144 Lindell Boulevard, #124, St. Louis, MO 63108.

Videos

Recommended by Friendship Press

NOTE: All resources listed below are ½" VHS format.

WELCOMING THE CHILDREN
    Sale: $39.95   1994   24:00
Rental: $15.00
This interactive video shows how congregations and communities are working for and with children, utilizing their own resources and partnering with other groups. Designed to be used in conjunction with *Welcome the Child: A Child Advocacy Guide for Churches*, the video focuses on **Section II, Making a Difference for Children: Step by Step.** The teaching format is enhanced by interviews with caregivers and marvelous moments of children in action in Florida, Tennessee, Puerto Rico, California, and Ohio.
    Available for sale from:
        Friendship Press Distribution Office
        P.O. Box 37844
        Cincinnati, OH 45222-0844
        (513) 948-8733
    Available for rental only from:
        EcuFilm
        810 Twelfth Avenue, South
        Nashville, TN 37203
        (800) 251-4091

Secondary Resources

AMERICA'S CHILDREN: POOREST IN A LAND OF PLENTY
    Sale: $39.95   1989   52:00
Rental: $20.00

Narrated by Maya Angelou, this video reveals the tragic neglect of our nation's most valuable resource — the child. Through the use of still photos and video, it conveys a poignant portrait of the insidious nature of poverty. We see some solutions in the equally moving portrayal of people in church and community organizations who are reaching out to give our children a future right now. Study guide included.

    Available for sale and rental from EcuFilm
    [see above]

BEYOND THE NEWS: SEXUAL ABUSE
    Sale: $19.99 US   1992   21:00
         $24.99 Can

Actors tell true stories of people who have survived sexual abuse — date rape, child abuse, and abuse by a leader in the church. Stories and feelings of perpetrators of date rape are acted out as well. The program features an interview with Carolyn Heggen, author of *Sexual Abuse in Christian Homes and Churches*. WARNING: This video is intended for adult audiences. Descriptive language and examples of sexual abuse are used. Study guide included.

    Available for sale from:
        Mennonite Media Ministries
        1251 Virginia Avenue
        Harrisonburg, VA 22801-2497
        (703) 434-6701

CHILDREN OF THE PROMISE
    Sale: $20.00   1992   20:00
Rental: $15.00

This video describes ministries with children in the United States and around the world — including the Browning Day Care Center in Browning, Montana, which nurtures children's cultural awareness and self-esteem; Camp Aldersgate in Little Rock, Arkansas, which devotes weeks to children with special medical conditions; and Moore Community House in Biloxi, Mississippi, where African American and Asian American children are shown abundant life. A program of the United Methodist Advance. Study guide.

    Available for sale and rental from EcuFilm
    [see above]

MILLIONS OF CHILDREN ARE HUNGRY IN AMERICA!
    Sale: $15.00   16:00

This overview of a two-year study in the United States describes programs that can prevent childhood hunger. Also known as "Campaign to End Childhood Hunger," it is available in several denominational film libraries.

    Available for sale from:
        Food Research and Action Center
        1875 Connecticut Ave., N.W.
        Washington, DC 20009
        (202) 986-2200

Also available for free loan from:
Church World Service Film Library
P.O. Box 968
Elkhart, IN 46515
(219) 264-3102

ON TELEVISION: TEACH THE CHILDREN

Sale: $49.00 + $5 shipping   1992   52:00

Children ages 6–11 spend more time watching television than they do in a classroom. This video is designed to help teachers, parents, and children scrutinize television's hidden curriculum. User's guide included.

Available for sale from:
California Newsreel
149 Ninth Street/420
San Francisco, CA 94103
(415) 621-6196

SPREAD THE WORD:
TEENS TALK TO TEENS ABOUT AIDS

Sale: $49.95   1992   27:00
Rental: $20.00

This video presents information, stories, attitudes, and feelings shared by teens whose lives have been affected by AIDS. It tells the story of teenagers who have AIDS and others who have close family members with the disease. *Spread the Word* provides teachers, parents, and religious leaders with a structure for discussion and action. Study guide included.

Available for sale and rental from EcuFilm
[see above]

WHO SPEAKS FOR THE CHILDREN?

Sale: $12.95   1989   28:00

Children and welfare mothers tell their own stories in this video developed by the United Church of Christ Office for Church and Society as part of this denomination's "Children in Poverty" initiative.

Available for sale from:
UCC Office for Church in Society
700 Prospect Avenue East
Cleveland, OH 44115-1100
(216) 736-2174

WHY WE CARE:
ABOUT CHILDREN AND EDUCATION

Sale: $29.95   1992   28:00
Rental: $18.00

Programs helping children to learn and to give are the focus of this video. In Indiana, Operation Classroom is giving children in Liberia and Sierra Leone the tools for learning, and at the same time giving children in

Indiana a lesson on being in mission. In Jamaica, we hear the story of children being touched by some very special people who care.

Available for sale and rental from EcuFilm
[see above]

WHY WE CARE:
ABOUT OUR FUTURE, OUR YOUTH

Sale: $29.95   1992   28:00
Rental: $18.00

Too many of today's youth run a gauntlet of violence, abuse, stress, and peer pressure just to make it to their 18th birthday. This program, an inspiring report from Appalachia and the streets of Detroit, looks at what committed Christians are doing to help and nurture some of those young people caught in a web that threatens their survival.

Available for sale and rental from EcuFilm
[see above]

Additional Recommendations from Children's Defense Fund

Center for Prevention of Sexual and Domestic Violence. *Hear Their Cries: Religious Responses to Child Abuse.* Seattle, WA: Center for Prevention of Sexual and Domestic Violence, 1991.

Children's Defense Fund. *Head Start Now! How the Head Start Program Benefits Children and the Case for Full Investment.* Washington, DC: CDF, 1993. $6.00.

Congregations Concerned for Children. *A Better Chance for Children.* Updated 1990. Rental or purchase from: CCC, 122 W. Franklin Avenue #218, Minneapolis, MN 55404, (612) 870-3660.

Evangelical Lutheran Church in America. *Just Like Me.* A 23-minute videotape drama for children about the realities of homelessness. ELCA Distribution Service, (800) 328-4648, $9.95 (code #69-5705).

McGinnis, James and Kathleen. *Building Shalom Families: Christian Parenting for Peace and Justice.* Credence Cassettes, 1990.

UNICEF. *341.* 1990. Available for $20 from West Glen Communications, Inc., 1430 Broadway, New York, NY 10018. Enclose a $20.00 check payable to the U.S. Committee for UNICEF. For a complete list of UNICEF audiovisuals, contact the U.S. Committee for UNICEF, 333 East 38th Street, New York, NY 10016, (212) 922-2646.

Unitarian Universalist Service Committee. *Promise the Children.* 1990. Available from: UUSC, 130 Prospect Street, Cambridge, MA 02139-1813, (617) 868-6600.

United Methodist Women. *To Love in Deed: United Methodist Women's Campaign for Children.* 1989. Available from: Ecufilm.

Vision Video. *Local Heroes, Global Change.* 1990. Augsburg Fortress #35-881-8516.

Readers' Survey

Your assistance in evaluating this guide will help us prepare improved materials for congregations. Please complete this questionnaire, detach, and mail in an envelope to CDF, Attn: Shannon P. Daley, 25 E Street, N.W., Washington, DC 20001.

Listed below are the six sections in this book. Please indicate how helpful each is to you as you seek ways to lift up and act upon the needs of children in your congregation, community, nation, and world.

	Not Very Helpful	Somewhat Helpful	Very Helpful	Did Not Use	Comments
Section I: The Eyes of Faith					
Section II: Step by Step					
Section III: Study into Action					
Section IV: Children of Every Nation					
Section V: Giving Voice to the Voiceless					
Section VI: Resources					

1. What was missing for you?

2. What was most useful?

3. What would you change or add?

Your name and position (optional) in the church/group: _____

Address and phone number: _____

_____

_____

Church's name, address, and phone number (if appropriate or different from above):

_____

_____

_____

Denomination (optional): _____

☐ Yes, I would like to become part of a growing network of religious advocates for children. Let my denomination know of my interest, and keep me informed of model programs and activities for churches, resources, events, and legislative updates.

☐ Send me information about the National Observance of Children's Sabbaths.